# SOCIAL CASEWORK

## A Problem-solving Process

HELEN HARRIS PERLMAN

# SOCIAL CASEWORK

**A Problem-solving Process**

**THE UNIVERSITY OF CHICAGO PRESS**

CHICAGO & LONDON

*International Standard Book Number: 0-226-66033-8*
*Library of Congress Catalog Card Number: 57-6270*
THE UNIVERSITY OF CHICAGO PRESS, CHICAGO 60637
The University of Chicago Press, Ltd., London

This is a book about social casework, about the dynamic components that are always to be found in it, and particularly about its process. My thesis is this: For all the range and diversity encountered in any individualized practice such as casework there may be found in it certain common elements and operations. The operations of casework are essentially those of the process of problem-solving. When this process is examined, it may be seen to be in congruence with the normal problem-solving operations of the human ego. This is not strange, because the latter is the model from which man has formulated the "logic" of his adaptive movements from dilemma to resolution in his social as well as in his psychological activities. In this book I try to identify the constant elements and the constant means in the practice of casework and to view them afresh within what has seemed to me to be a unifying and useful framework.

Casework's search for such structures for its processes has been a recurring one. This search has now alternated, now fused, with the search for a deeper and broader understanding of the materials with which casework deals. The need for structure is felt by the individual practitioner, by those who supervise and teach the practices of casework, and by the profession as a whole.

*Doing* is the practitioner's everyday problem. What to select to do, how to do, in what order and direction, by what means; how to operate with focus yet with freedom; how to be pliable yet precise; how to serve both the client and the community unstintingly and yet economically—these are among the questions with which the caseworker is daily beset. His need is for the knowledge that enables him to understand the nature of the client, problem, and agency in interaction and for the ethics, intention, and skills of helpfulness. But, beyond this, his need is for some dependable structure to provide the inner organization of the process in which he engages and to point out its general direction. In no sense is such a structure a stamped-out routine. It is rather an underlying guide, a pattern for action which gives general form to the caseworker's inventiveness or creativity.

There are those who look uneasily at any attempt to systematize so sensitive and individualized a performance as casework must be. They argue that, as casework comes alive in practice, it is an art and that spontaneity and responsiveness would be shackled by the caseworker's conformity to any preconceived system of its conduct. But others—and I am one of these—believe that the artist's creativity is freed when he has grasped firmly the essential structure and forms of his particular activity. Only when he has incorporated these into his practice are his energies fully released to feed his senses, perceptions, responses, imagination. In the art of helping by casework, too, this holds. The caseworker who possesses an organized idea of his constant means is free to listen, to see, to sense his client deeply, to relate to him warmly, and to think or act unhampered by anxious uncertainties about next steps or directions. "A science teaches us to know and an art to do," wrote William Jevons, the logician, "and all the more perfect sciences lead to the creation of corresponding useful arts." Thus the caseworker's practice may be buttressed by a systematization of knowledge about how to do what he is to do.

The daily problem of the teacher and supervisor of casework practice is how to equip the student and beginning practitioner as soundly and as speedily as possible to give the best possible service to clients. The time absorbed in developing its practitioners is a concern of every profession, but I think the problem of time is of particular concern in social casework because, at least to the present, we lose so many of our young practitioners (to marriage, to motherhood, to other kinds of work) while they are still more the consumers of the profession's training than the producers of its services. One haunting question, then, is how to prepare our neophytes more quickly and better to shoulder professional responsibilities and carry them with self-dependence and skill.

On one major answer to this question we are all in agreement: to push ourselves further to identify and systematize our knowledge so that it can be communicated in the large piece, so to speak, through generalizations of ideas and principles abstracted from the innumerable specific experiences of which practice consists. I think we would be agreed, too, that the most difficult knowledge to transfer from teacher to learner is that of how to do. What is to be known and understood, what is to be valued and striven for—these we have taken fairly firm hold upon and can transmit. But how the practitioner can put this knowledge to use, what he is to do in order to be of maximum help to his client with that economy of time and motion which is skill—these we are not yet so adept at transmitting. I say this, knowing that the art of doing cannot be taught in any complete sense. Only the principles by which it may be guided, the dynamic elements that operate in "doing," the general nature and direction of the process of being professionally helpful—only these can be taught and learned for the practitioner's creative use. These need to be named, ordered, and conceptualized beyond what we have achieved thus far.

It has been these several considerations that over the years have spurred casework practitioners and theoreticians to the work of systematizing their knowledge. As every social worker knows, the brilliant work of Mary Richmond in *Social Diagnosis* was the first and remains the outstanding single effort to order the processes of casework help. Selecting and applying some of the operational systems of law and medicine, Miss Richmond proposed one scheme of problem-solving: a study of the facts of the situation, a diagnosis of the nature of the problem, and, following in the direction pointed by this diagnosis, a plan and execution of treatment. For the first time caseworkers were given a framework for their efforts which formerly had been compounded largely of such good intentions and resources of agency and person as they could mobilize for their clients. We can imagine what the advent of this book meant to caseworkers of that time. It must have been like a child's experience of fumbling with a kaleidoscope; there he sees a jumble of bright bits of glass, colorful, interesting, but meaningless, and then someone comes along and says, "Turn it to the light and twist it a bit—so," and suddenly the jeweled bits fall into patterns—discernible, orderly, describable, with new and exciting significance.

Yet, despite this giant step to bring science to the aid of art, there remained troubling problems for practitioners. One difficulty was that clients would not stand still while the study was being made; another was that they would not always see eye to eye with the caseworker in the treatment plan that careful diagnosis prescribed. Moreover, it was clearly the caseworker and not the client who was active and purposive—it was the caseworker who investigated, who thought about what he discerned, who planned ahead, and thus, often, when he was ready with his proposals, his client was gone, in spirit if not in body. The means of problem-solving which *Social Diagnosis* proposed was limited by the times in which it evolved, for then our understanding of human behavior was in its embryonic stages. Thus it presented a problem-centered rather than a client-centered system, devoid of the means by which the client could be engaged and empowered to work on his problems. Mary Richmond herself was one of the first to see this. Three years after the publication of her book, she wrote in a paper presented at the National Conference of Social Work in 1920: "I place the study of *processes* first. . . . The processes common to all case treatment deserve our special attention."

But the identification of the "processes common to all case treatment" lagged behind the formulation of our working philosophy, including our ethical commitments, and the fluctuating but forward-thrusting efforts to organize the facts, hypotheses, and assumptions governing the subject matters with which we deal. The reasons for this are so multiple and complex as to forbid mention here. They are to be found in our professional history of the last four decades, when caseworkers as individuals and as members of a profession have undergone continuous and rapid adaptations and readaptations, now shocked by the impact of catastrophic world events, now excited and disturbed by the impact of great areas of new knowledge and ideas, always with the demand upon them for action, for doing, before their professional egos could see clearly or take the necessary time to achieve balance. This history deserves to be written; it would give us, I think, some new respect for our stature and our adaptive sturdiness.

There are numerous other reasons, too, that explain our reluctance or unreadiness to formulate the constant means of our process. One is the fear of "intellectualizing" what must remain a fluid, feeling experience. (Apropos of this, there is overdue among us the recognition that "intellectual" is not a bad word; it is a problematic state only when it is used as a defense against feeling, not when it illuminates and then modifies feeling.) A second source of difficulty lies in the fact that, as "doing" is experienced, it involves the whole person of the doer and therefore seems to elude capture for generalization. And, finally, of course, there is the fact that valid formulation waits on repeated tests of action that are consciously accounted for.

In recent years, at the same time as casework has avidly been absorbing the propositions of ego psychology and looking with new interest at the social sciences—perhaps heartened by the affirmations which those studies give to much that caseworkers have long known—its spokesmen have given increasing attention to the organization of our common methods and processes. Austin, Hamilton, and Hollis have made signal contributions by their classifications of casework methods; Gomberg and Towle, for all their differences, have identified with lucidity the sequential order as well as the constant elements in the helping process; the 1953 report of the Committee on Methods and Scope of the Family Agency takes another forward step in naming and classifying common goals and means in family casework. And all these essays, it must be remembered, spring not full grown from the foreheads of their Joves but have been brought to fruition by the practice and the recorded thinking of numerous fellow caseworkers.

So with this book. It is another effort in the profession's striving to establish the regularities of its means of service. In it I have attempted to organize what has seemed to me most useful and true in the characteristic practice and the common wisdom of casework.

Perhaps all that is "new" herein lies in the casting of the familiar into a framework which, it has seemed to me and to my colleagues, offers some fresh perspective and some firmer guide to the casework process. I know there are many roads that lead to Rome—the Rome, that is, of enabling people to cope with their problems in ways that are economical and sure. This book offers one possible road map to that goal.

When I started to trace the lineaments of this book, it was to be about the whole social casework process—the beginning, ongoing, and ending phases in casework's problem-solving. But almost from the start it took on a life of its own and began to defy management. Like that nightmarish squash vine in the children's story, it grew and grew and grew; and it not only grew but raced forward and doubled on its track; it leaped ahead of itself at times and at others stood stock-still, burdened with its own weight. When I complained of this unmanageable creature to one of my colleagues, she said, quite simply, "Why do you suppose so few books on casework have been written?"

So I came to realize that to write about casework presents the same difficulties as to learn casework. It is in itself a problem-solving task, because the subject matter is at once immense, complex, and in motion. The necessity both in learning and in teaching casework is to carve out some small cross-sections which contain the essential qualities of the whole and to view these microcosms as parts of a continuum. This recognition of the need to break down the subject helped me to cope with what for casework writers has so often been an unmanageable task and for readers a source of confusion.

The parts I selected to discuss were these: the dynamic components which make up the casework situation, with the helping process given special emphasis, and the beginning phase of casework as the cross-section in which these components could be viewed in interaction. The first part of the book deals, then, with what the casework situation consists of. (Its historical and social matrix and its working philosophy have not been included, because they have been cogently set forth elsewhere.) My choice of the beginning phase as the casework cross-section in the second part of the book was determined by the logic of "first things first" and by the fact that the process of engaging the client in taking and using help is paralleled in every ongoing aspect of casework. In ongoing phases there will, to be sure, be differences of depth, detail, and aim, but I think the reader will find that the underlying operations of problem-solving will be essentially the same, applicable across the board. Part III of the book offers two pieces of case material for illustrative purposes.

I first thought that this book should serve as a text and aid to students, to caseworkers young in practice, and to their teachers and supervisors as a sometime supplement to their guiding efforts. Now, as I view its complexity with something of the astonishment of a mother who suddenly finds that her child has grown man-sized, it occurs to me that it may have some usefulness also for the experienced and skilled "old hands" who now and again are re-freshed by considering old truths in new lights.

A book such as this is the product of the profession's work, yet it is inescapably a personal document too. Despite the discomfort of self-revelation, I believe I owe the reader this note: I have some-times been asked where I stand in relation to the two presently op-posing schools of casework thought. By practice, professional edu-cation, and conviction I am psychoanalytically and diagnostically oriented; perhaps I should say by natural bent as well, because I can scarcely conceive of my being able to think or act out of rela-tion to these systems. But I have not been inclined to make a virtue out of what is, for me, a necessity, and I have long cherished Whitehead's comment that "a clash of doctrines is not a disaster—it is an opportunity." The existence of the functional school of case-work offered me such an opportunity. By its separation and differ-ences from the main stream of casework thinking it forced me, along with many others, to a re-examination of the taken-for-truth theories and convictions with which I had worked, and, if by this examination some long-held assumptions and practices were opened to question, others were more clearly formulated and enhanced. Be-yond this, there were parts of functional concepts and principles which seemed remarkably useful in solving some of the casework-er's most perplexing problems. To me a number of them seemed "true," not because of the authorities who pronounced them or of the persuasiveness of their rationale, but simply because they came true in practice—they worked. Such practices and guiding principles as worked were, of course, those which proved to be in consonance with my basic orientation—those which modified but never violated it. I suppose, then, my stand may be called "eclectic," not, I hurry to say, in the frequent use of that term when it is equated with some magpie collection but in the sense of choosing ideas or principles from diverse systems of thought toward the formation of a coherent, integrated, whole system. I am not sure I have achieved this whole, but I am sure I do not want to strive for a fixed gospel.

As I have said, a book such as this is the product of all the professional nurture and experience the author has had. It is a humbling yet heart-warming thing to ask one's self, "To whom do I owe?" —humbling because one suddenly knows one's self to be heavily beholden to so many other people, heart-warming because one feels one's self to be part, thereby, of a goodly company. I cannot begin to name the people—the teachers, mentors, colleagues, students— who come to mind as I ask myself, "To whom am I grateful?" They are those who have warmed and sustained me; those who have, as with the turn of a key, opened whole new vistas of understanding to me; those who by their challenge have pushed me into the discomfort of further thought or effort.

Most immediately I owe thanks to my colleagues on the faculty of the School of Social Service Administration of the University of Chicago. In my eleven years of teaching there I have found myself in a climate that is at once benign and brisk, in a faculty which is creative and hospitable to ideas yet rigorously critical of them, taking part in ongoing dialogues which have been exhilarating, exhausting, and rewarding. It is with difficulty that I limit myself to singling out from my colleagues these few who are directly related to this book. To Dean Helen Russell Wright, retiring as this is written, I am deeply grateful for the unfailing stimulation of her keen and brilliant mind, for the enabling support of her interest, and for her unself-conscious exemplification of the purposive and staunch professional social worker. The person who has contributed most richly to this book and to me is Charlotte Towle, my colleague and friend. Beyond her ranging and deep thinking about casework, beyond the wisdom she holds and imparts, I have known her as a generously giving, sustaining, and creatively stimulating person.

To Mary Macdonald and Lilian Ripple, both of whom carefully read and criticized the first draft of my manuscript, my thanks for their astute, pointed appraisals. I owe a special note to Lilian Ripple, who helped me climb out of several technical pitfalls. Rachel Marks, Phyllis Osborn, Esther Schour, and Lola Selby each read one chapter of the manuscript and gave me many useful suggestions.

Finally, and most, I am grateful to my family—Max, my husband, Jonathan, my son, and my mother, Annie Harris—who by their unfailing understanding and warm support made it possible for me to write this book.

HELEN HARRIS PERLMAN

## CONTENTS

### I. PROBLEM-SOLVING IN SOCIAL CASEWORK

1. The Components of the Casework Situation . . . . . 3
2. The Person . . . . . . . . . . . . . . . 6
3. The Problem . . . . . . . . . . . . . . 27
4. The Place . . . . . . . . . . . . . . . 40
5. The Process . . . . . . . . . . . . . . 53
6. The Caseworker-Client Relationship . . . . . 64
7. The Problem-solving Work . . . . . . . . . 84

### II. CASEWORK IN CROSS-SECTION

8. Person, Problem, Place, and Process in the Beginning Phase 105
9. Content in the Beginning Phase . . . . . . . 114
10. Method in the Beginning Phase . . . . . . . 139
11. Diagnosis: The Thinking in Problem-solving . . . 164
12. The Client's Workability and the Casework Goal . . 183

### III. TWO CASES

13. Two Cases: Mr. Grayson and Mrs. Whitman . . . . 207

### BIBLIOGRAPHY

Bibliography . . . . . . . . . . . . . . . 241

### INDEX

Index . . . . . . . . . . . . . . . . . 263

# PROBLEM-SOLVING

# IN SOCIAL CASEWORK

# 1 THE COMPONENTS

## OF THE CASEWORK SITUATION

To attempt to define social casework takes courage or foolhardiness
or perhaps a bit of both. So many knowledgeable caseworker-
writers have attempted it, so many definitions have been produced,
and yet at some point in every caseworker's professional life he
faces and struggles to answer with some greater clarity and precision than existing definitions have provided the question of what
casework is. And no wonder. Social casework is a phenomenon at
once complex, dynamic, and in evolution. It is complex by virtue
of the varied knowledges which feed it, the ethical commitments
which infuse it, the special auspices and conditions of its practice,
the objectives and ends which guide it, the skills which empower
it. It is complicated further by the fact that it deals with materials
which are in interaction and change among themselves and also
in response to the injection of casework itself. As it is experienced,
practiced, or thought about, the social casework situation is a living
event. As such it almost cannot be contained within a definition.
Yet we must say what it is if we are to communicate understanding of it; at the very least there must be established between
writer and reader the premise from which discussion proceeds. This
definition, therefore, is ventured herewith:

*Social casework is a process used by certain human welfare agencies to help individuals to cope more effectively with their problems in social functioning.*

Whatever the imperfection in this definition, it has this small merit: it embodies the four essential components of casework in their relationships to one another. As the definition upon which all that follows has bearing, it calls for some elaboration.

The nucleus of the casework event is this: A *person* with a *problem* comes to a *place* where a *professional representative* helps him by a given *process*. Since this is the heart of almost any situation where a person seeks professional help, the distinctive characteristics must be delineated.

Who is this person?

The *person* is a man, woman, or child, anyone who finds himself, or is found to be, in need of help in some aspect of his social-emotional living, whether the need be for tangible provisions or counsel. As he begins to receive such help, he is called a "client."

What is the problem?

The *problem* arises from some need or obstacle or accumulation of frustrations or maladjustments, and sometimes all of these together, which threatens or has already attacked the adequacy of the person's living situation or the effectiveness of his efforts to deal with it.

What is the place?

The *place* is a social service agency or a social service department of another kind of human welfare agency. It is a particular kind of social agency and department in that it is set up to deal not with social problems at large but with human beings who are experiencing such problems in the management of their own personal lives. Its purpose is to help individuals with the particular social handicaps which hamper good personal or family living and with the problems created by faulty person-to-person, person-to-group, or person-to-situation relationships. This agency purpose and functions come to life in the person and professional performance of the caseworker.

What is the process?

The *process*, named "social casework" to denote its center of attention and its individualized aspect, is a progressive transaction between the professional helper (the caseworker) and the client. It consists of a series of problem-solving operations carried on within a meaningful relationship. The end of this process is contained in its means: to so influence the client-person that he develops effectiveness in coping with his problem and/or to so influence the problem as to resolve it or vitiate its effects.

It is the process of social casework that is the concern of this book. But, because this process injects movement and change into human living situations, it can be understood only as we understand the nature of the materials upon which and with which it works—their effect upon it and its effect upon them. Therefore, the caseworker must grasp the nature of the person who is a client, the nature of his problem, and the nature of the place which contains the problem-solving means. And then (although in reality there is no "then"; there is only "at once") we must perceive and understand the totality of these three ingredients, which is different from the sum of the parts, because interaction among them is continuous. When each of these ingredients has been held to examination on its own part and in its relationship to casework, the process itself may be viewed and analyzed as to its structure, its dynamics, and, chiefly, its usefulness to a person in need of help. This is the task to which the next chapters are set.

# 2 *THE PERSON*

The client of a social agency is like all the other persons we have ever known, but he is different too. In broad ways he is like all other human beings; in a somewhat more limited way he is like all other human beings of his age or time or culture. But, as we move from understanding him simply as a human being to understanding him as *this particular* human being, we find that, with all his general likenesses to others, he is as unique as his thumbprint. By nuance and fine line and by the particular way his bone and brain and spirit are joined, he is born and grows as a personality different in some ways from every other individual of his family, genus, or species.

No one of us can ever know the whole of another person, though we may sometimes delude ourselves to that effect. The reason for this lies not only in the subtle dimensions and interlacings of any personality but also in the shift and reorganization of new and old elements in the personality that take place continuously just because the person is alive in a live environment and is in interaction with it. Nevertheless, the person *is* a whole in any moment of his living. He operates as a physical, psychological, social entity, whether on the problem of his neurotic anxieties or of his inadequate income; he is product-in-process, so to speak, of his constitutional makeup, his physical and social environment, his past experience, his present

6

perceptions and reactions, and even his future aspirations. It is this physical-psychological-social–past-present-future configuration that he brings to every life-situation he encounters.

Fortunately, the caseworker's need to know and understand any individual human being is circumscribed by his purpose—to enable this person, his client, to find some effective way of solving or coping with his problem. To do this, he does not need to take a complete account of each person's dimensions and dynamics. The nature of the problem brought for help will determine, among other factors, what kinds of knowledge are necessary and how "whole" the understanding of him needs to be. But, whatever the service the client asks for and whatever the agency is set up to do, the essence of social casework help is that it aims to facilitate the individual's social adaptation, to restore, reshape, or reinforce his functioning as a social being. To do these things is to affect a person's behavior— the behavior which he acts out and that which is harbored within him—and, therefore, certain understanding about the forces and meanings of human behavior is essential for every caseworker. From among the great stores of knowledge about people, I select the ideas that follow as of major import to the social caseworker.*

*The person's behavior has this purpose and meaning: to gain satisfactions, to avoid or dissolve frustration, and to maintain his balance-in-movement.*

From the moment of the beginning of life the human being drives to gratify his felt needs. At first these needs are elementary ones—for physical and affectional security. But, as the person develops, the things he wants and needs, shaped by his perceptions, proliferate. His quest is for food to satisfy mental and emotional as well as physical hungers and for security in its manifold forms of money, love, status, and interests. The strength and the particular direction of the drive for satisfactions will differ for different people, of course, depending on their energy stores and on the culture group which most potently influences their idea of what is to be desired. But, in

---

* Readings listed for this chapter in the Bibliography in themselves and in their references lead the reader to a wealth of facts, theories, and assumptions about human attributes and functioning.

Italic numbers in parentheses which appear throughout the text and the footnotes make specific reference to the works listed, chapter by chapter, in the Bibliography.

whatever forms this drive finds expression, the human being strives by his behavior, the ways he thinks, feels, and acts, to achieve that internal sense of comfort or satisfaction which makes him feel in tune with his world, balanced, and open to new experience.

Inevitable in human life are those difficulties, assaults, obstacles, requirements—great and small—which impinge upon us and intrude between us and our ready gratifications. Even the baby, whose mother lends herself fully to protecting and nurturing him, will one day hear the words, "No," "You may not," and "You must," and it is not too long before he becomes aware that things and occurrences, as well as other persons, cannot always be bent to his desires. When in any stage of our development we encounter frustrations or obstacles to our drives, our behavior is responsive. We are irritated or blocked or made anxious or afraid, or sometimes we are agreeably excited and challenged. In any event, we make efforts to cope in some way so as to regain our sense of "dynamic stability."° Depending, again, on what we want and how much we want it and upon our reservoirs of energy and our capacity, we feel, think, and act in ways calculated (unconsciously as well as consciously) to restore our sense of security and relative mastery. Sometimes we retreat from a difficulty, sometimes we detour around it by relinquishing one goal and pursuing a substitute, sometimes we compromise and accommodate ourselves to the problem, sometimes we attack it head-on or by strategic maneuvers of thought and action—but always our effort is to solve the problem which obstructs our balanced forward movement in living.

A once popular song said, "Every little movement has a meaning of its own," and, while the lyricist was probably attempting to explain only the behavior of romance, he expressed a basic truth about all behavior. The person who comes to the social agency for help can be known and understood only through the search for meaning in the "little movements" of his behavior. The way he feels, thinks, and acts in the presence of the caseworker and others, the accounts from him or from others about his behavior outside the casework situation, how he has behaved in the past, how he conceives of behaving under different circumstances projected in fantasy—from some or all of these sources, the caseworker may draw inferences as

° This phrase is Alexander's (1).

to what his client is striving for or against. By his every movement, internal and overt, he will be saying, "I want something, and I act (in the ways I can) so as to get it," or "I fear or am blocked by something, and I act so as to protect myself against or to manage it." Often his behavior will reveal that he is caught between wanting and fearing, both at once, which is the essence of conflict. And sometimes the caseworker will encounter the client who has experienced more frustration than satisfaction in his efforts to fulfil his life-needs, and his behavior will show that he finds his crumbs of security in resignation.

Influenced by the success or failure of his behavior to gain his ends, each person develops certain patterns or characteristic ways of functioning by which he deals with himself, other people, and the situations outside himself in his pursuit of his conscious and unconscious goals. These patterns of his behavior, or this characteristic expression of himself, we call his "personality."*

Thus the client's personality is the particular organization of his drives and their particular expression through his feeling, thinking, speaking, and acting behaviors toward the end that he feel secure, balanced, and adequate. Whatever he does, appropriate or inappropriate as his behavior may seem, bad or good as its effects may be, it is at any given moment his way of trying to get what he thinks or feels he needs and wants, or of wrestling with what he thinks or feels is blocking him, or of defending himself against being hurt. Only as the caseworker understands and works in relation to these motives, their driving powers, and the adaptive and defensive maneuvers of his client's personality can he hope to effect changes in the way his client will function.

*Whether a person's behavior is or is not effective in promoting his well-being depends in large part upon the functioning of his personality structure.*

* Despite the fact that the word "personality" is on the tongue of every one of us daily, probably subordinate only to the words "love" and "money," it eludes definition. One definition has recently been put forth by the Special Commission on Psychodynamic Principles, of the American Psychiatric Association: "Personality is the organization of attitudes developed and utilized by a given person in dealing with his environment, particularly with respect to interpersonal relationships, and in dealing with his own internal tensions or pressures" (*The Psychiatrist: His Training and Development* [Washington, D.C.: American Psychiatric Association, 1953], p. 24).

The forces of the human personality combine in three major functions: (1) the life-energies that seek satisfactory outlets; (2) the check system, automatic or voluntary, that halts, modifies, or rechannels these drives to make their ends acceptable to their owner and his environment; and (3) the organizing and governing operations that control the negotiations and balances within the person himself, as between what he wants and what he can or ought to do, and between himself and his physical and social environment. The names Freud gave to these are the "id," the "superego," and the "ego."* The harmonious, concerted action of these forces in us makes for personal and social balance and competence; their discord or faultiness is revealed in behavior that is personally thwarting or socially unacceptable.

The id may be thought of as the life-force in the individual, that combination of energy and felt need which drives him to want and to will, to need and to strive. It combines motor power and directedness. Its purposes are not always recognizable or acceptable to the ego's scrutiny or to the superego's bias. They may be operating without the person's conscious awareness or volition, or they may be admitted to consciousness if they pass the censoring eye of the superego or if the ego takes them in hand to cover their nakedness with garments of rationality and propriety. At bottom, all our motives are in the interests of our own biological and psychological survival. What we drive for or are impelled to do is to be judged as "good" or "bad," not because it is energized or directed by id impulses but rather on the basis of whether the behavior into which it is translated is at once personally constructive and socially acceptable. As a person's behavior achieves his goal, he experiences satisfaction

* Sometimes these concepts have been written and spoken about in misleading ways, often as though the id were the personality's netherworld, a kind of black hole inhabited by uncontrollable imps; as though the superego were its upper regions inhabited by archangels who wagged threatening forefingers at those imps; and as though the ego were some area in between, where conscious man lived in constant harassment by the conflict of the forces of evil and good. It is interesting that, in thinking of the id, ego, and superego, we so often do so in the framework of those legendary and religious conceptions wherein man, pushed by Satan and pulled by God, struggles to maintain his human balance!

In the discussion that follows, the intent is, briefly, to explain not the psychogenesis but the psychodynamics of personality functions. The determinants of effective or maladaptive functioning are discussed in writings dealing with the growth and development of personality, many of which are listed in the Bibliography.

both unconsciously and consciously, and this gratification may permeate and modify the nature of his drives. He feels a release of tension, a remobilization of energy, a fresh sense of readiness. Conversely, as his behavior results in the frustration of drives, as what he wants and wills toward is not gained, this is registered within him as an increase of tension or a depletion of energy.* When unconscious drives defy control or modification because they have consistently been frustrated, they will skew and vitiate what the conscious mind bids the person to do. When, however, they have found gratifying and socially acceptable outlets, they become compatible with the ego's government, and their strength and purpose give energy and direction to the person's daily strivings.

The unconscious functioning of the personality is not that of id impulses alone. The superego, or conscience, is also largely unconscious by the time we reach adulthood. Some portion of it always remains in our consciousness, to be sure, probably that part which is the result of conscious learning, such as ethical values and principles; and many of its functions, also, are readily available to conscious awareness. We hear the "still, small voice" at points when wanting and "oughting" come in collision. But largely, in the stable person, the superego does its work unnoted. It is a dynamic system of the prohibitions, expectations, standards, values, and ideals which govern a person within himself in relation to other individuals and to his society. It operates to inhibit and guide the individual, so that his thinking, feeling, and acting behaviors are socialized. It is a learned function of the personality, starting with the first frown or the first glad approval of the parent for some act and developing through observations and experiences of cultural "musts" and "mays." It is taken into the person sometimes as though through the pores of the skin and at other times through discussion and guidance from loved and respected persons.

On any given day of an adult's life this socializing function of his personality operates continuously and noiselessly by its automatic punishment-or-reward system. The time schedules we keep, the way we eat, dress, and talk to other persons, the respect we show for the

* Social caseworkers and psychiatrists, both most familiar with people in periods of frustration or despair, know more of the effects of unhappy experience upon the individual's unconscious functions than of the benignly modifying effects of happy and successful experience.

property and rights of others, our expectations of ourselves on whatever task we engage in—all these kinds of behavior are indications of our incorporation of societal standards and ideals. We become conscious of our drives and our conscience chiefly at points of conflict; that is, at points when something we want to have or to do is clearly at odds with what is acceptable socially or personally. Then we become aware both of the id's inner push and of the superego's warning signals, usually in the form of unpleasant tension.

For example, a student may sit in a classroom of others, writing an examination. It never occurs to him to look at the papers of those on either side of him, because he long ago was taught, and took into himself, the idea that this is cheating and is wrong; he is quite unaware of the automatic working of his superego and considers his behavior "naturally" honorable. Suddenly, he is faced with a question he cannot answer. He feels a push of panic—"Your survival is at stake," says his id. Now he becomes aware of his conscience, because it, too, is speaking out in the form of feelings of discomfort or in actual thoughts. "Don't cheat," it says; "it's shameful," or "Better to keep your self-respect than get a grade," or "Suppose you get caught." (Actually, three qualitatively different conscience voices have spoken here: the first is that of stern parental injunction; the second is that of the owned "better self"; the third is the voice of a conscience which is more in the mind than in the heart—it *knows* wrong and avoids it for fear of external punishment, but it does not *feel* wrong.) In any case the student will be aware of some inner struggle between what he wants and what he expects of himself or what is expected of him. In this struggle between his now-conscious and opposing pushes, the one to attain a passing grade, the other to maintain his standard of self-respect, his ego will be arbitrator. If the ego aligns itself with the id impulse to get what is wanted at any cost, it will need to throw up a number of protective defenses against the guilt with which the superego will flood the personality—rationalizations ("Everybody does it"), projections ("The question's not fair"), denial ("I'm really not copying, just getting the general idea"), and so on. Depending on the powers and qualities of his personality functions, this student's ego may succeed in defending him against his superego, and he will feel justified and in balance again; or it may only partially succeed, and he will continue to feel an undertow of uneasiness and guilt which is his "punishment" by the superego. If his ego aligns itself with the superego, it will take measures of defense against the id's demands—suppression ("It would never occur to me to cheat"), reasoning ("In the long run I would be the loser"), sublimation ("I'll make up for this failure in other ways")—and in reward for this alignment the superego will flood the personality with feelings of goodness, pride, and integrity. Depending on how much he sacrificed, the student may feel gratified and in balance or may vacillate between gratification and frustration.

This example reveals another aspect of the superego that is largely conscious and is of considerable import in guiding behavior: the ego ideal. This is the person's mental image of himself, a kind of composite of his standards, self-expectations, hope—the self which he stretches to be. When the person's ego ideal is charged with motivational energies—in other words, when id and superego have some friendly connections with each other—the "I want" empowers his aspirations, and there results a constructively motivated person, less driven by fear than pulled by hope and expectations of achievement.

The effectiveness of an individual's behavior and his internal sense of balance are adversely affected under several conditions of superego and id functioning: when his superego is rigid and overpowering to or in continuous seesaw conflict with his impulses, or when it is insufficient in quantity and inadequate in quality to bridle impulse. The first of these is seen in constricted, anxious personalities, whose freedoms and powers are weakened by consciences which are no still small voices but are giants astride their backs. These persons have taken into themselves a prohibiting, punishing, parental system, because in their formative years submission seemed safer than any self-assertion. Such persons must often be helped to feel that there are allowances for human beings as well as requirements. At the other extreme are those persons whose consciences seem defective or corrupt, who may know right from wrong but are deterred more by the appraisal of possible consequence than by any automatic internal check upon their drives. Such persons must often be helped (if they will lend themselves to it, because it is their very distrust of those who nurtured them which resulted in their rejection of social guidance) to find that acceptance and expectation can go hand in hand or that self-control can be less painful than control from without. Most people fall in between these two extremes. The range is from the person who most of the time is on friendly terms with his superego because it contains approvals as well as restrictions and because at points of conflict it is subject to the judgments of his conscious mind to the person who is caught in chronic conflict, now between unfulfilled wants and a rewarding superego, now between fulfilled wants and the punishment of guilt.

Operating to resolve or to quiet conflict within the self and to mobilize and express drives in ways that are satisfying to the self and to the external world is that organization of personality functions called the "ego." Because ego functions are in large part conscious, we recognize them as "I." The "I" or the ego may be said to occupy the driver's seat in the personality vehicle, utilizing, yet guiding, the motor and energy forces, perceiving the signs and portents of the destination aimed for, of dangerous curves, of obstacles in the way, and maneuvering in relation to them—performing, in short, to keep the personality in balanced forward movement.

As a person behaves in order to express his needs and gain his ends or to cope with obstructions to those ends, some self-awareness and awareness of the relation of himself to what operates outside him is a first essential. This awareness sparks off certain organization of reactions, feelings, ideas, and motor responses which aim to maintain stability within the person as he makes some shift or takes some action in relation to what he wants to get or to avoid. These operations are usually described as the ego's perceptive, defensive-adaptive, integrative, and executive functions.

The ego's perceptive functions are fairly readily understood. We are aware that we "see" not alone with our eyes but with all our senses while, at the same time, drawing on our store of former perceptions. Furthermore, we can look both outward and into ourselves. Spontaneously, as the ego perceives, it seeks the meaning of what is perceived. The multitudinous interpretations which may be made may be cast roughly into two categories according to their effects upon the ego: those interpretations which arouse pleasant and those which arouse unpleasant tensions in the personality. The former are met either by a maintenance of the personality's dynamic stability or by some shifts and reorganizations of operations which may be termed adaptive; the latter are met by protective operations. Both functions of the ego, the adaptive and the protective, are commonly known as "defenses" (see Anna Freud, 6; Alexander, 3; and Towle, 16).

It is a frequent misconception that the person's use of defenses indicates malfunctioning. Defenses (and, perhaps, if some more constructive-sounding name had been given them, their connotations would be clearer) are essential to the maintenance of balance; they are to be found in all forms of organic life. In the human being they are, of course, highly complex, and they range from those that promote growth to those that retard it. Protection and defense may be said to be one kind of adaptive measure. They are the ego's fencing, guarding, parrying, feinting, moving with fine footwork, in the simultaneous effort to protect the personality's integrity and maintain its balance-in-movement. There is no defensive maneuver which the well-adapted person has not used at one time or other as a means to regain balance and ready himself to make some shift or change. Rationalizations, denials, projections, reaction formations, overcompensation—these and many others are used by every one of us in any day's living as momentary stays for protection against inner or outer assaults upon us.

The adaptable person may have a whole variety and range of defenses ready to give him temporary balance. When they are transitory, when they give way in the face of indications that there is nothing too fearsome about the problem to be faced, they may be said to be "good"—that is, useful to the integrity of the personality.

There are persons, however, in whom the ego protection systems have become so rigid, persistent, and chronic that, like walls, they constrict the ego's boundaries and bar its adaptive maneuvers. They distort the person's perceptive powers and thus may result in behavior which is inappropriate to the reality. These unyielding, intrenched defenses occur in persons who have been subjected to attacks or deprivations of an emotional and psychological nature which, corrosive or traumatic, have left them feeling helpless and hopeless. Defense becomes their way of life and their chief mode of keeping themselves held together. The energy that potentially was for the ego's use in change, movement, and adaption becomes channeled into maintaining a protective system. Like Don Quixote, such persons see every windmill as a fearsome giant, and they must fight or flee it. The kinds of defenses they use are the same as those used by all other people. The difference lies in the inappropriateness of their use and in the degree of their persistence and pervasiveness. When the ego's chief resource seems to be protection, when in the face of evidence that there is nothing to fear, its protective devices remain rigid and repetitive, then we may suspect that there has taken place some atrophy of ego functioning and that defense against disintegration has become this personality's chief task.

If the ego's protective defenses may be thought of as its temporary or fixed avoidance of an encountered problem, its positive, adaptive operations may be considered the efforts to absorb the meaning of the problem, to grapple with it, and to make or undergo the changes involved in coping with it. Adaptation is that fine co-ordination of motives and capacities which enables a person to make some tolerable compromise between what he wants and what is realistically possible and to maintain his sense of wholeness and balance at the same time as he makes changes in himself or in his situation. It involves many powers that as yet are more readily identified than understood—perhaps because the phenomena of man's healthy resourcefulness and resiliance have only begun to be studied. These powers include the person's basic sense of adequacy and purpose; the pliability of his defenses; the span of his perceptions and skills; his tolerance of tension; and his ability to discriminate and to make connections, to judge and to choose among alternatives.

The test of adaptation, of course, is the person's ability to take some action, inner or overt, that is directed and appropriate toward resolving the problem he faces or toward achieving the desired goal. Adaptive resources, thus, are expressed in the ego's taking some action, inner or overt, that results in the satisfactory accommodation or modification of the relation between the person and his problem. As this occurs, integration takes place, or, it may be said, the ego digests and uses for its further growth its experience of mastering a problem.

Thus in oversimplified terms it may be said that the ego is the personality's problem-solving apparatus. The strong ego is the result of the person's progressive experience of being more successful than unsuccessful in the mastery of everyday tasks from early childhood on. The ego may be considered "strong" when it is not sealed off from the id or superego but can admit, tolerate, and control their demands; when it has developed, adequate to its owner's age level, a range and combination of operations by which it can differentially respond to differing situations; and when it can protect itself adroitly as it works out its operating arrangements between inner demands and the demands of reality. The ego may be considered "weak" either when it is defenseless—when it has no way of holding off or containing tensions and is empty of adaptive competences—or when it is so rigidly protective as to be unable to see out from its walls (its perception function diminished), unable to exercise its communicative and governing powers (its adaptive means constricted), and unable to find means of behavior that are satisfying both subjectively and objectively (its executive powers enfeebled or distorted).

The necessity for the caseworker to understand the structure and functions of the personality is apparent. His client's behavior, like that of every other human being, is propelled and shaped by them. It is only as the caseworker grasps what his client is driven by, toward, or from, as he understands what inhibits or releases his energies, and as he can appraise the fixed or flexible qualities of his client's protective and adaptive powers that his helpfulness will be characterized by skill as well as good intent. Even in so mundane a decision as whether or not to go to a clinic or whether or not to keep the next appointment with the caseworker, the client's id, superego, and ego are in operation. And, were the caseworker to be involved in helping the client to make such a decision, he would need to use his knowledge of how to facilitate an ego's perceptions, how to lower defenses or to sustain them, and how to exercise his client's adaptive capacities of thinking, judging, and choosing, which lead to action.

*The structure and functioning of personality are the products of inherited and constitutional equipment in continuous interaction with the physical, psychological, and social environment the person experiences.*

On the issue of whether nature or nurture is more potent in the formation of the human being, there is general agreement today that both what the person is equipped with at birth and what he experiences from that moment combine to create his individuality. Moreover, it is assumed that these two factors do not simply exist together but that the person's biological being will affect strongly what he experiences and how he registers that experience and, conversely, that certain experiences will affect his biologically determined makeup. (How much weight may be ascribed to the influence of psychic, social, or physical factors in the molding of the personality no one yet knows.) At every age and in every phase of living the personality is being shaped and infused by social relationships and, in turn, is affecting them. The circles of our society widen about us, from the primary unit of baby and mother to the family group, to the neighborhood, to school with its teachers and children, to groups of peers, to groups of employers and fellow workers, to religious, civic, and recreational interest groups, to love relationships, and to the formation of a new primary unit in marriage and parenthood. Within the continuous give and take of all these relationships the endowments we bring into the world are nourished or starved, developed or dwarfed. Our ideas of what we need and want, our standards of behavior and our valuations of status, achievement, and even security, our sense of psychological well-being or imbalance—all these are fashioned by what we absorb from interaction with the attitudes and ideas of the people with whom we grow and live. Moreover, the channels and opportunities through which our physical and psychological selves can be both enhanced and expressed lie in our environment. And the environment, it must be remembered, is no "state of affairs"; it consists of the continuous interactions of people, of circumstances and conditions, of ideas, of institutions. To human beings it is always personal in import. Even to the impersonality of weather we react in psychological, not only physical, ways; and in ancient days, when man's social environment was relatively simple, he cast his physical environment into social-personal terms and made gods of the physical forces which shaped his life.

The importance in casework of conceiving of the individual as the product of the particular reciprocations of nature and nurture that have taken place in him is several fold. It leads, first, to that understanding acceptance of people which is basic to a casework relationship. It accounts for the particular behavior, constrained or relaxed, effective or inadequate, appropriate or unrealistic, which his client brings into his transactions with the caseworker. But, more than this, it alerts the caseworker to the recognition that his client brings with him not just his problem and his person into the interview but also a host of unseen and vital people and circumstances. Except as the caseworker comes to know, in relation to the client's current problem, what these are and how they act upon the client, he cannot know whether and to what extent they may be dealt with, how their bad effects may be vitiated or their good effects enhanced (see Pollak, *12*). And this leads to a corollary idea of considerable import in casework.

*A person at any stage of his life not only is "a product" of nature and nurture but is also and always "in process" of being in the present and becoming in the future.*

It is true that as we come to adulthood we are less plastic, less fluid, in our responsive and learning capacities than we were as children. Certain ways of responding, because they seem to have served us well, become habitual, "built in" to our personalities. By adulthood we tend to have characteristic responses to life-experiences, to react in ways that may be said to be typical for us. Yet within those gross patterns the possibility for growth or change remains as long as we live. (Change may be regression or deterioration, or it may be progress and betterment; growth is assumed, here, to mean the consolidation of constructive, desirable changes.)

This is not just a matter of faith. ᵀt is something we know by observing everyday people in everyday life about us (including ourselves): we are well or sick, vital or weary, happy or sad, not only because of what we were yesterday but also because of what we experience today. Today, as in all our yesterdays, we are trying to maintain our equilibrium at the same time as we are trying to cope with present problems or to pursue future goals. As what we experience today engages our emotions as well as our minds and bodies, it causes some change to take place in the nature or manner of our response. It may fortify old patterns of reaction, or it may cause some reorganizations of our typical responses; sometimes it may call forth feelings or behavior so different from the usual response as to seem quite new. Within the boundaries of the total personality which past experience has determined, change or growth continues to take place in response to current living experience. At the same time that the individual is "being" a product of his past, he is "becoming" a product of his present. The old saw recognizes this continuum in life and time when it says, "Today is tomorrow's yesterday."

The significance of this concept for the caseworker is this: It says that what happens to the individual today may be as vital to him as what happened yesterday. It says that those physical, social, and interpersonal situations he encounters in his operations today as worker, parent, spouse, student, or client will have an impact upon him and will be responded to in ways that will affect his development either morbidly or benignly. This means that the social caseworker must know the actualities of the client's current living situation, the realities by which he is being molded or battered today. The caseworker will need to consider the changes necessary in those realities so that the trauma and thwartings in today's living do not intrench old problems or create new emotional maladjustments in the client and to discover those resources in the client's environment which may enrich his living.

Moreover, our awareness of the impact upon a person's total personality of today's emotionally charged experience immediately sharpens our understanding of the potentials for helping or hurting people which lie within the casework interview itself and the client's experience with the agency. The client's communications with the caseworker and his experience with the agency may become potent factors in modifying or reorganizing his ways of feeling and acting so that his "being" becomes different from what it was before he entered the agency's door. Indeed, the value of the casework relationship and services may well be questioned if the current living experience of an individual is not understood as having potentially as vital an impact upon him as many experiences of his past.

Conditioned by his past and affected by his present, a person is also strongly affected by his future. All of us know this to be true of ourselves. What we can do today, how we feel, what we think, is determined not alone by our backgrounds or by current circumstance but also by what we are aiming for, what we are hoping for, what we are aspiring to have or do or be. It becomes possible to bear famine today if there is promise of a feast tomorrow; to live with pain if we know that surcease is ahead of us; to work slavishly if it will yield reward; to deny ourselves, postpone satisfactions, and make sacrifices if we have reason to hope for some gratification or achievement. Our drives and efforts, in short, are strongly shaped and directed by what we wish to become or to get in the personal future we conceive. This future may be a very near one—"this evening"—or it may be a remote one—"when I finish school" but it is a conception that is always potent in governing our feelings and actions. Hope sustains us in any unhappy present while we look forward to some betterment, and aspiration stretches us, so to speak; it keeps us reaching for some image or idea of ourselves or our situation. Thus our present is shaped by the struggle to achieve or maintain that future image.

As tiny children we begin this shaping of our present by our ideas of future rewards. The toddler who shakes his own head against his impulse to pick up an ashtray is already giving up a present pleasure in anticipation that his future, the next minute, will bring him the reward of his mother's approval. Even very old people maintain this "future orientation." Their day's aches and pains or the boredom of inactivity are mitigated somewhat by the hope that this medicine, that change of weather, or this change of scene will help, or they are sustained by the aspirations they have for their children and grandchildren which, if achieved, will accrue to their gratification.

Some people, it is true, at any age have lost both hope and aspiration. Usually this has occurred because of one of these circumstances: their current life-situations have repeatedly been so demanding of their total life-energies that they have had no chance to lift their eyes from their struggle to maintain survival, or throughout their past experience they have found no assurance that there was any use for them to postpone momentary pleasures or any reason to hope that tomorrow would bring anything different from what they are or have today. Of course, every mature person has moments of loss of "future orientation," caused by total involvement in some present crisis (as in a sudden bereavement, when the goal pursuits of a whole family may be set aside), by the irresistible pull of some momentary temptation, or by some devastating events which deplete energy and hope. But every person who is not basically infantile or chronically resigned tends after a time to look forward again, to take some measure of what further he wants. Thus the way the child or the man deports himself and relates himself to other people or things is the result not alone of what he has *been* or what he *is* but also of what he conceives of himself or his situation as *becoming*.

The significance to caseworkers of this concept is this: To know whether a person can be helped and to know how he can be helped, it is necessary to know what he wants for himself in the future, what his aspirations or conceptions of "becoming" are. None of us will give up any form of behavior which gives us momentary satisfactions unless there can be kindled in us some flicker of a wish to be different or to have things different from what they are. It goes without saying that this wish must be tied to some real possibility in order to be sustained. But the conception of a better tomorrow and the wish to have it are basic to any mobilization of our efforts to change. The caseworker therefore must relate himself and his client not only to considerations of past and present difficulties but also to those forces of hopefulness, of aspiration, and of self-image which keep the person struggling, reaching, stretching himself. The caseworker needs to know from the client what he would wish to be or do if he could, what he would hope for, and what his idea is of how he would like things to be. As he speaks of these, the client knows himself better and can catch some glimpse of how he can move forward to achieve his ideas of having or becoming.

*The person's "being and becoming" behavior is both shaped and judged by the expectations he and his culture have invested in the status and the major social roles he carries.*

Every person occupies some position in a social category of status and role. His status at any time is that combination of his sex, age, economic class, and so on, and certain expectations of responsibilities and privileges accrue to it. His social role consists of the major function he carries at a given time with its broadly designated behaviors, responsibilities, and rewards.*

---

\* For a more exact definition of role and status see Linton (*11*) and Parsons (9).

The roles we carry tend to multiply as our relationship with people and community life becomes more complex, but among them there are always a few which are of primary significance. These significant roles our culture (or subgroups in the culture) invests with general ideas of what a person is supposed to put into his role and what he has a right to expect out of it. He is considered to be carrying his role appropriately or poorly as he conforms to or deviates from the expectations of him, and he considers himself rewarded or cheated as the persons and circumstances in interaction with him in a given role meet *his* expectations. Thus a man in the role of father is supposed to feel an act in certain ways toward his children, a woman in the role of wife to behave in certain ways toward her husband, and a child in the role of student to operate in certain ways toward his teachers and schoolwork. In return the father expects that his children will react to him in the ways children "are supposed" to act toward a father, the woman will anticipate certain reciprocal behaviors from the husband, whose role is in interaction with hers, and so on.

Except as a person is disoriented by emotional disorder or mental incapacity, everyone brought up within a given society comes to know what the general requirements of his status and role are supposed to be. This is part of the external reality that the healthy ego perceives and takes in, that it shares with the superego, and that it works upon in order to adapt impulses to standards. All of us try to "live up to" some concept of ourselves in one or more vital social roles. Failures may result in feelings of shame and inadequacy; success, in feelings of gratification and effectiveness. Either may be felt by the person internally as he judges himself, but he will also be judged by others whose reactions to his social operations will have their impact upon his sense of identity and worth.

Any one of us may experience, at one time or another, some conflict in carrying out our social roles. In a complex society such as ours the individual needs agile and free-wheeling adaptability to make the numerous role shifts required of him even in the course of one day. A man may be a father, a son, a husband, an employee, a club member, and a client of the caseworker all in the space of a few hours, and in each of these roles he must subordinate certain feelings and behaviors and bring others into dominance. In some instances conflict within the person may be caused by his recognition of what his role calls for and his emotional inability to meet it. ("I know my child is supposed to have love and affection," says an unhappy mother, "but I've never been able to be demonstrative.") In another instance a cause of conflict between two persons or between a person and society may be the refusal or inability to conform to the expectations inherent in status and role. ("He forgets," says the indignant wife, "that he is my husband, not my boss.") Still another conflict may arise between the person's internal strivings and his effective carrying-out of his role when he has not had adequate opportunity to learn the role or when peculiar conditions have constricted such learning. An example of the former is the migrant who moves from one culture to another; an example of the latter is the adolescent who is reared in an institution and is only partially prepared to emerge into self-dependent living. Perhaps one of the most familiar examples of difficulty created by the combination of shifting roles and of insufficient knowledge by which adequately to carry one of them may be seen in the beginner in social casework practice. In one hour he is a student and in the next hour a mentor, and, as mentor, he feels understandably uncertain and awkward with the heavy obligations and authorities vested in his role. Conflict in being and doing what one is supposed to be or do in any given role may, then, be the symptom of conflict between inner motivations and self-judgment or between inner motivations and social judgments, or may grow out of a lack of knowledge as to performance requirements.

At the same time as a man's social roles may present hardships they are, it must be recognized, the forms in which he finds self-expression as a social being. As such they are both the test and the rewards of growth. When a person's feelings and ideal of himself are compatible with each other and with the social reality, and when he is clear about permissions and obligations, his role is a source of gratification and of expansion of his personality. When he feels adequate or happy in the performance of one of his major roles (e.g., husband, mother, professional person), he has some sense of mastery, and it becomes possible for him to bear or struggle with frustrations in other aspects of his living. When he has some diversity of social outlets in peripheral roles (the man who feels small and insecure at work but gains stature as he enters the union hall, the child who has few companions but is teacher's helper after school, the woman who is a bed-ridden invalid but is recognized for her handiwork), a person has a chance to gain small gratifications which may yield some compensation for his larger frustrations, and these lesser but satisfying roles serve to buoy up his sense of self-worth and self-expression.

The relation of the concept of social role to social casework practice may readily be seen. The person who is a client comes to the caseworker at a time of maladjustment in one of his vital social roles. This is what his problem usually is: he is unable to carry one or more of his life-tasks with balance and gratification, either because he brings to it an inappropriate pattern of functioning which results in disturbance or ineffectiveness or because social circumstance thwarts or undermines his functioning. Thus the caseworker must understand his client in relation to those social operations in which he is encountering problems. To help him, the caseworker must himself be clear as to what, realistically, the role's requirements are, its firm requisites, and the range of variations permissible within it. Then, within this objective frame of reference, the individual client's behaviors must be viewed and assessed as to the nature of the maladaptation—whether it stems from conflict between what he wants and what he can be or between what he wants and what he must be, from some unrealistic interpretation of what his role embraces, from some lack of preparation to engage in the necessary behaviors, or from the loss of external supports.* Furthermore, it is as the caseworker takes full measure of his client in his roles *other* that that of client (for this role, too, has its special attributes) that he will be better able to see the potentials in this person and in his milieu for gratifications in social functioning.

*The person who comes as client to a social agency is always under stress.*

Whatever the nature of his problem—whether it is due to failures or pressures in his environment, to warfare within him, to frustrations in carrying some valued social role, to obstacles which have

---

* A helpful framework within which to think about all this is to be found in Cottrell (5), Clyde Kluckhohn *et al.* (9), Florence Kluckhohn (10), and Linton (11).

intruded themselves between his drives and his goals—the client is under stress. The client's stress is twofold: the problem itself is *felt* by him (not merely recognized) as a threat or an actual attack, and his inability to cope with it increases his tension.

Therefore, the caseworker who knows that his client inevitably feels threatened or off-balance also knows that his defensive-protective operations will be in full play. At the same time his effort to obtain agency help may be seen as an adaptive move. The greater the client's sense of duress and tension, the more overwhelmed and helpless he may feel. The problem-solving functions of his ego are likely to be at least temporarily disabled or constricted. Furthermore, as the caseworker understands the network of intercommunication within the physio-psycho-social structure of man, he will remember that stress in any one aspect of functioning will affect other aspects and likewise that relief from stress in one aspect of living may lighten the burden in another. His aim from the first, then, will be to make it less necessary for his client to protect himself (both against his problem and against the fears of agency or of change) and more possible for him to resume or reinforce his efforts to cope with his problem.

The ways in which the caseworker may serve both in the client's protection and toward his adaptation and balance will be discussed in later chapters. But first the nature of the client's problem needs to be examined.

# 3 *THE PROBLEM*

There is probably no problem in human living that has not been brought to social workers in social agencies. Problems of hunger for food and of hunger for love, of seeking shelter and of wanting to run away, of getting married and of staying married, of wanting a child and of wanting to get rid of a child, of needing money and of wasting money, of not wanting to live and of not wanting to die, of making enemies and of needing friends, of wanting and of not wanting medication, of loving and of being unloved, of hating and of being hated, of being unable to get a job and of being unable to hold a job, of feeling afraid, of feeling useless—all these, and the many other problems of physical and emotional survival as a human being, come to the door of the social agency.

The prospect of relating to and attempting to help with such varieties of problems would be bewildering, indeed, were there not some ways by which human problems could be made amenable to systematic thought. Basic to understanding human problems, of course, are the growing funds of knowledge about human beings and their society. It is knowledge, to be sure, that, no sooner grasped, leaps forward again to excite new pursuit, and this is both the gratification and the frustration of trying to work on problems-in-change. Indeed, this is one of the reasons why specializations have arisen both across and within professional fields and why many social agencies are set up to deal only with certain kinds of problems, so that, by carving out particular categories of human difficulty, it may become possible to study them more fully and work with them more effectively. But, even within a given agency and within specific categories of problems, it is helpful to recognize that there are certain characteristic ways in which human problems may be viewed by the caseworker. They are these:

*The problems within the purview of social casework are those which vitally affect or are affected by a person's social functioning.*

The problem may be one of some unmet need—economic, medical, educational, recreational—which hampers or undermines a person's adequate living. Or it may be one of stress—psychological, social, physical—which causes the person to be ineffective or disturbed in carrying his social roles. Whether such needs and stress occur singly or in combination, it is the person's inability to muster the means by which to maintain or achieve social comfort and adequacy which brings the problem within the locus of casework's concern.

This focus upon the problems a person is encountering in his social secureness and his functioning adequacy is one distinguishing mark of social casework. It implies that the primary focus of the social caseworker's help is upon the difficulties the person is having in behaving in socially accepted or constructive ways or upon the assaults he is experiencing from circumstances impinging on him. The client of the caseworker typically sees his problems as lying in some interacting relationship between himself and some other person or persons or between himself and his circumstances. The help he seeks, typically, is for some readjustment of the self he is in relation to the demands and expectations of the social role he carries— as spouse, parent, student, worker—or he wants help in the readjustment of some parts of his social situation so that he can maintain or achieve the equilibrium necessary to his daily pursuits. When, as is sometimes the case, the client finds that his inner problems exert such power over his problems of social functioning that they are not susceptible to his management, he may need to be considered a patient whose first need is for psychotherapy. Then referral to psychiatric or psychiatrically supervised help may be in order. (Conversely, the psychiatrist may turn to social casework services when he deems his patient to be psychologically ready to place his social re-adjustment in the center of his attention and to engage himself dif-ferently in his person-to-person, person-to-situation relationships.)

The importance of the caseworker's orientation to the client's problem as lying in his inability to function satisfactorily in one or more of his major roles or in his inability to meet the deprivations and assaults of his life-circumstances is that it helps the caseworker chart his focus, his work plan, and his goals. It means that he will constantly keep before him the need to enable his client to cope with the frustrations and gain the potential gratifications in his day-by-day living. And, since this living takes place in dynamic interac-tion with other persons, social circumstances, culturally determined expectations and permissions, the caseworker will take full measure of these forces in each case in order to know how they need to be influenced and utilized in the interest of the client's best social adaptation.

*The multifaceted and dynamic nature of the client's problem makes necessary the selection by caseworker and client of some part of it as the unit for work.*

It is quite possible to understand the nature of a problem in the whole, but it is rarely possible to work on it in the whole. In case-work, as in any other problem-solving activity, the overt action must be partial, focused, and sequential even though the mental compre-hension and plan may be total. In part this is because perception is contained within the individual, but adaptation and overt action involve conditions and forces outside the individual which compli-cate those tasks and in themselves pose problems. Therefore, faced with having to do something with his client about a problem, the caseworker must ask and answer the question as to what part of the problem should be placed in the center of attention—what comes first, what is of primary importance, what is most accessible to modification.

Three main considerations enter into the choice-of-problem focus: what the client wants and needs; what the caseworker's professional judgments points to as possible and desirable solutions; and what the agency is for and can offer. Each of these merits discussion.

1. The problem is the client's problem, and his impetus is to get help with it as he sees and feels it. He may see it with perfect ac-

curacy, and he may see its solution possibilities clearly too. He may
see it with clarity as one of a constellation of intimately related
problems or as the end result of certain underlying problems, but
he may be unready or unable to face up to it fully enough to want
help with anything more than the resulting problem he presents.
On the other hand, he may not see the problem correctly at all; that
is, he may bring for help a situation which is really tangential or is
of secondary importance. This may happen when the real problem is
too frightening to face or when the person is beset by so many difficulties at one time that, like a trapped creature, he seeks all and any
exits. The problem as the client sees it, then, may truly be the central problem, or it may be a peripheral one on which he has centered
his concern. Whichever it is, common sense tells us that, since we
can help with a problem only through the person who has it, we
must, at least at first, start with the troubled person's center of
concern, with what he feels is crucial. Sometimes the caseworker is
so clear in his own mind that the problem the client presents is not
the "real" one, or he is so eager to establish his own speculations
about the problem's sources, that he starts to focus upon the areas
of his, rather than the client's, interests. When this happens, he may
find that he has gained full comprehension of the problem but has
lost the person whose problem it is.

This first center of concern is not necessarily the basic problem;
it is, rather, the one the client finds uppermost in his anxiety at a
given time, his problem of the moment. Sometimes the problems of
the moment may be found to be repetitious derivatives of other
problems, perhaps more basic ones. In such instances the caseworker
may need to help the client move to a more realistic perception of
the problem to be worked on and the solutions to be sought. This
help to perceive and focus differently rises out of the knowledge and
perspective the caseworker brings to bear upon each case. The caseworker must start with the client where he stands. Like all of us,
the client will more readily see another point of view or accept a
different interpretation if he is led to it rather than having it thrust
upon him.

2. The leadership given by the caseworker to help the client
select and center on one of his several problems or on some aspect
of one of them is based and dependent upon his professional knowl-

edge and judgment. From the moment the caseworker begins to relate to a specific client, he views him in the light of his understanding of and experience with personalities of this kind, with problems of this kind, with solutions or goals of this kind. Simultaneously, to be sure, he seeks to establish the uniqueness of this particular person in relation to his particular problem in relation to this particular form of help, but his judgments of specific qualities and his expectations of possible outcomes rise out of his profession's accumulated experience with this kind of person, problem, place, and process. This is what enables the caseworker to know better than the client not what problem seems most crucial or hurts most but what in general its significance is, what in general can or cannot be done about it. This is what justifies the caseworker's taking responsibility to help his client move from, let us say, the peripheral problem he has put forth to its more vital core or, at other times, to move from what is a "hard-core" problem to some outer aspect of it which in the caseworker's judgment seems more malleable; in either case, it is to give aid and direction to the client's focusing on his problem. Except as the caseworker helps to sort and select the problem to be worked on at a given time, the client may flounder endlessly among cause-effect intricacies or the multitude of instances in which the problem is reflected but not taken hold of.

A brief illustration may be seen in Mrs. Redd's problem. Her fifteen-month-old baby was hospitalized in a diabetic coma, and when Mrs. Redd presented herself to the medical social worker several weeks later, referred by the child's physician, she was depressed and in a panic. She was having a recurrence of old and fearful symptoms of emotional disorder—sleeplessness, weight loss, neurodermatitis. She felt she could not face the prospect of endless years of a diabetic regimen. Her focus was upon her need for help as a nervous, upset woman. The caseworker, however, helped her to shift this focus to herself as a sick baby's mother who could get help in learning the first steps in diabetic management.

The caseworker managed this gentle but firm shift of focus in ways that need not be delineated here; the basis of this shift was the caseworker's general knowledge and preliminary appraisal of the situation. We may assume he saw the situation something like this: The *basic problem* in Mrs. Redd is possibly a neurotic character disorder. This is not amenable to change by the casework process, nor can any therapy notably affect it in less than years. The *causal problem* probably lies in Mrs. Redd's old and current parental relationships. These cannot be undone. The *precipitating problem* is the baby's illness and all the normal and neurotic fears it excites. This is a reality with which the mother will have to cope. The *pressing problem* is the child's imminent release from the hospital to a helpless mother. The *problem-to-be-solved* is this mother's insecurity in relation to her immediate handling of her sick child. This, then, is the first focus into which the problem is cast. Guiding the caseworker's thinking was general knowledge about personality dynamics and expectations, about the ways current problems excite old ones, and, on the other hand, how the resolution of today's difficulties may cause old ones to subside, how equanimity is more readily achieved when the problem to be solved is seen, not as total, but small piece by small piece, and so on.

One further factor determined this caseworker's focus, and that was the agency's function. The medical social work department of a hospital has as its purpose the helping of patients (or relatives) to deal with such social and emotional problems as interfere with medical treatment. This is its caseworker's directive.

3. Each social agency or each social work section of another type of welfare agency (such as a hospital) is set up to meet certain kinds of human problems and needs. Not only does an agency declare its special area of service in its name ("child guidance clinic," "family service agency," "public assistance department," and so on) but in its interpretations of itself it makes its purposes explicit. Sometimes these purposes are quite specific and limited, such as those of a child placement agency that gives its help in relation to children who must leave their own homes. Sometimes the purposes are more general, such as those of a family and child welfare agency where almost any problem which arises in family life might be considered for service. Whether or not any agency is able to function in line with its avowed purposes depends upon whether it has the means, the services and resources, including skilled staff, by which to translate intent into action.

A clear conception on the caseworker's part of what his agency is for and is able to do serves immediately to help focus what is often a most ramified problem. It helps to say, in effect, "We will concentrate on this rather than that part of your problem, since it is this which we are equipped to understand and help with most efficiently. If, however, our inquiry makes clear that it is that rather than this part which is the immediate and vital part of your difficulty, then our help will be to bring you together with the resource which deals with that part."

If, for example, Mrs. Redd had proved so upset as to have been unable to relate herself to her baby's needs, referral to psychiatric help might have been necessary, with the focus shifted now to Mrs. Redd herself. Or, if Mrs. Redd had been able to mobilize herself to take the child home and meet the child's special physical needs with some competence and with gratification at the results and if, then, she had shifted her complaints to her conflict with her mother, the medical caseworker might well have considered whether or not a family agency would have been the more appropriate place for work on the newly emerging problem of intrafamily conflict. Had a referral to the family agency taken place, it would, hopefully, have followed on Mrs. Redd's recognition that her problem had shifted to another area of her living, on her wanting to be helped with it, and on her understanding, through discussion with the caseworker, of the special relevance of the family agency's services to her new problem-solving task.

*Problems in any part of a human being's living tend to have "chain reactions."*

To put it another way, any single problem that creates social or emotional maladjustment in an individual tends to arouse or highlight other problems in contingent aspects of living. This is because, while in the study of man he may be compartmentalized and analyzed as a biological or psychological or social entity, man lives as a dynamic interrelated whole, reacting to and upon the dynamic whole of his environment. Whatever hurts or skews one part of his living will have its impact and reverberations in other parts.

For example, both in technical and in popular books on marriage it is often emphasized that the capacity for good sexual relationship on the part of both the man and the woman will hold a marriage firm despite other hazards. Yet the fact is that a problem such as loss of income may arouse such tensions as to dull the sexual appetite, or the feeling in a man that he is a poor provider may so lower his self-esteem as to make him impotent, or the fear of a pregnancy which is economically unsupportable may raise barriers to the love relationship. From these maladjustments new problems may arise, such as the man's increased insecurity about finding a proper job or the woman's increased irritability with the demands of her children upon her. Every one of us can offer examples from everyday living of how "for want of a shoe a kingdom was lost" and of how the wants or fulfilments, the frustrations or gratifications, of yesterday affect our today and tomorrow.

This chain and fanning-out of cause and effect and cause would be a discouraging thing for the caseworker to face if it were not for two mitigating facts. One is that, just as a number of aspects of a person's life can be thrown askew by the maladjustment of one, so may a number of aspects right themselves by the adjustment of that one part; just as many parts of the somatic-psychosocial whole of living may be adversely affected by one problem, so may they be benignly affected by the resolution of that one problem and the restoration of balance.

For example, an adolescent girl who has carried her defiance of her parents into the schoolroom, provoking her teachers by brash comments and truancy, has promised her caseworker, whom she likes, that she will try to attend classes and behave herself in them—just this—although there are many other areas in which she needs to change. She goes to class regularly (supported and appreciated by the caseworker for her effort) and finds that the teacher has stopped picking on her (partly because she has stopped being provocative and partly because the teacher is co-operating with the caseworker). She grudgingly admits that some of the "stuff" in class is interesting. Her parents are delighted (holding their breath, meantime) that she is no longer truant and that they are no longer beleaguered by the school. Their tensions about the child lessen, she feels less "pushed" by them, and they voluntarily increase her allowance. She feels somewhat annoyed at this "bribe" but mostly gratified at their recognition of her responsibility. She shares her feelings with her caseworker and concludes that maybe her parents *do* have some feeling for her. She returns home in a tolerant frame of mind, decides maybe she will "give the teacher a surprise" by turning in her homework on time—and so forward, not without slipbacks to be sure, but with a benign chain reaction in the ascendancy.

Help by the social caseworker, then, in one aspect of the person's living, whether it be a one-time provision of money or a long-time provision of counseling, may serve to re-establish a person's whole sense of balance and adjustment.

*Any problem which a person encounters has both an objective and a subjective significance.*

However "ordinary" a problem might be, whatever its frequency of occurrence, however simple its solution may appear to the observer, it has particular, personal meaning to one who is involved in it. A problem may be *seen* and *understood* by an onlooker; it is always, in addition, *felt* by its carrier, and it is experienced with the particularity of individual difference. There are, to be sure, reactions common among all of us to certain kinds of difficulties, but the quality and intensity of our feelings and the ways in which we attempt to defend against or cope with them are different for each of us. Two aged men, both unable to work, both with no resources of their own, need money. This is a simple problem for which there is a ready solution in the form of old age assistance. Yet it may not feel simple at all to the two old men. One may feel depressed and humbled by the problem itself—that he is old, is found useless, is "dumped" by employers, and so on. He may be reluctant to apply for assistance, may feel "too proud" or unworthy, or even hopeful that the next day may bring a better solution. The second old man may, on the other hand, take the problem with equanimity; he accepts his aging and feels he has the right to be "given a hand," but his anger and anxiety are aroused by the solution proffered—he cannot see why he must prove residence in his state or how he is expected to manage on so little money.

The significance of this understanding—that problems have subjective as well as objective import—is that what any given person can or will do about his problem will be greatly affected by his feelings about it. Thus, the caseworker must elicit and often deal with such feelings so that they may implement rather than obstruct the client's work on his problem. At the same time the caseworker must remain firmly aware of the objective reality of problem and solution, for only so can he help his client see it straight and cope with it effectively.

*Not only do the external (objective) and internal (subjective) aspects of the problem co-exist, but either one may be the cause of the other.*

All of us encounter situations in our social living that, by our momentary or chronic inability to deal with them, create internal problems in us. We say we are "upset" by them, which is to say more technically that we are disequilibrated. Should this imbalance occur frequently or were we to feel under constant threat of upset, our characteristic reactions to and upon our social situations would be fashioned thereby. When circumstances or situations beset or attack an individual chronically and when, chronically, he is engaged in trying to get his footing only to find himself always in peril, the reactions those circumstances call forth tend to become crystallized and built into the personality. Thus a person might bring to every new situation the anticipation that it will go badly for him, and he may react pessimistically or anxiously or with hostility, even when nothing in the objective situation calls for such reactions. All "personality problems"—that is, problems of intrapsychic maladjustment—were once a spontaneous reaction to a problem which the person encountered outside himself.

For example, a little boy begins to know very early that he lives in a hard world. His world consists of a mother and father who are rough and harsh with him. He reacts spontaneously to protect himself. He may withdraw from the situation by trying to keep out of the way or by holding in the things he wants to say or do, or he may fight back in the few but effective ways that a child has—refusing food, bed-wetting, kicking the cat or the neighbor's children. If the situation continues to work upon him in the same way and he must cope repeatedly with it, his developing personality will be absorbing this situation along with his now chronic ways of feeling and reacting to it. He will be "internalizing" the problem. Now when he is ready to enter school, though the teacher may be a warm and gentle woman quite unlike his mother and though he may encounter no objective reason for withdrawal or fighting in the schoolroom, he will be likely to bring his established forms of reaction and behavior with him. He will excite hostility in other children and bewilderment or dislike in the teacher. Thus his internal problem, now a personality problem, will be the cause of a new situation; it will create certain circumstances of teacher and child reaction to him. Unless he is given help to reverse this vicious circle, this little boy will become an adult who constantly creates situations in which he is hurt or must fight, and his perception of the external world and his actions in it will be colored and patterned by his inner problems.

Things which happen to people cause or affect what happens in them, and, conversely, conditions which occur within people cause or affect their outgoing actions. The significance of this idea for the caseworker is several fold. First, it focuses the caseworker's attention upon the cause-effect interaction among the person's psychic, physical, and social experiences and leads to some ideas of where the problem ought first to be attacked; second, it lights up the fact that the casework process is in itself a "happening," an experience injected into the client's life which will have its emotional and social repercussions, good or bad. The very way a caseworker receives a person in need may make him feel worthy or unworthy, reassured or angered, and this surge of feeling in turn will cause his overt behavior to take certain forms. The services the caseworker has to proffer, those he may sometimes think of as commonplace ("just money," "only homemaker service"), may, for the person who lacks them and wants them, have intense emotional meaning; similarly, the relationship and counseling help the caseworker offers may infuse the client with fresh energy to tackle his social situation anew or give him another view of it or tolerance for it.

*Whatever the nature of the problem the person brings to the social agency, it is always accompanied, and often complicated, by the problem of being a client.*

Being a client entails asking for help, taking it, and using it. This sounds like a bald statement of the obvious. Yet it bears some analysis as to why a person's bringing of his problems to a social agency and his engaging himself in working on a solution are so often fraught with difficulty and discomfort and why the understanding of this is important.

Reactions to asking for personal help are as varied as people themselves, and they are heavily affected, too, by the attitudes in their social group as to the rightness or wrongness of certain needs. There was a time when, to ask for financial help, the individual had all but to prove himself a victim of some catastrophe or to admit to moral bankruptcy, and to ask for help with a problem of personal maladjustment was an admission that he was weak-willed or crazy. Within relatively few years, community attitudes about seeking personal help have undergone tremendous change. The concept of the individual's right to basic security, the popularization of psychiatry, and the open recognition of the pervasiveness of emotional disturbances (indeed, in some circles, the fashionable necessity to have one!) have tempered and changed attitudes about asking for many kinds of assistance. Yet, while "disgraceful" and "pitiful" are all but abandoned adjectives in our thinking about asking for help, there persist certain common emotional reactions to that request when it is made of a social agency.

For many people, to cross the threshold of a social agency is to walk into the unknown. A person may know an agency's general purpose, to be sure, but what that purpose will mean to him specifically, what will happen to him, what be required, and so on, are uncertain. Uncertainty inspires fear in all of us. Moreover—and this, too, is more characteristic of asking help from a social agency than from other professional resources—there is the disquieting internal question as to reciprocation. Adults in our culture are accustomed to returning some form of payment for what they get—whether in money, services, or friendship—and in a situation where none of these is required the question arises: What *is?* Gratitude? Obligations? Loss of rights? And complicating these unknowns may be particular anxieties, ranging from the fear that the request will not be granted to that peculiar fear that it may be granted but at too great a price.

When by the attitudes and words of the caseworker many of these problems of "asking" have been dispelled, there remains the problem of taking and using help. Every social agency has certain conditions under which help is given—conditions set by considerations of monetary and psychological economy and usefulness. The conditions themselves are not necessarily troubling; indeed, they are often comforting in their good sense and certainty. Yet they are set by other persons and are indications of their control. Further, the helping person, by virtue of his ability to be of assistance, is seen by the client as possessed of more powers than he. This is as he wants it. Yet to feel subject to the powers of another person is disquieting to adults, and in some it arouses periodic struggles of opposition, while in others it arouses yearnings to relinquish responsibility. All such feelings about taking help may create a number of problems in the ongoing work between client and caseworker. These feelings will be seen in resistance, covert or open, in expressions of hostility, in self-abnegation, or in unrealistic helplessness.

Social caseworkers have been more concerned than most other professionals about the problem of help-seeking and help-taking. Perhaps this is because they are committed to the proposition that a man must be sustained in his sense of security and self-worth if he is to maintain or assume his appropriate responsibilities. Experience has made them aware that a person's feelings and conceptions of himself in relation to a source of vital help affect how he sees and uses that help and, further, that the way help is proffered and interpreted and demonstrated will free or trap the person's energies and abilities to work on his problem. Caseworkers therefore keep attuned to and attempt to deal with those reactions in the client which are induced by and complicate the solving of the problem brought for help.

The problem brought by the person to the agency, then, is likely to be complex, ramified, and changing even as it is held to analysis. It may be given some boundary when the caseworker views it as a problem of the client's needs and strivings as a social being, related, in turn, to culturally determined ideas of the individual's social needs, privileges, and effective functioning. It becomes more manageable to him who bears it and to his helper when some part of it is carved out for a working center at a given time. Because a person is always in action upon and responding to his problem, there are both subjective and objective factors which the caseworker must take account of, along with the recognition that these factors may in themselves become causal. Casework help in problem-solving provides, among other things, an intervention which breaks or modifies the cause-effect chain of difficulties. Since this intervention may in itself prove problematic to the client, the social caseworker must seek to understand his means and processes as astutely as is possible so that he may facilitate rather than complicate the client's problem-solving efforts.

# 4 THE PLACE

The place to which the person comes for help with his problem is known as a social agency. When such an agency gives services of material aid, situational change, counseling, and psychological help, or any combination of these on an individualized case-by-case basis, it takes its designation from its working method: it is called a social casework agency.

Social casework agencies differ one from the other in a number of ways, but there are three major factors that determine their classification: their source of support, their source of professional authority, and their special function and area of concern. Every single agency combines these factors in its makeup, and their particular combination will affect the focus, range, and conditions of the agency's services and its casework help.

Agencies are supported either by public taxation or by voluntary contribution. Tax-supported agencies, called "public" agencies, include not only the great income-maintenance programs such as Aid to Dependent Children, but also child welfare, correction, and physical and mental health programs. The so-called private agencies, private only in the sense that they are maintained through the voluntary contributions of individuals or groups, provide services of these same kinds. Both public and private agencies may use casework as the method by which their services are conveyed to the people who come to them. But their policies and procedures, and the range and flexibility of their programs and methods, will be affected in many ways by their sources of support. The legal framework within which a tax-supported agency operates, the rights and requirements which govern the giving and taking of its services, the open or subtle climate of political temper and citizen opinion to which it must be sensitive, the equality of opportunity that it is charged to offer to every eligible applicant—all these factors will bear upon the extent and limits of its help. So too for the voluntary agency—the sanctions of its supporting group, its charter, its discretionary rights, its applicant population, and so on, all bind or release, shape and color, the kinds of service it gives to whom and under what conditions.

A second factor that classifies casework agencies, whether public or private, is the source of professional authority. Some agencies carry primary and full authority and responsibility for their social welfare functions; others, because they are part of another human welfare organization, derive their authority and responsibility from the host agency. The former may be called "primary," the latter "secondary," social agencies.*

In the primary agency (typically family and child welfare agencies) the program and resources available may be varied, ranging from those designed to cope with social maladjustments caused by physical and economic breakdowns to those caused by personality disorders. Such agencies are manned by social workers, the identification of all the staff is with the social welfare purposes of the agency, and the basic method of giving help is by the casework process. When other professional persons are drawn into the pri-

* These terms were originally settled upon (with some dissatisfaction for want of better ones) by the casework faculty of the University of Chicago's School of Social Service Administration in our work of developing a course on the relation of agency settings to casework treatment (see Perlman, 7). Using "primary," we had no intention of designating importance; we meant, rather, that the agency was primarily set up to provide social aids, material or psychological, to human well-being. By "secondary" we implied no value judgment either but only that the social services conveyed were auxiliary to the host agency's foremost function. Sometimes, to be sure, as in many psychiatric clinics, social caseworkers outnumber the psychiatrists and actually carry much more of the case load than does the primary profession. Yet in the psychiatric setting the basic authority and responsibility are vested in the medical profession.

mary social agency, whether on a temporary or permanent basis, their services and skills are auxiliary or supplementary to those carried by the social workers; they operate as aids to the social workers, who carry the responsibilities which are primarily vested in their profession and agency.

Other kinds of welfare organizations—hospitals, schools, clinics, courts, nurseries—frequently incorporate a social casework agency or agent; that is, they may have a social work department or a single social caseworker as part of their structure and function. In such settings social work is in an auxiliary position. The use of social casework by these organizations came about through the recognition of two facts. First, while a person's manifest problem may be one appropriately brought to the non-social work agency, as sickness is brought to the doctor or as truancy is brought to the school principal, the problem may be caused or affected by social or psychological circumstances which call for the particular knowledge and resources of the social worker. Second, people are often unable to make use of the services that are available to them. Thus, the school child who is exposed to teaching but cannot learn; the hospital patient for whom bed rest has been prescribed but whose home does not permit this luxury; the mother who is suspicious of the clinic psychiatrist in relation to her child—all these call for a function which will implement that for which the organization is set up. This implementing function has long been social casework's. As part of a host organization, then, a social casework department or a representative of social work operates to provide enabling and auxiliary services to some allied but different service. It may be seen that what the social caseworker will do—the range, focus, and emphasis of his operations, the conditions which may limit or enhance his services, and the authority and responsibilities he carries—will be affected by whether his agency is primary or secondary as well as by whether it is supported by public or private funds.

The third characterizing feature of the social casework agency is the nature of its particular function. Primary agencies, both public and private, may define certain areas of social need as the particular field in which they give service and in which they develop expertness of knowledge and special problem-solving resources. There are, for example, many multipurpose child welfare agencies, but there are also many agencies specializing only in certain aspects of child welfare—the child adoption agency, the foster-home placement agency, the children's institution, the child guidance clinic. The reasons for specialization of function in social casework agencies are the same as those which underlie specialization in other professions—chiefly, the magnitude and complexities of modern social organization and the growing breadth and depth both of knowledge and of awareness of the yet-to-be-known problems. As it becomes impossible for any one human being to know all there is to know about meeting personal and social needs, so it becomes impossible for any one agency to contain in its program and give in its service all the kinds of welfare aid. Agencies therefore may develop to meet and to advance knowledge about particular kinds of problems, and the personnel of such agencies develops particular experience and expertness in understanding and dealing with these problems. Specialization in social casework also occurs because in the secondary setting casework help is related to the work of some other profession, such as medicine, education, or law, and to its specific knowledge and purpose. Whether the agency is highly specialized or is multifunctional, however, the agency function—what it is for, what it is set up to promote or prevent—will determine the caseworker's focus and emphasis, the services he has to offer, and the goals toward which he works (see Gomberg, 3).

These three factors, then—the source of support, the professional authority, and the particular function—are the determinants of major differences among casework agencies in regard to the clientele they serve, the services they offer, the goals they set, and the conditions and directions of their helping process. Yet, despite their differences, there are certain generic ways of thinking about all social casework agencies which may help the caseworker to know his agency more surely and to use it more effectively in the service of his clients.

*The social agency is an organization fashioned to express the will of a society or of some group in that society as to social welfare.*

An agency embodies a society's decision to protect its members against social breakdowns, to prevent their maladjustments, and/or to promote the development of better or higher levels of human functioning (see Towle, 10). To these ends, interest and financial support are mobilized to provide service and opportunity in organized form. To protect from, to prevent, and to promote conditions or happenings implies that the supporting community has assigned values to them and that certain social states or operations are held to be undesirable and others to be good. The social agency, then, stands for what its supporting community holds to be desirable for its whole membership. It is one means by which to maintain or achieve social standards and values.

This has importance both for the client and for the caseworker. Whether the client conceives of the agency as "we" or, as is more often the case, as "they," he sees it as the expression of society's intent toward him and others like him. From the very physical setup he encounters on entering the agency's application room he will draw some sense of whether his society has respect for the likes of him or not. The attitudes he encounters, from switchboard operator to caseworker, will convey to him whether he is considered as "in" or as "out" of the community the agency represents, and his feelings will be affected thereby. If the agency's help is meager or hedged about with restrictions, he will be inclined to feel pitted against society or that portion of it which supports this kind of succor and to separate himself from identification with it and its alleged purposes. If, on the other hand, the agency's help is of such quality as to accredit his human dignity and worth at the same time as it accepts his human frailty, he will be inclined to feel at one with a society which values him and demonstrates its helpful intent.

When the caseworker enters the employment of a social agency, he contracts to carry out the purposes for which the agency is set up and undertakes to further its social intents and values. He must remain aware that the agency "belongs" not only to its staff and board members but to the community which actively or tacitly supports and furthers its existence. He must remember, however, that the agency hires him for his professional competence, and part of this competence is judging the efficacy or inadequacy with which the agency actually meets its avowed social purposes. What is implicit, then, is that, at the same time that the caseworker carries to each of his clients the community's concern to sustain him in the ways embodied in the agency's function and services, he also brings to his agency his professional concerns that society (and the partial function of it which his agency performs) be conducive to the individual social welfare.

*Each social agency develops a program by which to meet the particular areas of need with which it sets out to deal.*

The agency program consists of the aids and activities by which intent is translated into provisions of help. The ways and means which an agency program provides will convey its function effectively or not, depending on a number of factors: money; the knowledge and competence of the agency staff; the interest, resources, and support of the community; the consistency between ascertained needs and the proffered means; and so on (see Lowry, 6).

For want of one or more of these means an agency's program may not fully sustain its purpose. It is not uncommon for an agency to have a stated purpose that is more future aim than present reality, because it has not yet developed the adequate means by which to achieve its ends. For example, the purpose of a public assistance agency is family welfare, but if there is a shortage of money and staff, if case loads are too high and budgets too low, these inadequacies will curb and restrict its purpose. Nor is it uncommon for a client to bring to a given agency needs which, while they fall within agency function, are not provided for by the agency program of service. For example, a private child care agency stated its function as the "care and treatment of the child who cannot adequately be cared for in its own home." Its program was largely one of foster-home care. When several extremely disturbed, all but psychotic, children were brought to its door, it found that its foster-care program fell short of carrying out its function—indeed, its public promise. Happily, the money and the enlightenment of the supporting board were available to extend and change the agency's program, and a treatment institution was developed to meet the newly evident and unmet needs.

This distinction between an agency function and its program has some importance for the caseworker. Where a client's problem belongs may be determined on the basis of function, but what can be done about that problem, how adequately it can be tackled, depends greatly upon the agency program which is supposed to carry out that function. While agency function may remain constant, agency program ought to be responsive to the changing needs of the community and to the profession's changing concerns and knowledge of problems and means of solution.

It is the caseworkers of the agency who, through their continuous contacts with people seeking solutions to their problems, first know the nature, impact, and extent of current social needs. They may choose to disregard this knowledge and to say or imply that, if their agency or others do not have the program or means by which to meet such needs, the services are thereby unnecessary. Or, with greater professional responsibility, they may continuously measure what the agency provides in relation to apparent necessity and transmit for consideration their facts and ideas to the agency personnel charged with developing program and policy. In the first instance, the caseworker may have lost—or perhaps may never have gained—his social work identity; in the latter instance, he sees his particular casework functions as an inextricable part of social work, and he promotes social welfare through such changes in his agency's program as enhance its usefulness to the community.

*The social agency has a structure by which it organizes and delegates its responsibilities and tasks, and governing policies and procedures by which it stabilizes and systematizes its operations.*

Structure, as it may be depicted on an organizational chart, is the agency's anatomy. The agency's body is made up of many members with differing purposes and powers, all dependent upon one another in the body's total workings. The board of directors or advisers, the executives, the supervisors, the caseworkers, the consultants and department heads—each carries certain tasks and certain stipulated "musts" and "mays." It is to the particular "job" that rights and responsibilities are delegated, and each person, as he undertakes the part of the agency's body assigned to him, undertakes to carry out its particular tasks, obligations, and authorities (see Follett, 2).

In the small agency where structure is simple and informal it presents few problems to the caseworker. He finds himself closely related to the total body of the agency, and his sense of this is immediate and constant. In the large agency, however, the caseworker may come to feel so far separated from the "top" or so isolated from persons with functions different from his own as to lose sight of himself as connected with anyone or anything except his case load and his supervisor. Often this is less the fault of the caseworker than of those whose responsibility it is to provide for open channels of communication among the various parts of agency structure. The importance of open, two-way channels cannot be overestimated, for, as has been implied before, it is in response to the caseworkers' perceptions and experiences of client needs that program and policy are in large part shaped (see Johnson, 5).

The functions in any formal organization must be designated and delegated so that responsibilities may be organized and carried out reliably and expertly. The structure of an agency identifies and assigns separate and joint responsibilities, authorities, and tasks to its personnel and demarcates the relationship among various functions in the total agency body. Collaboration among the workers of an agency—whether between caseworker and psychiatrist, supervisor and caseworker, executive and board members, caseworker and caseworker—depends for its effectiveness upon each member's clarity as to the particular functions he represents and for which he takes responsibility. It depends, too, upon his recognition of the difference of his functions from those of others and of how these differences may be dovetailed in the interests of the total job to be done.

When an agency function moves from noun to verb, so to speak, when the agency readies itself to convey its helping purposes, it becomes apparent that some systematic method of performing its business, some regulated ways of operating, are essential to orderly and consistent effectiveness. These ways and means are called "procedures." But, before proceeding, there must be some guiding principles and rulings that clarify the boundaries set by prudence or wisdom upon the carrying-out of agency purposes and programs. These formulations are called "policies."

The caseworker needs to understand the usefulness of agency policies and procedures in order to do his everyday job well. Sometimes they seem to him to be only "a lot of red tape," only a means by which he and his client are thwarted. Sometimes he cannot see the sense in a policy or cannot see what this or that procedural requirement has to do with him and his purposes. And sometimes caseworkers use agency policies and procedures as armor against thinking or exertion.

For the caseworker who "lives by rules," or for him who sees the client as having to be bent to the inexorable will of the agency, these basic premises must be reiterated: The social agency is established out of the community's concern to meet certain needs in people's living. Its form, its setup, its workaday philosophy, and the ways it does its work are all for the purpose of meeting those needs for the greatest number with the greatest efficacy. Thus, the test of policy and procedure is in their serviceability to the agency's clients. It cannot be assumed that "it's good because we always do it this way"; it must be able to be affirmed that "we do it this way because it's good."

In some agencies there are to be found parts of structure or pieces of policy and procedure that no longer have usefulness. Conditions outside or within the agency may have changed, but these functions and ways of functioning have persisted. They are like vestigial organs in the body of the agency. When a caseworker cannot honestly affirm some ruling, policy, or procedure as useful to the agency's avowed purposes with its clients, or to the agency's stewardship to its larger community, he ought to open it to question and discussion with the appropriate personnel charged with administrative responsibility. (It goes without saying that a caseworker's freedom to do this will depend upon whether administrative and supervisory personnel have established a climate that is hospitable or bleak to ideas that challenge the status quo.) Perhaps it can be explained and justified; perhaps it needs to be reappraised for revision or even cast out.

The caseworker who champs against structures as reins upon his free and perhaps more imaginative operations would do well to conjure up a mental picture of an agency in which any person might carry any job or in which the caseworkers might simply use their own judgments as to what should be done, for whom, and under what circumstances. The mental and emotional chaos this would create for the caseworker would paralyze him—nor would it be long before someone would suggest that "we ought to have a rule." The client would be totally subject to the judgments or biases of individual caseworkers. As for the community, it could find no agency to relate to and support, but only an aggregation of individual social workers under one roof. Whatever faults may characterize them in an individual situation (faults which must be subject to vigilant scrutiny), the structures, policies, and procedures of a social agency give form, orderliness, consistency, and dependable movement to an agency's services.

*The social agency is a living, adaptable organism susceptible to being understood and changed, much as other living organisms.*

Perhaps this stretches a metaphor. Yet, if it promotes the conception of likeness between an individual person's organization and that of an agency, it may serve to dispel the common tendency to think of agencies as fixed and static instrumentalities. If agency structure may be seen as its anatomy, its operations may represent its physiology, and the purposes, attitudes, and goal directions of its personnel and board are its psychology. Like other living organisms, it has a past history, and its present means and ends are fashioned by this. The circumstances of its inception, the persons who nurtured it, and the social situations it encountered will have affected an agency's present behaviors. If it has become fixated at some level of earlier development, it may be found to be operating inappropriately in the face of present problems. If, however, it has continuously and appropriately responded to changed demands upon it and changed conceptions within it, it is likely to be further adaptable. Like the aims of the human beings who make it up, the aims of an agency are determined by past, present, and future orientations and purposes. Its competence depends on the strengths and weaknesses of its staff members along with the presence or absence of resources in its environment—money, leadership, co-operation, and support. The society of which it is a product acts upon it to shape its form and operations in many ways, and by the agency's responsive reaction the community will be influenced in turn.

That the social agency "lives" in relationship to other social agencies and other welfare organizations also affects the scope and nature of its work. The help it gives is dependent upon other basic supplementary services in the community; its single- or multifunctional nature is determined by the absence or presence of other facilities, and its usefulness is likewise affected thereby. The more the administration and casework staff is conscious of the agency's purposes and services in relation to those of other community agencies, the greater is the likelihood that individual clients as well as the general community will be well served. The means to problem-solving expand as an agency keeps connected with other welfare resources.

*Every staff member in an agency speaks and acts for some part of the agency's function, and the caseworker represents the agency in its individualized problem-solving help.*

This has several significances for the caseworker. First, he is not an independent professional practitioner to whom an agency has given office space. No one, to be sure, would argue that he is—yet in practice it is not unknown that a caseworker may think of his clients as "belonging" to him, or may ally himself with his client against his agency, or, in some momentary combination of zealousness and loss of perspective, may act to circumvent agency policy. What a caseworker can do with and for his client derives both from his professional commitment and skill and from the agency which hires him. The specific purposes and conditions that govern what he does, however, derive chiefly from the agency he has contracted to represent (see Perlman, 8 and 9). Essentially, this is why the caseworker needs to know and understand his agency both in blueprint and in operation. "To represent" means "to speak and act for," and this is only possible when the caseworker has gained a grasp of his agency in some of the ways suggested.

Nor is it possible to represent that with which a caseworker finds himself at odds. In order to represent the agency, he must be psychologically identified with it, at one with its purpose and policies. This is not to say that the caseworker must feel "my agency, right or wrong." It is to say, rather, that his agency must have those major purposes and means which for the most part are compatible with the caseworker's professional philosophy and standards. The agency may not have arrived at its highest level of operation, but it may still be acceptable in its rudimentary stage if it is striving adaptively to achieve higher development. It may have certain outmoded procedures or policies that cry out for revision, but, if for the most part it is using appropriate means to achieve its desirable ends, it is possible to identify with it, accepting it as it works toward becoming better. However, where the social welfare of the individual or his society seems consistently to be held secondary to other considerations (see Towle, *11*) or where policies and procedures remain so frozen as to block rather than transmit the welfare purposes despite efforts to modify them, the professional social caseworker cannot in good conscience represent such an agency.

When the social agency is of sound and good standing, it holds many values for the caseworker himself. Every social agency banks a fund of knowledge about and experience with the particular problems it has set out to solve. The supervision and staff training programs that good social agencies provide are means by which this knowledge is transmitted. The practitioner who is young in life and professional experience may feel some confidence in venturing to deal with the complexities of human problems when he can readily draw upon those funds of accumulated and organized wisdom. Even for the experienced caseworker, he who feeds more into the agency's store of help than he draws from it, the agency's organized resources make it possible to provide services to clients and develop helping means beyond what individualized private practice could hope to provide.*

*The caseworker, while representing his agency, is first and foremost a representative of his profession.†*

Actually, in all instances where agency purposes and powers have been delegated to professional social workers for programming and execution, the agency itself is an instrument of the profession. But there are instances, as when a caseworker has points of difference with his agency, or when he is employed by an agency struggling to develop standards, or when he is working in a social work "department" of another kind of setting, when the caseworker needs to maintain vigilant awareness of his own professional identity and identifications. As a professional person he must know and be committed with feeling to the philosophy that guides the practice of the social work profession. This means that the social caseworker practices in the conviction that individual human welfare is the purpose and the test of social policy; that his attitudes combine open inquiry with dedication to the people and the purpose he serves; that he maintains "social consciousness and social con-

---

* An analogous condition may be seen in medicine, where even the private practitioner is concerned that he be part of a good hospital staff so that he may bank on the organized medical knowledge and resources which are necessary supplements to his individual practice.

† In this discussion the "professional caseworker" is considered to be one who has a Master's degree in social work or its equivalent in professional education and training—one who has consciously undertaken to prepare himself by the profession's educational standards for his practice of casework.

science"; and that he conducts himself ethically in all his professional transactions (see American Association of Social Workers, *1,* and Towle, *10*).

Along with these requirements of professional commitment, the social work profession has developed and incorporated a body of standards and values about what is good and what is bad for individual and societal welfare; of facts, ideas, and assumptions as to how what is good may be attained or how it is undermined; and of resources and skills by which to achieve the greatest good. These standards and values will change as cultural values and mores change; ideas and assumptions will surely change as knowledge about human beings and their living changes and grows and as resources and skills develop, shift, and adapt in relation to changed knowledge and ideas. But at any point in time the profession of social work, like all professions, upholds certain human values and standards. And at any point in time the social caseworker, as a member of the profession, upholds these same values and standards. He does so not in any parroting acquiescence or smug assumption that the term "professional" automatically bestows grace but in constant alertness to measure his daily practice and that of his agency against what his profession knows or thinks to be good. Hopefully, too, at the same time as he knows and acts on what he stands for, he also stretches himself to seek to know more and to do better than he knows and does today. Thus he not only will benefit the clients who get his help but will also feed back into the growing body of his agency's and profession's knowledge and expertness.

But now to return to the person with a problem. As he crosses the threshold of the social agency, he may see it only as an office where "they" will or will not be able or willing to help him. Even in the small agency, however, he is entering an organization representing a community of interest and values, structured, staffed, and implemented for conveying the means by which his problem may be solved. As its client, he will come to know the agency and its usefulness to him through the professional services of the caseworker. This help, whether it is to enhance his physical, social, or psychological welfare, or all three at once, is given by a process which combines certain professional methods and behavior. It is with the nature of this casework process that the next chapters deal.

# 5 THE PROCESS

The casework process is essentially one of problem-solving. Immediately it must be said that this idea does not imply that casework resolves all the problems brought to it, nor does it imply that it is upon the problems per se that the caseworker bends his major efforts. It is an idea, rather, that stems from a conception of human life as being in itself a problem-solving process, a continuous change and movement in which the human being works on so adapting himself to external objects or them to himself as to achieve maximum satisfactions. This is the work in which every human being engages from the moment of birth to that of death. It is both unconscious and conscious. It is concerned with problems, some small, some large, of two kinds: of replacing dissatisfactions or discomforts with satisfaction or comfort and of seeking to achieve greater or more satisfactions. When we say of a human being that he is "well adjusted" or psychologically healthy or that he leads a happy life, we do not mean that he or his circumstances are fixed in a kind of suspended perfection. We mean, rather, that the actual problems with which he is confronted are not so many or so overpowering but that they are susceptible to his management, and/or we mean that his modes of coping with his daily problems are competent and economical (see Jahoda, 5).

Much of our daily problem-solving takes place unbeknown to us. Our perception of a problem situation, our turning-over in our minds its causes and effects, our consideration and choice of some mode of dealing with it—all this may go on in us without our being fully aware that we are doing something as important-sounding as problem-solving. We may call it "thinking something over" or "trying something out" or "taking a chance"—and even taking a chance is a kind of problem-solving effort, albeit a poor one, because there is a skip from half-perception to trial action without the benefit of consideration and judgment. We become conscious of our problem-solving work when we encounter a problem too hard or too big to be dealt with in our usual ways. Then we struggle to marshal and organize our ego powers so that they will bear upon what it is we wish to work out. "Now, let's see," we say to ourselves, "just what does $x$ in this problem stand for?" "Now, wait a minute," we adjure ourselves, "don't make a decision until you've thought it over." "Where do I go from here?" we ask ourselves at the fork of a decision. And so on. What we are doing in these conversations with ourselves is attempting to direct our powers to seeing more sharply, to probing and sorting our interfering feelings and thoughts, to considering more imaginatively and precisely, and to adapting or choosing the most effective action. These are major, common kinds of ego operation, and they are involved in all human problem-solving efforts.

Happily for all of us, there are some life-problems that "solve themselves" or are solved for us. Changes occur in events or circumstances that re-establish our equilibrium and make it unnecessary for us to move, to change, or to adapt. But there is no adult human being who will not have, in the course of any one day, some dilemma he must consciously solve, whether it be as frivolous as what to wear or eat or as serious as familial or international relations. It is when we encounter a problem that defies our coping efforts or that requires for its solution some means we cannot command that we turn to persons whose perspectives, expertness, or resources may be of help. This is why persons come or are sent to social caseworkers when they are experiencing inability to cope with their problems of social or interpersonal stress.

*In order to understand what the casework process must include in its problem-solving help, it is necessary to take stock first of the kinds of blockings which occur in people's normal problem-solving efforts.* These six are among the most common:

1. A problem cannot be solved if the necessary tangible means and resources are not available to the person. A client, for instance, may see and assess his problem and its solution accurately and may lack only the material provision for it.

Social agencies contain and supply many of these provisions. Sometimes, however, the use of them or their very nature may present another problem, and the client may need the caseworker's help to adapt, compromise, and come to terms with the differences between his ideas and the reality of the means of solution.

2. Sometimes people are unable to solve their problems simply out of ignorance or misapprehension about the facts of the problem or the facts of existing ways of meeting it. The father who looks on his son's stuttering as "just a bad habit" or the youngster who believes that his masturbation will result in his insanity are examples of the former; the girl who finds herself pregnant and thinks only of a drastic way out or the woman who, recently widowed, thinks she must place her children so that she can go to work to support them are the simplest examples of the latter. Missing knowledge and facts, like missing pieces in a puzzle, may make a problem impossible of solution.

In such situations the caseworker may provide the necessary knowledge, interpretation, or means by which the facts of the problem and of the potential resources may be known. In some instances the provision of necessary knowledge may be enough, but in many instances it is necessary first to clear away or lower the emotional blockings that prevented the person's "knowing" in the first place.

3. A problem is difficult of resolution when the person who has it is depleted or drained of emotional or physical energy. He needs to mobilize himself—"pull himself together"—when he must plan and act according to plan. Energy is essential to such mobilization. Where there is physical exhaustion, as may occur in illness, malnourishment, overwork, or emotional exhaustion, as may occur when a person has struggled with conflicts and has found them too much for him (he is "played out," "washed up," "a wreck"), the

person's capacity to "see straight," to think clearly, or to organize himself to do something may be at low ebb.

In these circumstances it may be necessary for the caseworker to provide such physical or psychological supports as will restore the person's equilibrium before he can begin to face up to and tackle his problem.

4. Some problems arouse high feelings in a person—emotions so strong that they overpower his reason and defy his conscious controls. Sometimes these feelings are realistically called for, as great grief at a death or great anxiety over serious illness. In other instances they may be "overreactions," caused by the problem's bringing to life old, dormant emotions that add their strength to the present ones. High and strong feeling disintegrates a person's capacities—"it pulls him to pieces." It is said that he is "blind with rage," "torn with grief," or "frozen with fear," and in these everyday phrases are expressed accurately the disabling effects of emotional disturbances. When the problem sets off a conflagration of feeling, a person's thought processes, delicately attuned as they are to his emotions, become clouded and tumbled about.

In such instances the caseworker needs both to relieve the person's feelings and to lessen the impact of the problem so that the person may begin, with casework sustainment, to try to "see straight," to analyze the situation in its effects upon him and his upon it, and to think of alternative adaptations.

5. The problem may lie within the person; that is, he may have become subject to, or victim of, emotions that chronically, over a long time, have governed his thinking and action. In such instances the person's feelings are not necessarily acute and high but may run long and deep—so deep, perhaps, as to be almost unknown to their owner. Yet they remain alive and active, thrashing about in the unconscious mind, vitally affecting what their victim sees, how he thinks, and how he acts. "I see the situation clearly," says a man—as, indeed, he may—"but I can't seem to do anything about it." "I understand what you mean," says a woman, "but, when I try to carry it out, it just doesn't come out right." When this occurs repeatedly, when, despite his good effort and strong wish and despite the absence of realistic provocation of his feelings, a person remains in the grasp of stereotyped reaction, it is the mark of neurosis.

Somewhere in this person's past a problem of great emotional import to him was left unsolved, pushed under, as it were, buried but far from dead. It will affect the way he sees or thinks about or tries to deal with his present-day life, especially as some part of it resembles his original problem.

Sometimes the turmoil this storm center creates is quieted by the modification or resolution of other problems in the person's life. Sometimes more radical forms of help than social casework need to be recommended, such as psychoanalysis, which, as one of its differences from casework, seeks to make the unconscious conflict accessible to the consciousness of its owner. But most often casework may need to help such a person live with himself, not to resolve his basic emotional problem but to modify it enough so that he can manage his impulses more effectively. This may involve helping him to recount, review, and appraise his actions and reactions in relation to persons and situations in his current living, to identify his typical behavior, to assay its values, to choose and experiment with different and more appropriate modes of action.

6. Some people find problems difficult of solution because they have never developed systematic habits or orderly methods of thinking and planning. Such persons, characteristically impulsive, or products of life-experiences that have kept them constantly "running to stay where they are," tend to see living as a series of unrelated episodes, as "happenstances." They tend therefore to react to problems in catch-as-catch-can ways. If theirs is a predominantly optimistic disposition, they are sure that somehow things will work themselves out; if pessimistic, they are resigned to their fate, or they worry about the situation in circular, fruitless ways. They do not readily see cause-and-effect relationships and consider themselves acted upon rather than potential actors in relation to their problems. In some instances these blindnesses have become ingrained in the personality (again, neurosis); in others, however, the difficulty lies chiefly in the person's lack of experience in organizing his powers to grapple with problems.

When this latter is discerned as the difficulty, the caseworker needs to promote repeated exercise in the steps of problem-solving, in the hope that these steps may become habitual: looking at the salient facts, appraising their meaning and their possible solution, and moving toward action which is planned out of knowledge and forethought.°

As these conditions that make it difficult and at times impossible for persons to work through their problems unaided are understood, it becomes clear that the help needed will be more complex than can be provided simply by reason plus resource. Problem-solving with the person whose inner or outer resources have failed him must involve engaging and working with his own motive powers, feelings, attitudes, ideas, and behavior in their interrelatedness to the nature of the problem itself and to the existing resources. How to manage all this is the professional problem the caseworker faces. He can do so only if he has some systematic idea of how to get hold of a problem (and then how to help his client get hold), how to understand it (and then how to help his client understand it), and how to work on it (and then how to engage his client in work on it). In short, the problem-solving process called "casework" attempts to inject into its client's life-process its methods of operation and its resources of knowledge and organized provisions by which the client's own problem-solving struggle is substantially aided. Sometimes as a result of this the specific problem is solved; sometimes it is only modified, but enough so that the person can live with it reasonably well; sometimes the person's work on his problem results in his feeling differently enough about it to enable him to cope with it even if it persists.

*The intent of the casework process is to engage the person himself both in working on and in coping with the one or several problems that confront him and to do so by such means as may stand him in good stead as he goes forward in living.* These means are, in the main: (1) the provision of a therapeutic relationship that sustains the client and affects the nature of his emotional relation to his problem; (2) the provision of a systematic, though always flexible, way by which the client may discuss and work over the nature of his problem, his relation to it, and its potential solutions; and (3) the provision of such opportunities and aids (those of communication and/or of resource) as will further exercise and implement the client's adaptive action upon his problem.

° These major kinds of casework help are succinctly though differently designated in *Scope and Method of the Family Service Agency* (7).

A more complete discussion of each of these will take place in following chapters. However, they bear some further introductory expansion here.

Problem-solving that involves a troubled person's use of himself requires first of all that considerable help be given him to quiet, dilute, or transform those confused feelings in him that thwart or distort his adequate functioning. This kind of help permeates the casework process of problem-solving, and it is this that signally differentiates casework help from those other problem-solving processes as are chiefly intellectual. It is provided in a number of ways, the most constant of which is the establishment and management of the relationship between the caseworker and his client. The expressed and demonstrated warm interest of the caseworker, his wish and ability to be of help, his sustaining and sympathetic attitudes, his responsiveness and his knowledgeability—all provide a kind of safety island to the person who is in trouble. In this safe medium of understanding and sustainment the client may begin to feel secure and steadied enough to face up to and grapple with his problems.

But the nurture of the relationship is not all. It is necessary that the fullest capacities and potentials in the client himself be utilized and that he be fully engaged in the effort to work out his conflict or problem situation. The reasons for this are both practical and philosophical. "We learn to do by doing," says the educational maxim, and it holds here as in all life-situations that the development of the ability to take action on the basis of forethought is developed and fortified by exercise of that ability. It is possible for one person to think for another and to provide him with some ready solution. But under those circumstances he remains only the consumer rather than the producer of the solution. Then two things may happen: his self-responsibility is weakened thereby and his dependence on someone outside himself is deepened; and ready-made arrangements of ideas and actions often fail to fit the needs and capacities of him who is to use them, and therefore his use of them may fail. An example of the former is the "good" client who, like an obedient child, does what the person in authority suggests or requires and continues to hang on to that person as his source of strength and direction. An example of the second is the client who, while he consciously wants to do that which has been suggested, is somehow unable to carry it through—he "means" to go to the doctor, just as the caseworker said he should, but "things happened" in such a way as to make postponement necessary, etc. Only the exercise of a person's own powers in problem-solving, then, develops self-direction and self-dependence. Furthermore, it is only thus that those resistances or disabilities within the self which might block appropriate action are fully recognized and opened to modification.

Beyond these practical considerations is the democratic tenet that each individual has the right to self-determination: within the limits of reality, each man has the right to be "master of his soul" and of his fate. This "right" is his. The concern of the caseworker must be that he be helped to use it to his best welfare. To determine what he shall be or do in contrast to just blindly being or doing requires, again, the conscious use of man's rational powers.

Thus it is that the casework process of problem-solving within a nurturing relationship includes, also and always, the fullest involvement and participation of the person himself. To help the person to help himself, the caseworker, then, strives to stimulate, elicit, and encourage the person's own activity as a feeling, thinking, and doing person. To activate a client to feel through and think through his problem, a professional helper must have a clear idea of the efficient, orderly way to go about it.

*All competent problem-solving, as contrasted with trial-and-error methods, contains three essential operations.*\* *Urgent pressures will often dislodge their logical sequence, but any conscious effort to move from quandary to solution must involve these modes of action:*

1. The facts that constitute and bear upon the problem must be ascertained and grasped. Such facts may be of objective reality and of subjective reaction, of cause and effect, of relatedness between the person and his problem, of the solutions sought and of the actual means available, and so forth.

2. The facts must be thought about. That is to say, they must be turned over, probed into, and reorganized in the mind—examined

---

\* The core material in this section and in others where problem-solving is the subject was first presented in a paper read at the National Conference of Jewish Communal Services, May, 1953 (see Perlman, 6). See also Dewey (1 and 2), to whom I am heavily indebted for the development of my ideas of problem-solving.

in their relationships to one another, searched for their significance, viewed in their resemblance to and difference from like configurations known elsewhere, and connections made between facts of drives and of goals, of obstacles and of aims, and so forth. In short, the fact must be played upon and organized by ideas—ideas springing from knowledge and experience and subject to the governing aim of problem resolution.

3. Some choice or decision must be made that is the end result of the consideration of the particular facts and that affects or has the intent of resolving the problem. Such a decision may take the form of the selection of a course of overt action or, more subtly, of some change in the person's responsive relationship to the problem. Either conclusion must be tested for its validity by some action upon the problem—by some different attack upon it or by some changed internal or overt behavior in relation to it.

The reader will readily recognize that these three operations almost parallel the logical steps long known and practiced in casework: study (fact-finding), diagnosis (thinking about and organizing facts into a meaningful goal-pointed explanation), and treatment (implementation of conclusions as to the what and how of action upon the problem). But the study-diagnosis-treatment formula has presented a persistent stumbling block in casework. To the practitioner it has posed many difficulties. Among the obstacles to the usefulness of this formula is that it has tended in practice to produce more problem-solving activity on the caseworker's part than on the client's. What seems to happen is that the client becomes subject to the caseworker's efforts, and this despite valiant efforts to conceive of the client as participant from the first. The idea of problem-solving seeks to inject, not a fundamental change in the structure of the casework process, but a difference of emphasis and dynamics.

Problem-solving implies that both the caseworker and his client are simultaneously and consciously, though differently, engaged in problem-solving from the first. In problem-solving activity there is no implication that treatment waits on study and diagnosis. Rather, the client's adaptive mechanisms are involved from the beginning in working upon the difficulty he has brought. Fact-finding jointly with the client may in itself be an operation which clears and orders his perceptions. The client's sharing and working-over of his feelings, and the impetus and help given him to know and think about his attitudes, behavior, needs, and goals, are in themselves an experience and exercise of adaptation. (The by-products of both of these ongoing activities yield the caseworker a large part of what becomes his diagnosis.) And the taking of next steps out of considered choice, the planning of action, or the internal settlements arrived at involve all the executive and integrative functions of the ego. The dynamic difference, then, between the study-diagnosis-treatment idea and that of problem-solving lies in the latter's use of operations parallel to those of the ego in the problem-solving process. Of this more will be said later.

*Finally, for the solution or mitigation of many problems there must exist certain material means or accessible opportunities which are available to the needful person and which he can be helped to use.*

Money, medical care, nursery schools, scholarships, foster homes, recreation facilities—these are the kinds of resources that any person may need in order to resolve a given problem in his daily living. That the caseworker should know about these resources or know how to become informed of them is patent; that he should be able to pick them over imaginatively in their relation to the client's problem is essential. But, even when such resources are carefully culled, there often remains the problem of helping the person who needs them to use them well. Just as a man who is thirst-parched cannot take all at once the water his body needs, or as the man who is starved may have to be carefully readied to ingest food, so persons who have great need of another kind of sustenance may not be able simply to take hold of it and use it. From the toothache to the resources of the dental clinic is a simple problem-solving step indeed; from loneliness to the resource of a group activity seems an obvious move to make; yet in these or in like situations what looks like the ready solution to the problem may in itself present a forbidding obstacle to the client. It may become necessary, then, that the caseworker help the client to grapple with the problem that the solution presents to him. Frequently, in addition to this, it is necessary that the caseworker turn from direct work with his clients to trying to modify or prepare the instrumentality of help so that it may become more hospitable and usable to the troubled client. In short, the casework process will involve not only knowing and imaginatively using environmental resources but also working directly with them in order to make them usable by the client.

In summary, then, the casework process is a problem-solving process in that it employs the orderly, systematic methods which are basic to any effective thinking-and-feeling-toward-action. Since the problems with which it deals are those of the individual's social living, their solution must take place by and through the persons involved in those problems. For this reason casework attempts to help its client perceive and appraise himself and his situation and mobilize himself to act in consonance with his understanding. In cognizance of those potent emotional factors that may variously block or promote the person's functioning, casework provides an emotionally freeing and sustaining "climate" and bond which is known as the casework relationship. It is within this relationship that caseworker and client both strive to seek ways to dissipate or cope with the dilemma. These ways are to be found in environmental means and resources and within the client himself. In either or both circumstances the caseworker, deeply attuned to the individual person, offers support and stimulus to that person to exercise and use his actual or latent powers and means to move from conflict to resolution, from stalemate to decision and action.

Both the therapeutic relationship of casework and the conscious, adaptive operations which its problem-solving work involves are complex phenomena. In operation they are inseparable one from the other, mutually interdependent and sustaining. But, to grasp fully their merged action, each needs to be viewed in its separateness. Therefore, the nature of the caseworker-client relationship and of the problem-solving work as the major methods in the casework process will be separately discussed in the ensuing two chapters.

# 6 THE CASEWORKER-
## CLIENT RELATIONSHIP

*Vital relationships between people rise out of shared and emotionally charged situations.*

For the growth of any living thing two conditions must be present: nurture and the exercise of innate powers. This is true of the simplest plant that thrives on sun and rain and soil and that, in turn, husbands and spends its energies to protect itself and to grow. It is true of all animals, including man, but by virtue of man's complexity his nurture and exercise are likewise highly complex. In order that he achieve humanity, he must be nurtured not only physically but also psychologically, and the responsive exercise of his powers as he struggles to grow and adapt will be expressed not only through his body but also through his mind and through that compound of psychological behaviors we call "personality." The climate for the growth of human personality, the nutriment for its development, and the stimulus for its subtle adaptations are emotion-charged relationships with other human beings. Mothering is the first vital relationship the human young know. Later fathering joins it, and then relationships fan out with many other human beings and living things, some of them long term and vital, some transient and tenuous. And throughout his life each person seeks (and feels secure only when he has found) a relationship with one or more other human beings from which he can draw the nourishment of love or sustainment and the stimulus of interaction.

This is why the casework process, like every other process intended to promote growth, must use relationship as its basic means. The labors of mind and body involved in problem-solving may feel less arduous when they take place within the warmth and security of a strong relationship; the will to try may be spurred and sustained by the helpfulness and hopefulness it conveys; and far below the surface of consciousness the person may absorb from him to whom he feels related that sense of oneness and yet of separate worth which is the foundation of inner security and self-esteem.

We reach adulthood, having lived all our lives in relationships, taking their existence and purpose so much for granted that, except when we are suddenly bereft of a meaningful relationship or as we become involved in a new one, we are scarcely conscious of what they mean to us and what powers they contain. So, on becoming caseworkers, when we encounter the concept of relationship and want to understand and use it wisely, it suddenly seems strange to us (just as is the case when we lift out some word in our everyday vocabulary and look hard at it, or when our attention is focused on some article of furniture with which we have lived for many years), and we feel peculiarly gauche in its presence, unsure as to how to deal with it consciously. The task we face, then, is to examine it carefully in all its familiar and its unfamiliar facets in order to know of what it is composed, to know what its purposes may be, and from there to know both its therapeutic problems and values.

In the sense in which we speak of "relationship" in social casework (and it is probably the concept that appears with greatest frequency in all of casework's oral and written discussions), it is a condition in which two persons with some common interest between them, long-term or temporary, interact with feeling. It is not made up, as is sometimes assumed, merely of being together in time and place, or of a pleasant and comfortable intercommunication, or of long-term proximity or acquaintanceship between two persons. Relationship leaps from one person to the other at the moment when emotion moves between them. They may both express or invest the same kind of emotion; they may express or invest different or even opposing emotions; or—and this is the situation in casework—one may express or invest emotion, and the other will receive it and be responsive to it. In any case, a charge or current of feeling must be experienced between two persons. Whether this interaction creates a sense of union or of antagonism, the two persons are for the time "connected" or "related" to each other.

We know this phenomenon well in our everyday lives. Take your relationship with John Doe, who has lived next door to you for years. You see him once a day or so; you smile, and so does he; you exchange observations about the weather or about some newspaper headlines; he asks you to keep an eye on the house while he is on vacation, and you are glad to help him out. You remain "related" to him in time and space and intercommunication; you think of him as a nice person; but, if you never see him again, you will feel neither better nor worse. Then, one day, he comes to ask you to sign a petition on some political issue about which you have strong feeling. You express that feeling—you are for this issue or that candidate— and he expresses, in turn, his same feeling about it. Now, suddenly, you see and feel him more as a person of import to you, as a person with whom you are, if only temporarily, involved—as a person with whom you feel an at-oneness. You are in *positive relationship* to him. You may suddenly find charm in him that you never saw before, or admire his qualities of mind and character, or even impute certain attributes to him which may or may not be there. Even though, from that time on, you may resume your casual commentaries about sun or rain, something will remain in you of the experience of having shared feeling with him about an issue of importance to you both, and you will remember him as one who was meaningfully related to you if on only one issue.

Now turn this situation about and say that you are against what he is for, and you express your feelings of opposition, and he responds, also with feeling, against you or your point of view. Again you are psychologically related; you see and feel him as a person of importance because of his difference from you and his potential danger to you or what you stand for. Now you are in a *negative relationship* to him; you may impute stupidity to him or be strongly repelled by him, and, though you may never speak of this again and may resume all the superficial courtesies of neighbors, he will never lose the special significance he assumed in the moment when you met about an issue that was charged with mutual antagonism and that connected you by currents of feeling.

This, then, is how all meaningful relationships come into being, all feelings of being at one or at odds with another person: some interest or concern is temporarily or continuously shared between two persons, and for both, or at least for one of them, it is emotionally charged. When only one has feeling invested, the other must recognize, receive, and respond to that feeling; when that reception and response are understanding and accepting, the surge of relationship has a positive quality; but, when they are blunted or rejecting, the relationship becomes antagonistic or defensive.

The application of these ideas to the casework situation becomes immediately apparent. The client comes to the caseworker with some life-problem in which he finds himself helpless. To come to some solution of the problem is the business between him and the case-worker, and this is the center of their joined concern. The person who carries the problem always has emotion invested in it—guilt or anger at having whatever difficulty it is, frustration at finding himself helpless, uneasiness at having to take help—and, as long as he conceives of himself or his situation as being maladjusted, he has emotional involvement in it. It is when his feelings are expressed, or when the caseworker reaches out to release them and they are responded to receptively, attentively, and sympathetically, that an emotional span is flung between client and caseworker which is the beginning of relationship.

As that relationship develops, it will be seen to have many elements in common with all good relationships and sometimes, for reasons to be touched on later, some of the elements of problematic relationships, too. As the positive relationship is used consciously by the caseworker as both climate and catalyst for problem-solving, it will be seen to have some special elements that are essential in any professional, therapeutic relationship.

*All growth-producing relationships, of which the casework relationship is one, contain elements of acceptance and expectation, support and stimulation.*

"Acceptance" means that warmth and fulness in giving one's self to and receiving another person which says to him, "I like you; I lend myself to you to meet your needs, to know and understand you; and I will not engulf you because I respect your right to retain your own identity." It is a nurturing quality, a readiness to lend one's self to the needs of another. But within all growth-producing relationships some elements of expectation must also be present, and they are to be found even in the most "giving," most loving, relationships. "Expectation" means the anticipation—sometimes implicit, sometimes explicit—that the love which is being given will result in some responsive behavior. Even in the love that we believe to be most selfless and most giving—that of a mother for her baby— there are elements of expectation. She expects him to come to recognize her, to smile at her; bit by bit she expects him to give up or take on some modes of behavior because he reciprocates, in his rudimentary way, her love for him. All through the development of the child, he experiences acceptance and expectation from his parents. To put it in other words, he receives nurture and stimulus—nurture to grow from within himself, stimulus to mold that growth to the prevailing forms of social living.

By the time adulthood is reached, a person's major personality structure and patterns have been set, and the process of growth and change is both slowed up and confined within fairly close limits. But even the well-adjusted individual still needs and seeks the sustenance and the stimulus of good relationships. At times of crisis this need is even greater. All relationships that naturally or by conscious intent contribute to an individual's growth must contain these essential components of support and stimulus, acceptance and expectation. They go hand in hand. So, in the casework relationship, a constant medium is provided that is accepting, nurturing, and supporting at the same time that the stimulus of problem-solving work is injected to promote the client's efforts to feel, to be, or to act in the ways leading to his better social adjustment. This combination of tenderness of feeling with firmness of perspective and purpose is best sustained if the caseworker keeps before himself and his client the problem that is at the center of their mutual concern and the work that must be done to cope with it.

*The identifying mark of a professional relationship is its conscious purposiveness growing out of the knowledge of what must go into achieving the goal.*

In everyday life the formation of a relationship may be an end in itself—that is, the gratifications sought and found in another person may be the be-all and the end-all of the relationship (although there will be by-products of growth or regression as inevitable results of interaction). But a professional relationship is formed and maintained for a purpose recognized by both participants, and it ends when that purpose has been achieved or is judged to be unachievable. The mutual concern is the resolution or modification of the problem the client is encountering, and it is assumed that the professional person has the knowledge, competence, and authorization to be helpful to that end. Whatever personal rewards or frustrations may accrue to the professional helper from such relationships are irrelevant to his management of them, for the need of the client is the central focus. The social caseworker, in short, is involved in the relationship with his client not out of kindliness or for his own gratification but because he knows how to be of help and is charged and authorized by his agency with giving help. Thus, the idea that one "gives a client a relationship" is fallacious; rather, the relationship develops out of the professional business the caseworker and client have to work on together.*

Another element of the professional relationship requires elaboration: the element of authority. "Authority" as used here does not mean domination or wilful impositions. It conveys rather the meaning of carrying those rights and powers that are inherent in special knowledge and are vested in special functions. Sometimes, in their zeal to affirm the client's own rights and powers (and perhaps in their valid humility), caseworkers have spoken and acted as though to deny that they had any experience or knowledge of greater usefulness than that of the client himself. To a person who feels helpless this is indeed a sorry kind of equality! A person in need of help seeks someone who has the authority of knowledge and skill to help him; he goes to someone who knows more or is better able than himself, and it is the client's very assumption that the caseworker carries this authority which infuses the relationship with safety and security and strengthens his response to guidance.

---

* Sometimes that "business" may be of problems in interpersonal relationships; then the client-caseworker relationship may itself become a locus of experiment and scrutiny.

In the course of being helped, he may come to take some of this kind of authority into himself, but even this is contingent in part upon his being helped to affirm his own strengths by someone whom he regards as more knowing (in the area of his trouble) than he (see Studt, 6, and Wolberg, 8).

A second aspect of authority within the caseworker's relationship is that vested in his particular functions by the agency's purposes and program. The import of this is that the caseworker often stands for a societal figure to the client, as a representative of the "they" with whom the client either wants to be identified or from whom he feels withdrawn or cast out. In either instance, he imputes to the caseworker who represents the "they" certain standards and powers. In many instances he does so correctly, and we may say, then, that he enters the relationship with a realistic perception. In other instances he may conceive of the powers vested in the caseworker as greater or less than they are. Whichever it is, his responses in the relationship will be conditioned by his clear or distorted conception of what the caseworker represents and is authorized to do.

Finally, it must be said that relationship takes two persons, both free to respond to each other. Some clients are not so free; some are more and some less needful of relationship. The common problems encountered in forming and maintaining a working relationship will be discussed below, and some signs by which capacity for relationship may be known will be found in chapter 12. For our purposes here it is enough to note that any caseworker able to relate warmly and purposefully will find that each client differs in his needfulness, responsiveness, and use of the relationship.

From the moment he sets eyes on his first client, the social caseworker is expected to be "able to establish a good relationship." Probably anyone who is interested enough in people to choose a helping profession conceives of himself as so able. Yet, sometimes, at the moment when it is necessary to bring this essential state of relationship with his client into being, it looms as a frightening hurdle to the caseworker. He may try to resolve this problem by being as innocuously pleasant as he can, as acquiescent as is possible, treading softly and cautiously, and hoping desperately that somehow something will "click." Sometimes that "click" does occur, quite spontaneously, out of capacities or needs which the client brings or out of qualities of warmth and receptiveness in the worker, but sometimes it does not. Since a professional practice requires the development of processes that can be consciously repeated, controlled, and transferred from situation to situation, it seems important to recapitulate, if only in rough form (for the subtleties defy capture), the entering means to a good relationship.

*The casework relationship begins as the client shares some part of his problem and as the caseworker demonstrates that he feels with the client at the same time that he has professional competence to bring to dealing with the problem.*

In the problem that the client brings to the social agency, both he and the worker are involved, though very differently; the client is in need of help, and the worker is the instrument of help. The client is emotionally involved both with the problem and with his necessity to look for outside help. It is necessary, then, that his feelings be recognized and received sympathetically by the caseworker. The worker therefore begins with an attitude that says, in effect, "I am here to receive you, to understand your difficulty, so that I can be helpful to you." Most often, the client will begin to tell what is troubling him, but sometimes he may remain silent and inarticulate or talk about trivialities or side issues, or he may not know where to begin. When this happens, the worker must help him to focus on the business that is the reason for their coming together, the matter of their concern. What are the facts of this problem he faces? As he tells them, all in a rush or haltingly, organized or confused as the case may be, the caseworker expresses to the client by words and by responsive attitudes his recognition that the client *feels* about those facts. He feels badly, or angry, or afraid, or mixed up—in short, he feels in any or all of the understandable ways a human being might feel when faced with this problem. It is as the worker accepts the complete naturalness of the client's being emotionally involved, responds to his expressed feelings, helps him to express those he is trying to push under, and receives those feelings understandingly that the emotional tie is drawn between the client and the worker. The worker demonstrates that he is at one with the client—that he is feeling, not *like* him, but *with* him.

As emotion expressed and received spans the distance between client and caseworker, they are united in their common endeavor of problem-solving. To this endeavor the worker's contribution is his difference from the client—that is, his function and role are different; his perspective, his capacity to understand and execute, his resources, his position in relation to person, problem, place, and process—all are different from the client's and necessarily so. It is his *different* way of approaching a problem, shaking it apart and thinking about it as he guides the interview that begins the client's experience of a special way of tackling his difficulty. New ways are not easy to undertake; they demand patience and change, and the client's reluctance to grapple with the new way of working on his problem would be very great indeed except for his feeling of relationship which underlies and supports his efforts. The business upon which he and the caseworker labor may involve long work together, as in helping a woman to become a better mother, or it may be a one-time problem, as in helping a runaway decide to return home. Since some emotional involvement is inevitably a part of wanting and not wanting, striving and resisting, being able or being unable, the caseworker will continuously need to relate himself both to the objective difficulty and to the client's emotional involvement in it. As he does the latter, relationship bonds will be affected—strengthened, diluted, intensified, strained, as the case may be—but their existence will provide casework's essential condition of "togetherness."*

*The casework relationship may have several therapeutic values.*

The essential condition of togetherness does not express all the therapeutic values that the relationship provides. A meaningful bond between two persons is actually a communication channel operating largely on an unconscious level, and through it many subtle feelings and values both emanate and penetrate. This is why relationships have been from time immemorial so potent a factor in influencing and modifying personality, and it probably explains, too, how it is that therapeutic successes may occur in all kinds of differing schools and schemes of treatment. Out of the social casework relationship, these healing and ameliorating effects may be anticipated:

In our everyday world of hurried and harried people, the warmth,

---

* For some indicators by which a client's response to relationship may be gauged see Towle (7).

respect, and sensitive attentiveness the caseworker offers are not commonly found. They may seem even more rare to the person who feels at odds with his world, and, therefore, these qualities of relating may be especially prized by him. Moreover, as he experiences the caseworker not only as a person he likes but also as a representative of the agency, the "they" of society may seem to him more hospitable too. "There is a person, there are people, who care about me."

To be cared about is in itself a sign of one's worth; to be cared about by someone for whom one has respect and liking enhances the personality. All of us know ourselves by our reflections in the eyes of other people who seem important. When those eyes reflect an image that is likable, respectable, understandable, then our self-esteem is raised and secured. So it is with the client.

Yet something further may occur in the undercurrent of non-verbal intercommunication in a relationship. As the client tells of himself and his feelings, he gives over or deposits something of himself in the caseworker; as he feels at one with the caseworker's responses, he begins to take back into himself some of the caseworker's attitudes, qualities, and values. Sometimes this is a conscious effort, one that all of us have made at times when we have been strongly identified with some other person and when our attempt has been to pattern ourselves after such ways as seem admirable or effective. But most often this incorporation is unconscious. Not only in childhood but also in adulthood, although our capacity to change becomes limited and restricted in many ways, we take into our innermost selves the attitudes and behavior of people who nurture us psychologically. Thus, a client may be nourished and fortified by his feeling of union with his caseworker that not only has augmented his sense of wholeness but also may considerably alter his inner reactions and overt behavior. The Philosopher in James Stephens' *The Crock of Gold* understood this deeply when he said, "I have learned that the head does not hear anything until the heart has listened, and that what the heart knows today the head will understand tomorrow."

To feel accepted, nurtured, and understood endows us with energy. This is because insecurity, shame, and anxiety consume psychic energy—energy used in the continuous erection, repair, and maintenance of protections and defenses against discomfort. In a relationship that offers warmth, sustenance, and assurance, some of these energies are released from their defensive tasks. They may be invested elsewhere—perhaps in the service of experimentation with change and adaptations in thought or action.

As these alterations occur, a good casework relationship may be seen to have healing and corrective values for the client. We approach new relationships in the manner for which old relationships have prepared us. If we have experienced potent relationships largely as attacking or critical, we come to new ones warily and defensively; if we have experienced security and acceptance, we come to them with confidence and trust. Experience with a caseworker of a dependable, sustaining relationship through troubled times and conflicted feelings builds into the client some faith in the potential good will of other persons. This, together with his enhanced sense of self-worth, enables him to venture to relate himself to the people he meets and lives with in less anxious, more positive ways. In effect, his adequacy as a human being is expanded.

*Relationship needs and difficulties from outside the casework situation may intrude into and complicate the casework relationship and may have to be dealt with.*

Up to this point, those attributes and effects of the working relationship that may be said to be fundamental and constant in all casework have been discussed. To every client, the caseworker offers himself in a sympathetic, honest, warm, respectful, and attentive way that stems from the purpose of his professional functions. But not every client will respond alike, nor will every client react appropriately to such a proffered relationship. The nature and management of some of the problematic responses the caseworker may encounter must be given cognizance.

There are some persons who come to social agencies whose experiences in the years of their most fundamental development were so devoid of emotional nurture and warmth that they were left starved, and their "stomachs" for relationship, so to speak, became atrophied and shriveled. And, to carry the analogy a step further, their capacity now to take in nourishment is constricted and shallow (see Ackerman, 1). They relate thinly and tentatively, and their use of the caseworker is likely to be limited to meeting material need or to wanting problems solved for them. Poorly nurtured, they lack the psychic energy to engage themselves fully with either persons or problems. As adults they have much of the psychological dependence of young children, but they lack the accompanying potentials for response and growth through relationship. Whether or not these persons are seen as schizoid personalities, as passively dependent parents of unwanted children, as derelicts, the probability is that the acceptance and support aspects of helping will need by far to outweigh the expectation aspects. The caseworker who works with them will need to bulwark his patience with understanding of reasons for unresponsiveness, with realistic anticipation of outcomes, and with conviction about the values of meeting social needs.

There are other persons who have experienced enough of loving to long for more, and yet they have been so hurt or betrayed by their sources of love as to carry a deep disbelief that they can really find acceptance from anyone. Often this is combined with a denial of their need of anyone that may express itself in delinquencies or brash attitudes about being an outcast, or it may be combined with an excessive need of others and express itself in relationships so demanding, so really voracious, as to frighten off other persons and thus, ultimately, to leave the needful one again betrayed, again hurt. Over and over again such persons will test and goad the caseworker to prove that he, too, will turn against them, that he is "like all the rest"; or repeatedly they will attempt to woo or wangle him into giving to them more of himself—his time, his compassion, his effort— than is valid or possible. Such persons, roughly classified, are seen as having "character disorders" of the psychopathic or neurotic type, and it is perhaps in this group of persons that the connection between personality functioning and the use of human relationships can most clearly be viewed. With them the caseworker must always be keenly alert to the meanings and usages of relationship, but, more than this, he must be firm in its management. In such relationships acceptance of the person must never falter—and this is a taxing requirement, indeed, because the person often behaves in attacking, demanding, irritating, even shocking ways—but the element of expectation must also be held firm, the expectation that there must be labor as well as love, that there must be giving as well as taking, and that limits must be faced and taken into the self. Many times in the course of work with such clients their use of the relationship must become the focal problem to be grappled with.

But even those relationships that begin by being "good" may, in the course of a worker's and client's work together, undergo changes of tone and quality. In a sense, it is erroneous to speak of "establishing" a good working relationship as though, once achieved, it will remain unchanged. When two people operate together about matters that are of vital, intimate importance to at least one of them, and when, as in all problem-solving situations, there are ups and downs, good days and bad days, external irritants or palliations all operating simultaneously, even the most stable relationship may undergo shifts and changes. Thus not only must the caseworker "establish" a good working relationship but in the course of a case it may be necessary to re-establish it, or, as is sometimes said, to "work it."

The most frequently encountered necessity to "work" a relationship occurs with the phenomena called "transference" or "transference reactions."* To any emotionally charged relationship each of us brings conscious and unconscious feelings and attitudes that originally arose in or still belong to other, earlier, important relationships. This is readily understandable, for no one of us comes newborn to new relationships. "I took an immediate dislike to that woman," we say, or "I feel instinctively drawn to that man" or "There's something about the way she looks at you," and we tend to attribute these reactions to our intuitive talents of discernment. The probability is that we are drawn to or repelled by persons who unconsciously remind us of others we have already known who made

* These terms have been used in our speech and literature to connote so many different qualities of relationship that their explicit meaning as used here must be stated. As the reader has already discerned, the term "relationship" has been used here to embrace all the realistic, appropriate, emotion-laden bonds that unite caseworker and client in their common endeavor. That all meaningful relationships hold within them transference elements—that is, qualities of attitude, feeling, and need transferred from other, earlier, relationships—is taken for granted. It could not be otherwise if man is seen as being a product of his past as well as his present. "Transference," then, is used herein *not* to mean that the client relates meaningfully to the caseworker but to mean that affects or reactions are expressed that are inappropriate to or uncalled for by the casework situation, that appear so irrelevant or in such exaggerated degree as to seem to refer to some other situation. For greater precision I use "transference" to refer to some persistence of this problem and "transference reaction" to refer to the occasional, transitory flare which often occurs even with the client who maintains his realistic relationship fairly well.

See Alexander and French (2), Garrett (4), and Wolberg (8).

their mark on us or that the nature of our needs at a certain time clothes persons in the attributes of those who met or failed to meet our needs in the past.

These transferred elements of attraction or repulsion, yearning or defensiveness, liking or dislike, occur spontaneously, and they may emerge at any point in a relationship—at the beginning or any time along the way. In casework they present no particular problem if the client is not so heavily subject to them that he sees and reacts to the caseworker as though he were some person with a function other than that of professional helper. When the client reacts inappropriately, with excessive or distorted feelings, to what is called forth, we say that a "transference" or a "transference reaction" has taken place. It may occur in a relatively simple situation, as with the excited man who rushed into the public assistance office for the first time and shouted at the intake worker, "You people never do anything for a man and his family!" He would have been totally unable to say what this intake worker looked like, how she greeted him, or what she said, because in that moment of desperate need he projected to or transferred into this worker the image of the denying persons he had known before when his need had been great. Transference may occur too after an interview that has been deeply satisfying and has called up echoes of submerged wishes to be more fully and continuously satisfied. "You are like a sister to me," says a grateful woman; "I'd like to come more often to see you." It may arise when some vitally wanted aid has been given or denied, when the client suddenly feels a surge of overwhelming gratitude or helpless frustration and reacts "childishly." ("Why can't we drop all this professional stuff and just be friends!" pleads the woman who wants the caseworker's affection but not his help in work on her problems.)

Transference or transference reaction may also manifest themselves not in spoken expression at all but rather in the way a client momentarily or consistently reacts toward the caseworker. He may be obedient, helpless, approval-seeking, resistant, or defying. Any one of these responses, we must recognize, may have been called forth by the stimuli coming from the caseworker. They may be considered transference reactions when, on their examination in the light of the actual role and operations of the caseworker, they have not actually been provoked. They can be understood, therefore, as behavior that is symbolic of relationships to other potent persons in the client's past or present life.

Some persons chronically infuse new relationships with strong transference elements, but all of us are prone to transfer irrational elements into relationships with others, especially when we are at low ebb or feeling helpless. This is because under such circumstances we regress both to wanting parental nurture and to fearing parental domination. People who come for help to a social agency are always in what is at least a temporary state of helplessness and with, therefore, lowered feelings of adequacy. It can be anticipated that transference reactions and feelings may surge high in them.

In casework practice our effort is to maintain the relationship on the basis of reality; that is, to keep both client and caseworker aware of their joint purpose, their separate and realistic identities, and their focus upon working out some better adaptation between the client and his current problem situation. Transference manifestations need to be recognized, identified, and dealt with as they occur, but the effort is to so manage the relationship and the problem-solving work as to give minimum excitation to transference.* Characteristically, the caseworker process seeks out and utilizes those ego powers of the client that are conscious or readily available to consciousness and that are responsive to expansion or intrenchment as they are tested and exercised in present life-experience. A client's loss of his sense of reality as to the purpose and nature of his relationship with the caseworker may set off a whole chain of unrealistic responses in him—the rise of demands and expectations that cannot be fulfilled, the yielding to dependency pulls that are inappropriate to adulthood, the temptation to relinquish his present problems and roles, the striving to maintain the warmth and safety of this satisfying relationship as an end in itself, and so on—all of a backward-moving kind. What happens is that the unconscious need and drive to have the caseworker be someone other than who he is affect the client's perception. This distortion of perception, this "double vi-

---

* In a different helping process, psychoanalysis, transference is often encouraged for purposes of intensifying a relationship with the analyst, bringing its irrational elements under scrutiny, analyzing its meaning, etc. Such a method draws upon the patient's irrational, unconscious drives and strivings, and its aim is toward a basic resolution of the patient's relationship difficulties.

sion," tends to rouse the emotions that belong to a different image. These feelings, in turn, further muddy or distort the client's vision so that the other functions of his ego that depend on clarity of perception are likewise disabled, and his sense of helplessness is increased. This is why, when momentary or repeated transference reactions dominate the client's relationship, they must be dealt with.

The principle underlying the control or management of the relationship is that the client needs to be helped to see afresh what it is he and the caseworker are together for—what their business is—and what the conditions and means are by which the client's conscious purpose can be achieved. This may be done in a number of ways, directly or indirectly. In any instance, the worker's acceptance and understanding of the naturalness of relationship distortions (rather than an accusation that the client is feeling or acting inappropriately) provide the necessary security for the client to face up to what he himself may then find "foolish" or inappropriate in his behavior or feeling.

Primarily, the caseworker avoids the rousing of transference or deals with its spontaneous emergence by maintaining his clarity of direction, role, and purpose. When, as sometimes occurs with the best of us, one of these is lost in some bypath or floundering, the caseworker does well to share with the client his recognition that they have gone off the track or that they must come to a full stop and take stock again of what they are aiming for and how to get there. A second and always present means for the control of transference is the use of such conditions and boundaries as give dependable form to the special kind of "business" we conduct. The time limits of the interview, the frequency of interviews, the stipulated place for transactions—these mark professional from non-professional communication. The content of the interview—what is talked about, what is ruled out or put aside as irrelevant or postponable, what the worker's responsibility is and what the client's—continuously identifies the difference between a professionally purposive communication and "just talk" that blurs focus and goal. The tendency of a client to lose hold on his present role and problem mounts high when he dwells upon past experiences, upon his earlier unfulfillments. So when in his spontaneous narrative or by the caseworker's direction the client is led to remember and recount past events and emotions, the caseworker, for several reasons (the avoidance of transference among them), must always be alert to helping the client relate this past to its significance for the present problem on which they must work.

There are instances, however, when the caseworker has managed well enough but when the client's needfulness still distorts the relationship. Occasionally, then, the caseworker will need to place his recognition of this fact directly and openly between him and the client; to point out, gently and understandingly, the realistic difference between himself and the image in which the client casts him; and to suggest that it is in the interest of the client that they attempt to keep this difference clear. Two brief examples illustrate this:

> To the woman, quoted before, who wished to "drop all this professional stuff" (and whose behavior over a number of interviews had acted out this wish) the caseworker explained, simply and sincerely, that, were he the woman's friend, he could not be her helper and that, in order to help her with her manifold problems, certain conditions different from friendliness would have to be maintained.

> In another case, that of an anxious depressed young woman, the caseworker has noted that she begins each interview by a searching regard of the worker's face, as if she sought to identify exactly who the worker was. She makes, too, constant references to what her mother would think or say of her behavior under this or that circumstance. In the fifth interview "she felt that I called her 'Mrs. O.' on purpose, looking directly at her then. She somehow wants me to call her by her first name 'as if I were a child.' We discussed how this would be fitting into what she *wished* rather than what she *needs* to solve her current problem and to feel more comfortable. I commented that it looked as if she needed to know who I was, too. I was not her mother. To this she smiled and said she . . . knows she is 'unrealistic.' " Of course, this does not end Mrs. O.'s unrealistic relationship tendencies; rather it establishes a beginning recognition of them between the caseworker and her which can be referred to and worked again when necessary.*

This management of the rational and irrational elements in relationship sounds so reasonable and simple as one sets it down or reads about it. Yet, as anyone who has experienced it knows, it is one of the most difficult, discipline-demanding operations in any therapeutic process. To talk with a man about his relationship with his wife or with a mother about her relationship with her child is to

---

* I use this excerpt by courtesy of Marjorie Browne.

hold the position of listener, observer, discussant, thinker—and outsider. But when one's own relationship, the client's and the worker's, must be dealt with by action and/or speech, then the caseworker is involved himself as actor and as acted upon, and this becomes difficult indeed to observe or even think about objectively. So what of the caseworker in all of this?

*The caseworker, too, has relationship reactions, and part of his professional skill is the management of them.*

The caseworker, in the foregoing discussion of what he must be and do, how he must observe and feel with the client and yet be responsible for the control of his and the client's feelings, and how he must carry forward the business at hand, sounds almost superhuman, an Olympian in mufti. But the fact is that the caseworker too is only a human being, subject, like his client, to feelings of anxiety, dislike, lovingness, and vulnerability. He may be strongly attracted to certain of his clients, like the struggling, optimistic, handicapped father of a family, or strongly repelled by others, like the bragging, swindling delinquent; he is swept with compassion for the hurt child and enraged at the child's parents; he is made uneasy by the person who says, "Just what is a social worker for, anyhow?" and is warmed by the one who says, "Things always seem better after talking to you." He would be less than human if he did not respond with feeling, and he would be less potentially capable as a social caseworker because, in large part, his ability to respond to others grows out of freedom to feel and intimately to know his own emotions. Moreover, not only may the caseworker be expected to have "natural" reactions to emotion-exciting situations but under certain conditions he, like the client, will unconsciously transfer into his relationships certain positive or negative reactions that are realistically uncalled for—distrust or hostility, for example, or strong feelings of attachment. This phenomenon is known as "countertransference," that is, a transference on the part of the helping person. Any subjective involvement on the part of the caseworker with his client or the client's problem may be part of a real countertransference, or it may represent only a single instance of loss of professional objectivity.

The need for achieving objectivity is readily apparent. If he remains involved in his own feelings, the caseworker is in no position to perceive with any clarity or judgment the feelings and needs of his client or his client's difference from him and from other persons; nor will he be ready to lend himself freely to enabling his client to progress. How, then, can he deal with this paradox that he must feel, yet not too much, be "warm" and yet objective, be free and yet controlled?

Perhaps the first step toward this goal of self-management by the caseworker is the simple one of honestly facing himself and his feelings. To deny that he *has* feelings, to insist, as many beginners do, that they love all people or, like children whose relatives pin them with a query as to their favorite parent, to insist that "I like them both the same" is to push out of awareness of facts of his own feelings. What is pushed out of awareness and denied existence is not accessible to conscious analysis and control. Therefore, the first step to objectivity is to recognize his subjectivity, to be self-aware. Once recognized, his feelings may be subject to change or, at the very least, to control.

Control involves the conscious assessment and laying-aside of those feelings that have no helping value in the business between client and caseworker. Obviously, this is more easily said than done. One of the aids to doing this which casework agencies typically provide is supervision. Within supervisory conferences the caseworker may be helped not only to identify his subjective involvements but, through their expression and discussion, to dilute their intensity, to separate them from the casework purpose, and to subject them to restraint. His impulsive sympathies, impatiences, protectiveness, angers—any of the emotions that certain situations or certain people evoke in us—will lie more quietly under their owner's stern eye with the promise of being "talked out" later if they cannot be acted out now.

But if conscious control of his subjective responses were the only means by which the caseworker could provide a therapeutic relationship, it might be feared, and rightly so, that his psychic energy might remain so tightly bound to the management of himself that there would be little to spare for his client's needs. Fortunately, this need not be the case. Again, since the caseworker is a human being (and it is assumed here a reasonably well-integrated one), his feelings are susceptible to change and modification, both consciously and unconsciously. Change in feelings occurs as they are subjected to scrutiny. They may diminish in intensity, or fall away, or become amenable to reason. Emotional change occurs, too, in response to new knowledge and understanding: the alcoholic who yesterday seemed immoral or derelict comes today to be recognized as a person who is sick, and our feelings toward him undergo considerable modification because of that different understanding; the rejecting, irresponsible mother comes to be understood as a child in the body of an adult, and our feelings toward her undergo a change responsive to what the mind has taken in. It goes without saying, perhaps, that such changes occur only in those caseworkers who deeply and consistently *want* to use themselves to understand and help their clients, not in those who seek only personal satisfactions in each relationship with a client.

Finally, subjectivity diminishes with experience. The repeated exercise of submitting subjective involvements to examination and analysis and the accumulated experience of sharing human want and anguish and passions begin to make it possible to take the impact of relationship with greater equilibrium. This is in no sense a "hardening" process. It is rather a mellowing process in which knowledge and acceptance of the differences among human beings, including ourselves, and security as to our professional purposes and capacities serve to steady and temper our emotional responses.

Even the most experienced and self-knowing among us does not achieve this once and for all. On one day, any day, we become aware—or have called to our attention—that we are responding to a client with our personal selves rather than with our professional selves; that we are reacting in the relationship in accord with our needs rather than with those of the client. On that day, again, we must come to a full stop, this time to rework our own feelings, alone or with supervisory help, to make sure that the relationship we offer the client is for his welfare.

Warmth, receptivity, sympathetic responsiveness; acceptance of the person as he is and expectation that, with help, he will strive toward change in himself or his situation; purposiveness, objectivity, and goal; the ability and willingness to be of help; authority of expertness and of charge—all these characterize the caseworker's professional relationship. Within this dynamic matrix of acceptance and expectation, security and stimulation, the conscious work of problem-solving takes place.

# 7 THE PROBLEM-
## SOLVING WORK

Perhaps the chief complexity of casework lies in the fact that its concern is always twofold: to promote the solution of the client's problems in social living and by this process to promote his capacity for growth. One eye of the caseworker must be kept on the object and the other on the subject, and it is small wonder that in this task of double perception the caseworker's vision at moments becomes blurred or strained. Yet we must hold to what we know to be true— that the conditions for the human being's social development are the use of his own powers in coping with the people and situations he encounters and the presence of pliant opportunity in his social environment. Thus, social casework attempts simultaneously to provide these two kinds of conditions: the resources and influences by which its client's social needs may be met and the modes which promote its client's personal and social effectiveness.

The first of these is readily recognized and identified; it is the oldest, most tangible, and most easily understood service. The second, less tangible and manifest, less readily demonstrable, is based upon the assumption that people's own powers are built up and enriched by their working on their social problems in the ways developed by professional social casework, because casework operates in full consonance with the functioning of the personality. The proposition has already been set forth that there is a striking parallel between the normal operations of the ego in its problem-solving efforts and the systematized work in which the caseworker engages his client. The problem-solving work, consciously undertaken by caseworker and client, guided by the caseworker's understanding, and promoted by the nurture and stimulus of the relationship, is the subject of this chapter.

To recapitulate briefly (for these are not easy considerations, and the reader's perceptions, too, may falter!): The functions of the ego —to perceive, to protect or adapt, to mobilize and to act—are heavily affected by emotional or environmental conditions. In the face of feeling helpless, a person's ability to recognize reality may be dulled or skewed. He may see some things acutely but blot out others; he may "lose sight" of important factors; he may fail to differentiate between actuality and his response to it. The ego's protective functions are activated immediately with a perception that records "danger." They normally operate to give the personality time and place to fence and reorganize itself in order to cope with a feared or actual assault; but those protective functions which arise as a result of faulty perception can lead only to faulty adaptation. This may take place by the erection of rigid walls of defense behind which the person barricades himself, thereby cutting off his perceptions and making himself incommunicado (to others and to his own inner communication system), or, at the other extreme, by the collapse of efforts at self-defense, with ensuing helplessness and relinquishment of the self to the mercies of fate. Somewhere between these extremes will be found the behavior of most persons in trouble, seeking with greater or lesser success to protect themselves against feelings of insecurity or inadequacy at the same time as they are skirmishing to find some way of bringing their problem under control.

As soon as the functions of perception and protection are enfeebled or rigidified, the functions of adaptation are affected. The healthy ego's adaptive powers are manifold. They consist of the selection of certain stimuli to be entertained and the casting-off of others; the placing of certain factors in the center of attention and the suppression of others; the governing of impulses in the light of conscious appraisal of reality requirements; and the churning of facts, sensory perceptions, ideas, and experiences (known and antic-ipated) in that process called "thinking." Sometimes consciously and sometimes unconsciously controlled, the ego's adaptive opera-tions include making connections, discriminations, and choices. Then decisions are organized for expression in behavior. If, however, adaptive operations are undermined or walled off by unrealistic per-ception or rigidified defenses, the action which the person takes is accordingly inept or distorted. Scrutinizer, organizer of inner re-sources, the ego is also the acknowledged executive of the person-ality. It controls, inhibits, or releases movement and action, and it determines, thus, what the person will do. Depending on the effec-tive or ineffective operations of ego functions, then, the person's problem-solving efforts will be useful or destructive to his social transactions.

As the client presents himself to the agency, one thing is certain: his behavior is his ego's effort at taking action which he hopes will lead to some different adaptation—either of the situation to his needs, of himself to the situation's demands, or both. In other words, his ego is already involved in problem-solving measures.

*The casework process sustains, supplements, and fortifies the functions of the client's ego.*

As has been said, the casework relationship itself may have potent effects. Even in its simplest form it provides for the client a kind of safety island where, for the moment, he experiences freedom from the traffic that bears down on him and on which he may view the hurly-burly with some lessened fear and better perspective. Within the sympathetic attentiveness of any good working relationship the client may experience some lowering of his tensions and therefore some greater freedom to see his problems and himself more clearly. When the relationship becomes charged with his trust in the worker and with his sense of the worker's stability and understanding of him, it yields even greater support and nourishment to his ego. As the client comes to feel at one with the worker, he unconsciously incorporates some of the worker's steadiness, faith, and confidence. Consciously, too, he may identify by trying to take on some of the worker's ways of viewing things, and he may stretch himself to try to do and to be what he believes the worker would hold to be de-sirable. He begins to perceive himself and his situation differently.

He feels the support of the bond which unites him to a person stronger and steadier in the area of his trouble than he. "The ego learns correct behavior through identification with others who have mastered it," Alexander says, and, again: "Identification is the basis of all learning which is not acquired independently by trial and error."*

Even in those situations where the client's need is chiefly for some material aids or arrangements, the caseworker by the quality of his relationship says, "You have nothing to fear from me. I am here to help you." As this attitude is consistently demonstrated, the client's defenses may be lowered. (The exception, of course, is found in the person whose defenses have become so rigid that he is unable to come out from behind them to test reality.) With the lowering of defenses against the source of help, the client sees himself more clearly, his problem, and the helping means. The energy tied up in defense is freed for adaptation; his sense of "belonging together" with the reliable helper fortifies his security; and so it is that he dares to risk the exploration of new ideas and new actions in relation to his problem.

Thus, much of the problem-solving work is on an unconscious or only partly conscious basis; that is, it "happens" spontaneously in the empathic interaction between caseworker and client. But all of it, let it be remembered, centers about some problem consciously brought by the client and affirmed by the caseworker—a problem to be solved by joint effort. Problem-solving must also include, then, conscious, focused, goal-directed activity between client and caseworker and for each on his own part as well. The work of problem-solving in the caseworker's mind must, if it is to be effective, be a systematically organized process. He will hardly play it out in its logical outline as he involves the client in it, because he will measure it to the client's capacities and needs. But he should be clear as to what must happen in order to move from dilemma to solution or from stalemate to decision; the facts that constitute the problem must be known, thought and feeling must be brought to play upon them, and choices and means for dealing with them must be considered and decided on. The work of problem-solving as it is ex-

* *Fundamentals of Psychoanalysis,* chap. v, "The Functions of the Ego and Its Failures." (See Franz Alexander [1] listed under chapter 2.)

perienced by the client, on the other hand, may be recognized by him chiefly as a stimulation to mobilize himself to think about himself and his situation in some protected and orderly ways.

*The first part of the casework process, as in all problem-solving, is to ascertain and clarify the facts of the problem.*

A fact, according to the dictionary, is "any event, mental or physical; an assurance, quality, or relation, the reality of which is manifest in experience or may be inferred with certainty." The facts to be ascertained in the casework process are just such facts of objective and subjective reality—events, qualities, relationships, situations, reactions, and behaviors that may be established by observation, documentation, and inference. They are the accounts of the nature of the problem as it actually appears to the worker and as it is both seen and felt by the client. They include the circumstances, the client's feeling and behavior responses to them, and the means or goals sought and available. They are the minutiae of "What is the trouble?" of "What brought this about?" of "What have you tried to do?" of "What, exactly, do you mean?" of "What do you want to happen?" and so on. They give to "difficulty" and "trouble" their tangible, specific forms, so that "help" and "solution" may be focused and appropriate.

Sometimes it seems that caseworkers tend to consider facts as dull matters to be got over as quickly as possible so as to "get on with the case." But "the fact is" that only certain facts can ever be established once and for all—facts of static happenings and things. Other facts are those of feeling and experience, those which record circumstances and forces in movement, those which are continuously emerging out of what is happening between the client and his problem both outside and within the casework process. Such facts as these cannot be gotten over with; they must continuously be attended to, drawn out, examined, taken into account.

The establishment of facts, whether objective or subjective, is actually the essential condition of comunication. Only thus can the caseworker and his client know that they are talking about the same things, physical or mental; that they mean the same things by the words they use; and that they perceive the same data as the base of their discussion. Facts, in short, establish the working reality.

Whether of situation, event, action, or feeling, the establishment of fact is a large part of the clarification process of which we speak so much in casework. Clarification is not often, as is sometimes thought, the result of a sudden flash of insight or interpretive illumination. It is more often the product of a continuous, repeated, step-by-step search for exact data and exact meaning. Particularly when problems involve psychological confusions and unrealistic perceptions, facts need the most careful pursuit. When Mrs. White says, tremulously, "I sometimes wonder if I'm capable of motherly feelings," a caseworker, noting the fact of her upset, may hasten to reassure her that indeed she is. But this only excites further anxiety in Mrs. White, because it brushes aside a whole group of facts which she needs to express and to look at with the caseworker's support. These are the facts of her ideas of motherliness (What does "motherly feeling" mean to her?), the facts about the feelings she has which make her anxious (In what "unmotherly" ways does she feel toward her child? What "unmotherly" things does she do?) and so on. Only as these facts of feeling and behavior are laid out between her and her helper can either of them be sure they are talking about the same thing when they say "motherly," and only so, too, can Mrs. White sort out and clarify that mass of resentful anxiousness she harbors toward her child. Only by this means can she come to *know* clearly rather than to *feel* vaguely the nature of her problem.

What this says, then, is that the continuous piece-by-piece eliciting of facts serves the client in several ways. First, it provides the essential condition to his realistic perception. Of course, he can report only what he sees, but supplementing or differing from his perceptions are those of the caseworker—clearer, broader, and more organized by virtue of knowledge, experience, and non-involvement in the problem. How the caseworker perceives may be a corrective to the client's vision, and thus the client's ego is aided in its testing of reality and preparation for action. Sharing and examining data with another pair of eyes, so to speak, helps the client come to see the difference or the connection between his actual situation and his interpretation of it, between his drives and the demands of reality, between his ends and their relation to the facts of the agency's means.

By telling about the facts of his situation and feelings and having what he tells accepted and reflected back to him with the caseworker's clarifying questions or comments, the client's perceptive faculties may be even further enhanced. When the real and the imagined are differentiated from each other, when obscurities of feelings or ideas are clarified, and when it is found that the anxious wish or fear when spoken out has no power of its own, then tension may be lessened and unreal fears diluted. Lowered anxiety results in clearer vision.

Of course the eliciting and clarification of facts must be to help the caseworker and the client in working on the problem, not to enable the client to "see all" or to satisfy the caseworker's sense of completeness. Thus, the caseworker may glimpse or grasp many facts which he will not attempt to have his client see, since they might overwhelm the defenses against them—defenses which say, "I do not see because at this time I cannot dare to see"—or since they are not truly relevant to the problem at hand. Or a caseworker may decide to postpone discussion of certain facts, waiting on the client's increased trust or stability or on other working considerations. Always the caseworker must exercise his judgment as to which facts are appropriate to select and explore, which are primary and of foremost relevance at a given time, and which—while they may be interesting—are of secondary importance or actually useless to the aims in the particular case.

The client and the caseworker cannot always establish all the necessary facts during the interview. In many instances it may be necessary to ascertain facts of personality and situation from other sources—other people in the client's life, professional persons who have knowledge of the client, documents, firsthand investigation of housing or school conditions, and so on. Only as the caseworker understands that what a person sees and how he interprets it is affected by the functioning of his ego powers will the caseworker himself perceive that it may be necessary to supplement or correct the client's view of fact through the use of collateral sources.[*]

*The second aspect of casework problem-solving grows out of and interweaves with the ongoing eliciting of facts: it is thinking through the facts.*

[*] For developed discussion of this point see Perlman (3) listed under chapter 9.

By "thinking" I do not mean at all the dispassionate "click-click" of some disembodied intellectual mechanisms. Perhaps some distinction lies between *thinking about* a problem, which is a kind of rumination or a play of ideas across it, and *thinking through* a problem, which requires coming to grips with it, probing into it, facing up to the feelings which it excites or with which it is charged, and working with the mind and also the spirit and the body to achieve mastery over it. Anyone who has thought through a problem knows the body tensions, the anxious conflict of drive and resistance, and the sweat and tears which may accompany this so-called intellectual process. Even working an abstract problem, such as an algebraic equation, may call forth this involvement of the whole self. It will do so when it holds some emotional value or significance to the person, as when passing a course or maintaining status or self-respect is involved. How much more, then, is the whole person enmeshed in thinking through a problem which is his own and affects his whole living! To "put one's mind" to one's problem is in no sense the same as to divorce one's mind from one's feelings. Rather it is to bring them together into communication, so that what is felt may come to be known and understood and what is known and understood may be experienced as true.

Enabling a client to tell his problem, its facts of situational and emotional import, is the first step in helping him. What accompanies or follows this is enabling him to think it through. This means help to the client to search for understanding of what his problem is made of, how his actions and reactions affect it, what different meanings may be imputed to it, and therefore what different significances it may have in terms of his reaction to it and possible decisions about it. It is helping him to shake the problem apart and view it in its separate and therefore often more manageable parts. It is helping him to select out from the massed pressure he feels those elements which are most important and to cast off others and thus move toward some more organized and economical approach to coping with his trouble. The client is led to express and explain, to make clear, to suppose, to recollect, to ruminate, to speculate, to consider, to anticipate, to see relationships—in short, to play the light of ideas across the facts in order to feel them, react to them, and understand them differently. As he wrestles with some fact of situation or feeling to submit it to reasoning or as he strives to bring his thoughts to bear upon his reactions, he is, whether he knows it or not, engaged in the internal work of adaptation.

The caseworker's help in this work is made up of several processes. It consists of guiding the client's "telling" and his discussions in such ways as to bring certain aspects of the problem into focus into the center of attention. One chosen center of attention may give way to another, found to be more vital or pertinent, but at any given time some focus is essential to seeing clearly and precisely. Moreover, because it is overwhelming to encounter any problem in its wholeness, with all its implications, this focusing is a way of partializing the problem-solving task. One thing at a time and a time for each thing is an age-old admonishment to ourselves to cut the task to manageable size. The caseworker gives further aid in making the problem manageable by the orderly, relevant nature of his queries. By this means a client's inner confusions may be reduced (see Irvine, 4, listed under chapter 5). Later chapters will present this help in more detail.

In this work of thinking through, the ego takes responsibility, so to speak, for the exercise of its consciously controlled functions. As a person turns over in his mind considerations of relationships (as among cause and effect, action and reaction, acts and consequences), as he concentrates on some aspects of a problem and excludes others, as he makes connections and isolates differences, as he conjures up the images of people and situations and anticipates their actuality and his behavior in relation to them, as he expresses and views his feelings in the light of reason, as he measures his strivings against his reality—as he does all these things, he is exercising his adaptive capacities in preparation for adaptation in his action. These exercises are both the means and the substance of conscious adaptation. By such means do all of us make choices of attitude and action, so that they will be, within the limits allowed to human beings, at once realistically appropriate and satisfying.

The caseworker's comments and questions give continuous stimulus to this process. As he distinguishes the more from the less important, as he suggests focus, as he raises questions that clarify and differentiate data, as by repeated comments he implies connectedness and patternings, he gives impetus and direction to the client's ego in its conscious fantasy-experiments with adaptation. This, indeed, is a major function of the human being's thinking process. Moreover, if, as in a long-term contact, the caseworker demonstrates over and over again the ways by which problems may be approached, the client may come to make these ways his own and use them after he has left the experience of casework and of the agency behind him.

As the mind and the heart of the client are freed to communicate better with each other (and are supported and encouraged by the caseworker's constant relationship), certain mellowing changes of attitude may occur, too; and, while his real problem may remain intransigent, it may be experienced differently by the client. His feelings of anxiety or frustration may undergo changes of quality and intensity due to their being aired and through identification with the caseworker's differing perspectives. Perhaps a brief example will illustrate in a homely way what may, as theory, seem to have qualities of magic:

Mrs. Black has come to the family agency, voicing her discontent with her marriage. In this fourth interview with the caseworker she bursts forth with anger and contempt that her husband is "a liar." "A liar" on the tongue of an angry wife may mean many things—habitual lying, one protective falsehood, etc.—so the caseworker asks what Mrs. Black means and what the facts are. Mrs. Black recounts a number of instances in which her husband tells falsehoods or, at the least, exaggerates—he didn't tell her until two weeks after he lost his job that he had done so, he exaggerated his status in his office, he bragged to her family about earning more than he did, etc. These "facts" spontaneously have meaning to the caseworker, but more immediate is the fact of Mrs. Black's feeling. His comment, then, is on how annoying this has been to Mrs. Black. Mrs. Black responds freely to this recognition, and she expresses further anger and scorn. She knows from the caseworker's sympathetic nods that he understands her feeling, is "with her."

Now the caseworker tests Mrs. Black's ability and willingness to gain some different perspective on these facts and to see connections. He asks Mrs. Black why she supposes Mr. Black acts this way, since there must be some reason. Mrs. Black makes a stab at going along with the idea the caseworker proposes, because she feels related to the worker and understood by him. She ventures that maybe Mr. Black "has an inferiority complex"—that he lies to build himself up. The caseworker comments that Mrs. Black has an idea here. He wonders, aloud, why Mr. Black would need to bolster himself. Mrs. Black responds to this stimulus to pursue her idea further. She says he was pretty much kicked around as a kid, pulled himself up by his own bootstraps—really, he told her when they were married that he had never felt "safe" before.

Now some feeling change is discernible in Mrs. Black as she is led by the worker to recount further facts of her husband's understandable insecurities and his dependence on her. There is contempt still, but it combines now with some indulgent compassion in place of anger. Her own feelings are being modified by her thinking. But the caseworker, knowing this may be short lived, asks her to push further in thinking about this, now in its significance for Mrs. Black herself. He suggests that, even though Mrs. Black understands it and feels sorry for her husband, it isn't always easy to live with a liar. Mrs. Black muses over this: "It's true, it isn't—but, yet, he's sort of like a kid—you feel sort of sorry—he's got his good points." The caseworker comments on her two-sided feelings, and by this he places them squarely in Mrs. Black's line of vision. Mrs. Black nods and muses over this.

The caseworker proposes that Mrs. Black wants to do more than feel sorry for her husband. He is stimulating Mrs. Black to work on the problem further, not to be content with the momentary sympathy she feels, because the caseworker knows that this can be supplanted by dislike again if it is not worked through from feeling to mind. He suggests that they ought to talk more about what happens between Mrs. Black and her husband when she finds him lying—what are the facts of what she says and does, for instance. Mrs. Black launches into an example, a vivid, mimicked account of what she said and did when her husband finally confessed he was jobless. The caseworker listens attentively, relating to Mrs. Black's feelings throughout. When Mrs. Black pauses, the caseworker asks what Mr. Black's response was. Mrs. Black says, triumphantly, "He just put his tail between his legs and slunk off."

The caseworker comments, as a matter-of-fact extension of Mrs. Black's remark, that her husband probably "felt like two cents." Mrs. Black does a double-take on this. "He sure did!" she says, and then (because she sees this more clearly now, having projected it and also borrowing the caseworker's perceptions) she catches her mouth says, "Lord! I guess I put him right back into that complex!" She squirms uneasily and defends herself against her own indictment by saying, "But, honestly, I got so fed up."

The caseworker appreciates her feeling sympathetically. But he comments, also, that Mrs. Black's interpretation is probably right. Mrs. Black asks, half-challengingly, half-pleadingly, "Do you suppose it's *me?*" The caseworker supposes it's both of them, Mrs. Black *and* her husband, in their interaction on each other. This is something to think about for next time.

It is not difficult to see the several changes that have occurred in this interview in the nature of Mrs. Black's feelings, her perceptions, her making connections, and her different grasp of the problem. Several dynamic factors are responsible, but prominent among them is the repeated impetus given Mrs. Black by the caseworker to submit the facts of situation and feeling to her thought. This may be considered a small cross-section of the way the caseworker, by comments, questions, suggestions, or even only half-spoken words, gives stimulus and direction to the client to bring feeling to thought and thought to feeling and to bring both to bear upon his problem situation; to scrutinize, cogitate, reflect, make connections—to work, in short, at readapting his ideas and powers in relation to his problem.

For the caseworker the ways in which his client responds and takes hold, feelingly and thoughtfully, of the struggle with his problem and its possible outcomes reveal what difficulties and resources may be counted on in pursuit of the problem's solution. He gets diagnostic signs, in brief, which he incorporates into his thinking about means and ends of further help. For the client, the work of guided discussion should clarify and deepen his understanding of himself, his difficulties, his ways out—all in relation to one another. This is *his* diagnosing experience; it serves as the base of his conscious organization of himself. At the same time it is an experience of being helped and of change, because feelings exposed to the light of thought and thoughts open to the powers of feeling and both worked over in a responsive, sustaining, goal-directed relationship cannot but modify one another. When such modification succeeds in harnessing emotional energy to reasoned purposes, some problem-solving activity will ensue.

*The conclusive phase of each problem-solving effort in casework is the making of some choice or decision.*

All this experiencing and thinking activity which casework promotes and sustains is a kind of dress rehearsal for the ego's executive action. Its action may be upon the internal organization of the personality, unobservable except in subtle ways which bespeak modification of feelings, lessening of tensions, and stabilizing of comfort; or its execution may take the form of outward behavior, in responses and acts; or both may occur. Either is the product of a "decision" made by the ego, sometimes unconsciously, consisting of the spontaneous coming-together of selected perceptions, ideas, strivings, and partial adaptations, and, often consciously, consisting of cautious choices made in the light of facts, their appraisal, and the attempt to anticipate possible consequences.

The making of choice and decisions from which some inner change or overt action will flow is the third step in problem-solving. To make this step, too, the caseworker must help the client. This help consists of keeping in constant view the questions of what the client wants or hopes for, what he can realistically get or have, and what he is really willing to invest in getting it. It involves the recognition, by caseworker and then by client, of the two-way pulls which operate in all of us at times, the client's wanting and not-wanting, the yea and the nay in him, and, beyond this recognition, the working-over of these feelings to bring one side of them to compromise and the other to affirmative ascendancy. It includes the joint examination of the alternatives and consequences of choice—"What will happen if I do?" "How will it be if I don't?" and so on—so that decisions can be made not blindly but with some measure of foresight. And it involves for both caseworker and client that delicately maintained balance between the struggle to be freed from "mortal coils" and the acceptance that for most of us choice is a privilege with limits.

Lest "choice" and "decision" sound heavy with portent, perhaps it should be said that the decisions the client must come to are often the small everyday ones and only occasionally major choices. More exactly, it is the small decisions along the way which, week by week, bit by bit, shape the full nature of choice. To illustrate this, Mrs. Black will serve again, as she comes in for her next interview:

She starts by saying, laughingly, provocatively, that she almost didn't come. She really didn't see that she was getting anywhere. The caseworker might have anticipated this. Mrs. Black was uncomfortable at the end of the last interview, for she had suddenly found herself to be an active force in a situation where previously she had considered herself to be chiefly a victim, and, moreover, she had begun to feel in herself the stir of guilt and conflict. But, the caseworker recognizes, Mrs. Black has made a decision, if only momentary, about returning. The caseworker says, "But you did come—you are here."

Mrs. Black says, "Yes," but does not follow through; she looks down at her gloves.

The caseworker ventures that perhaps at the same time that Mrs. Black thought she wasn't getting anywhere she was also hoping she might get somewhere. Maybe this is what brought her back? Mrs. Black says, lamely, "I guess so." The caseworker ventures further to suggest that, even though there is a lot in her marriage that "makes her sick," Mrs. Black still has some feeling that she'd like to make a go of it. He is, it can be seen, pushing Mrs. Black gently to face up consciously to her ambivalent feelings about her marriage. "Yes, it's true," Mrs. Black says, "but how—that's the point."

"*How* isn't easy to describe," says the caseworker. It would mean that she and her husband would both need to work on themselves and on their trouble together, both at home and here, with their caseworkers; and the hard part is that it's bound to be uncomfortable, because that's what happens when we start to look at ourselves. Probably the last interview made Mrs. Black uncomfortable. . . .

The caseworker is trying to help Mrs. Black see the conditions which she would be choosing if she decides to continue. Mrs. Black grimaces. "It was uncomfortable," she says laconically. Then, in a burst: "I felt like I was walking on eggshells all week! Every time I said something to Tom, I thought, 'What am I doing to him?' and believe me, that's no fun."

The caseworker relates to Mrs. Black's feelings heartily, "It's no fun at all—it's upsetting." And, yet, it shows that Mrs. Black has made one big step toward doing something about her marriage problem—she has seen that she's part of it. Mrs. Black's response is a long look at the caseworker, a look which says, "Do you mean that?"

"The other step you have taken," says the caseworker, "is to come back in spite of feeling angry, maybe, and uncomfortable, surely, so maybe you think we *can* help you." (The caseworker accepts her bad feelings and at the same time supports the constructive elements in Mrs. Black's action.)

"That's true," says Mrs. Black.

"Do you think, then," the caseworker asks, "that you want to try going on with me, even though there will be times when you'll be irritated with what we're doing or unhappy? I think we can work things out. But I suppose the question is: Is Tom's and your life together worth trying to save?" Again the caseworker has placed before Mrs. Black the consideration of choice—discomfort and the possibility of working out her marriage or the possibility of sloughing off the whole matter.

Mrs. Black does not answer directly. She nods her head slightly two or three times, then leans forward and says, "Well—I'll try. Let me tell you what happened when I got home last week."

She has made her first small decisions: to return to the agency and to work a bit further at her problem with some recognition and some ambivalent feeling that she is choosing the hard way. Now the small problem of to take or not to take help has been resolved, and her energies are transferred for investment in the larger problem of whether or not she can achieve more satisfaction in her marriage. But this, too, can be resolved only through a whole chain of small choices and decisions, arrived at by choosing lesser evils or greater goods as the basis for coping with dilemmas.

The preparation for settling on what to do or be today or tomorrow and for its testing in life takes place, then, in the dialogue between caseworker and client. Again, it is the caseworker who gives stimulus to the consideration of means and ends, of acts and their consequences, and of the positive and negative feelings that sway choice. Decisions that involve taking some overt action need one step more—they require the projection in the mind's eye and then in discussion of the anticipated things to say or do and the expected reactions. Every one of us, in preparation for meeting a situation in which we anticipate difficulty or danger, uses this form of fantasy. Whether this forethought and forehandedness serves us well depends, usually, upon several factors. We must see the facts, objective and subjective, realistically; we must comprehend the interacting relationships between ourselves and the situations to be dealt with; and we must be capable of conscious use of ourselves in line with what we know and understand. For the client, too, these factors hold valid, and his ability to be successful in his trials of action will depend upon his having achieved some different orientation to his problem and a better integration of thought and feeling about it. As he begins to find himself more ready to cope with his problem, there expands in him that sense of internal resource and hope which is the requisite to ongoing adaptations.

The proof of the ego's functioning adequacy is the person's ability to carry out into his living such action as is appropriate both to social reality and to his own consciously chosen goals. Often this step to action feels like a risky business, because it may involve behaving differently—in some instances, taking bold steps of speech or actions; in others, desisting from impulsive behavior; in some, uprooting habitual living arrangements; in others, upsetting long-established patterns of relationship. Here, again, the casework relationship makes it possible for the client to take these risks, for it offers him the haven to which he can return to share his small triumphs or failures, his satisfactions or frustrations, and, in addition, to prepare to sally forth again. As the person's trial actions succeed, as what he does or how he maintains balance gratifies him or as it evokes more satisfying responses from other persons, his ego gains in its sense of mastery. "Nothing succeeds like success" was never more true than as it applies to the ego. With proof of impotence it shrinks and retreats; with proof of ability it expands and grows venturesome.

Behavior that is rewarding is claimed by the ego as its own, and it tends to be digested into the ego's total organization. This is how patterns of adaptation become established; it is the condition for the consolidation of learning. Part of the client's reward for acting in new ways comes from the recognition and warm support of his efforts which the caseworker gives him. More valid and more vital than this, however, must be the gratifications he can get from his new ability to cope with his everyday living and from the responsiveness of those persons and things to which he bends his efforts.

There remains to be taken into account that group of persons who come to many social agencies for whom the work of problem-solving is largely the burden of the caseworker, because they themselves have little energy or capacity to invest. These clients are to be found among the senile aged, the near-psychotic, and those persons whose physical, emotional, or intellectual handicaps all but consume their small store of vital energies. Their ego capacities may be found so dwarfed, deteriorated, or volatile as to make intrenchment a virtual necessity for the maintenance of life. They may need their defenses as the dystrophied muscle needs braces. For them the caseworker may need to give more acceptance than expectation, more cushioning than challenge, more justification than questioning. Yet, even among these unfortunate ones, such problems as whether to undergo surgery or not, to go to live in an institution or not, even whether to go to church or not, may be worked through by the patient discussion with the person of the facts, the "whys" and "why nots," in the possible decisions to be made. This helps him to stretch the narrow margin of his selfhood.

And finally, a fact of which social workers scarcely need to be reminded: the reasons for a person's failure to solve his problems by adaptation and choice of action may lie not solely in himself but in his circumstances. There are situations in people's lives that are more crucial or more persistently eroding than the personality can bear, and there are other situations where to the person's experience of need and want there is presented only emptiness. No loss or debilitation of ego powers can adequately be assessed except as the conditions to which it is a response are known. Nor can the ego develop vigor or flexibility when it is starved or chained by an unyielding environment (see Towle, 5). This is why social casework, concerned with strengthening the client's ego, relates not only to the personality in its struggle to learn effective behavior but also to the social environment with which the person interacts. The caseworker's direct efforts to influence other vital persons in the client's life, his arranging for help from another source, the provision of such arrangements or moneys as are necessary to the maintenance of adequate living, the finding of and collaboration with opportunities and resources by which the client may expand the narrow circumstances of his life—by all these aids the caseworker empowers the ego.

As the person is actually less put upon, as his struggle against social odds is less overwhelming, as he can look about him and see that his environment holds some promise for self-fulfilment, his ego's integration is supported and its expansion encouraged. When real need is met, there is a lessening of defensive operations, and energy is freed for gaining new goals. Moreover, when provision for lacks or restitution for losses is at hand, real difficulty can be more readily faced by the ego, because it is freed from crowding anxiety and buoyed up by some hope. Thus even those services which to the caseworker may seem commonplace may, when they are missing, undermine the person's balance and may, when they are present, support and promote his ego's equilibrium and its sensitively geared functioning.

In sum, the ego's continuous task is that of solving the problems, small or great, posed by what the person wants, what powers of mind, spirit, and body he can harness to his purposes, and what his environment requires, gives, or withholds. Social casework's continuous task is that of helping the person who is encountering difficulty in his problem-solving to enhance his own powers, enrich his opportunities, and achieve his socially desirable ends. To this purpose the casework process of problem-solving offers the nurture and sustainment of relationship, the stimulation, exercise, and development of its clients' own feeling, thinking, and acting capacities, and the modification of social stresses and provision of social opportunities. In its structure, its operations, and its ends this professional process may be viewed as a knowledgeable and skilled counterpart of the ego's own good functions and task.

How this works in practice, the details of how the person with a problem can be helped in the social agency which uses the casework process, is developed in the chapters which follow.

# CASEWORK

## IN CROSS-SECTION

# 8 PERSON, PROBLEM, PLACE, AND
## PROCESS IN THE BEGINNING PHASE

"Well begun is half-done," says the old proverb. Perhaps nowhere is this more true than in the beginnings of an experience with a human being that is expected to have continuity and to produce change. In order that such an experience be well begun, it must contain at its start the essential elements and operations that characterize its nature. The human being not only receives and records experience but also reacts to and interprets it. On the basis of what he experiences and how it seems to him, he anticipates what it is to be from this time on and adapts himself accordingly. So it is important that the beginnings of any ongoing process should be as true to that process as they possibly can be. Otherwise, people feel impelled to begin over again, because what they have experienced has been a false start.

This is why the beginning phase of the casework process is of such importance. The client, if he is to know what he is undertaking and if he is to be enabled to organize himself appropriately, must have a true sample and demonstration of what is to be expected. This sample and demonstration should give him in capsule form the essence of the interaction among him, his problem, and the agency and the forces and means that will be brought to bear upon the difficulties at hand. If what the client is to experience in casework problem-solving is to be more than a laying-on of helping hands and a laying-out of helping goods, the beginning phase of this experience must involve more than a delineation of problem and an offer of service. If the experience is to be more than being understood and soothed, then the beginning must contain more than helping the client to express himself and proffering reassurances. If it is not to be simply a giving-over on the one side and a taking-over on the other, then it must from the first be different from this. If, to state it in positive terms, casework is to be a process which exercises the person himself in perceiving, thinking about, and acting in relation to his problem situation at the same time as he is fortified and sustained, then the beginning phase must so exercise and sustain him in good measure. When this happens, the client takes part from the first in using the agency's helping means; he can anticipate what the ongoing experience is to be like; he and the caseworker are "well begun."

The initial phase starts at the moment the client presents himself to the agency, whether by telephone, by proxy, through the intercession of someone else, or in his own person. It ends, as phase, when a kind of pact has been arrived at in the nature of a "trial engagement" between client and caseworker to go forward together in their problem-solving efforts. This pact may sometimes be reached in a single interview, but sometimes it may take four or five discussions before clarification, mutual understanding, and decision are arrived at. In this conception of the beginning phase its aim and end may be said to be this: to engage the client and his will to do something about his problem in a working relationship with the agency and its special means of helpfulness. When this has taken place, the ongoing phase ensues.*

### The Person in the Beginning Phase

At the door of the social agency stands the person who has a problem. It may be simple or complex, old or new, commonplace or peculiar, but it always has this significance to the person: it is something that he is experiencing as frustrating in his present living situation, and it is something that he finds he cannot cope with un-

---

* For a differing point of view see Scherz (8).

aided. Usually he has tried to wrestle with the problem on his own or with the help of persons and things in his normal social milieu. Depending on his ways of defending and adapting himself, he may have tried to deal with the problem in one of a number of ways: he might have resolutely pushed it out of sight and tried not to listen to its insistent pounding on the doors of his consciousness; he might have sought solutions for it, frantically or thoughtfully, and have exhausted his physical and social resources in trying to solve it; he might have turned it over and over in his mind and in talk with family and friends, only to find that it seemed to grow bigger and that he seemed to grow smaller in relation to it. The nature of the problem might hold some particular fearfulness for him; it might spell for him the loss of his feeling of security ("The bottom has fallen out of my world"), the loss of his sense of adequacy ("If I had any kind of guts, I could lick this thing"), or, worse, the loss of both. And the fears which the problem engenders begin to undermine the person further, to make him feel even more beset and helpless. So even a problem that is "simple" on its objective face is complicated for the person who owns it, because it gnaws at him, drains his confidence and hope, and takes possession of him.

Whatever else the person has been able or unable to do about his problem, his arrival at the agency—or even his tentative phone call—means that he has come to a decision to ask for outside help. He may not be at all knowledgeable as to what this place represents or does in so far as his problem is concerned; he may think of it as "The Relief" or "The Child's Welfare" or as some substitute for the psychiatric help he feels he needs but cannot afford; or he may be clearly cognizant of its function. But, however he conceives of it, he knows it is some organized resource outside himself and that his first step toward it represents a new effort on his part in dealing with his problem.

Yet this new effort does not always feel constructive and hopeful to the person himself. It may, on the contrary, be charged with feelings of desperateness and of relinquishing his own rights and responsibilities into the hands of others. Or the person may be permeated with such an overwhelming sense of urgency that the effort to seek help is felt as an effort to command preconceived solutions.

These feelings, of sinking dependency or of fighting self-assertion, mingle with the emotions that already surge in the potential client.

But even this is not all, for, as the person stands at the door of the agency, he is aware that a new problem confronts him—the problem of asking for and taking help from a stranger in an alien place. It is not "alien" when he supports it, say, as a contributor to the Community Fund, or as one who refers another person to it; it becomes "alien" when he needs it for himself on intimate, unhappy matters. The caseworker and the agency become "they" for him, that third-person plural which for all of us at times represents vague powers in society, that "they" onto whom we project our guilt and uncertainties. "What will they think of me?" the person wonders. "I should be able to manage my child myself." "Maybe they'll think it's my fault that I'm out of work." And, then, "What will they ask me?" "What will they do for me?" "What will I have to pay if I don't pay money?" The person begins both to feel and to think about the shame or guilt that adults in our society have learned to feel when they fall short of being self-dependent, self-responsible persons. He may defend himself by finding and clinging to the victimizing causes that bring him to help, or by self-condemnation so scathing that nothing "they" say can match it, or by suppressing his feelings and putting on the mask of indifference or briskness. But he can only wait to find out what the answers will be to his unformed questions as to what will be done to him and for him.

So, added to the original burden that he carries, the person, as he stands on the threshold of the agency, encounters a second problem—the feelings and the yet-to-be-known facts about the business of being helped. Something of this is true even of the client who is an "old customer" of social agencies. He, however, approaches the agency readying himself to expectations and actions that he has experienced in the past. He anticipates the "they" he will encounter, what they will say and how they will act; and the feelings roused by his earlier experiences with the same or other agencies will rise again to make him present himself, often inappropriately, as already resistant or already acquiescent or uneasy. In other instances, having had experiences which won his trust, he approaches the agency with hopeful confidence. In either instance, and even if he comes with the flare-up of an old problem, he is making a new beginning, and the caseworker may need to help him recognize this and the differences from the past which the present experience holds.

## The Problem in the Beginning Phase

The problem which the person carries to the agency, sometimes clutched to him tightly, sometimes distastefully held out at finger's tip, is something which troubles, hurts, or incapacitates him *today*. As today's problem it may be only one manifestation or only a side issue of a central problem of long standing, but it is seen by him and is most readily communicable in its tangible, socially recognizable form. Whatever its true nature, it will have some changed aspect for its owner as soon as he begins to share it and his feelings about it with the caseworker and as soon as the caseworker demonstrates his intent and ability to be of help.

But perhaps the uppermost problem in the beginning is not that which the person brings to the agency but that which he encounters at the agency's door. It is the problem not only of asking for help but of taking and using it. The fact is that for most life-problems there are no ready-made solutions which can be applied per se to dissolve the problem, and this fact is disappointing. It is complicated further by the necessity that the person become, not the agency's ward, but its partner in stipulated kinds of work on the problem; and this is often an unexpected arrangement, perhaps gratifying, perhaps frustrating. The degree of difficulty or ease will vary with the person's basic security and the problem's importance to him, but the business of becoming an active partner in work with the agency on his problem is the first difficulty to be solved in casework.

The problem in the beginning, then, is always a dual one. Which aspect of its duality will require most attention and emphasis will depend heavily upon how ready and able or how unmotivated and incapable the person himself is to go forward in work on the problem as he brings it.

## The Place and the Caseworker in the Beginning Phase

On its side, the social agency stands ready to receive and if possible to give help to the person whose problem brings him to it. The agency has a stated purpose, a special set of functions, structures, policies, and procedures, which, if they have validity, are the implements of its special welfare purpose. It is (or should be) peopled by persons with professional knowledge and skill in the management of human relations and in the use of such social opportunities as enrich the lives of the persons the agency is set up to serve.

In order that its particular kind of help be given relevantly and efficiently, the agency through its professional caseworker must gauge as early as possible whether the particular person applying for help is eligible for its services and can use them. First, the problem must be one with which the agency is equipped to help. Therefore, the kind of problem the person presents must be quickly appraised against this consideration. Beyond this, there are always certain conditions that govern the help-giving and help-taking relationship, either conditions that bear on the person's ability and willingness to undertake work with the agency or those that prescribe certain prerequisites of need, status, or procedure. Therefore, early in his discussions with the person applying for help, the caseworker must make explicit what these conditions are, so that the person himself may know and choose whether or not he wants help from this place on these terms and so that the caseworker may help him to make his decision on the basis of knowledge and thoughtful consideration.

The person, nursing his problem, rarely knows all this. He cannot know in advance whether the particular agency he has come to can give help with his particular problem, nor can he know whether the kind of help it gives and the conditions under which it is given will be acceptable or seem workable to him. One client, as he opens the door of the agency and gives his name to the receptionist, is so immersed in his anxiety that he scarcely sees even the physical aspect of the room. Another, alerted by his anxiety, tries to gauge what this place is like, and, from the manner of the receptionist and the appearance of the waiting room, its ugliness or pleasantness, the quiet orderliness or general carelessness which characterizes the office, he draws some conclusion as to whether this is a place that is helpful or not. But for any person the first vital experience of the agency in action in relation to him comes as he meets and begins communication with the caseworker.

The social caseworker is the social agency come alive and human.

The client's first glance seeks to take him in as a person, as a human being who has the power to help him or to hurt him. As the caseworker operates with security as to his professional identity and competence and with clarity as to his function in the agency's program, the client will come to see him both as a human being and as the agency's professional representative. As the former, he is compassionate, steady, knowledgeable, and ready to be of service. As the latter, he is empowered in his willingness and ability to be of help by his drawing upon the store of the agency's experience and expertness, by his having available the organized means and resources for helping, and by the agency's definition of its help and the conditions under which it can best be given and used. These give boundary, equity, and form to his generous helpfulness.

Now they sit, client and caseworker, across from each other, already saying many things to each other, although vocally they may have exchanged only courteously formal greetings. For all the things he may need and want, for all the sentences he formulated beforehand to say to the caseworker, the client, were he asked and were he able to be selective at this point of high tension, would say that he wants three things. He wants to be recognized and accepted sympathetically as a person in trouble. He wants to tell what his trouble is about and what he wants of the agency. And he wants to know *if* and *how* the agency will help him. ("Tell me plain," a client once said to me, "one, two, three.")

## The Process in the Beginning Phase

The process by which the caseworker will meet the three foremost concerns of the client as he begins his experience with the agency is the prototype of the whole. It begins with the caseworker's attitude of attentiveness and receptivity, and, as this attitude is caught by the client and he begins to feel safe in revealing his story and himself, he begins to feel the burgeoning of relationship and the securing sense that, in feeling, the worker is with him. But the relationship of trust and confidence grows not on acceptance and warmth alone. It depends for its sustenance on the demonstration that the caseworker not only *wants* to be helpful but *knows how,* and this becomes manifest in the ways the worker begins to help the client tell his troubles. He is not only an attentive listener; he is also an active inquirer. He asks for facts by which he and the client can get clear what the trouble is made of, and he helps to sort the more from the less important facts. His comments and questions stimulate thinking about the problem in relation to the client's self, in relation to possible solutions, and in relation to the particular agency. Within this part of the process several helpful things occur simultaneously: the client is helped to tell his troubles, to release his feelings of pent-up burden; he feels supported by the caseworker's attitudes; his confidence rises as he sees that the caseworker has some systematic way of going about tackling his problem; and, by the relief of sharing his burdens and by the perspectives which the caseworker's questions and comments provide, he begins to see his problem in some different light, not necessarily more rosy but certainly more clearly illuminated and defined.

Out of the facts of the problem and out of the client's verbal and behavioral responses the caseworker's understanding grows to reveal what inner and outer resources the client brings to the business of solving his problems. To test the client's ability to take and use the agency's help, the caseworker must do two things which are vital to beginning: he must answer the client's often unspoken question as to whether the agency can give help and under what conditions, and he must help the client decide to involve himself in co-operative efforts with the agency.

The caseworker answers the client's questions, not "one, two, three," but as discussion of the problem makes it sufficiently clear that this, indeed, is a situation with which the agency is equipped to help and that certain practices and procedures have particular relevance to ongoing help. Because the client, feeling the urgency of his need and the inevitable disappointment that there is no panacea for him, may waver and be unsure as to whether he wants the means and the ends available to him, and because real participation rises out of free choice, the caseworker may need to engage the client in the work of deciding whether or not he wants what the agency can offer him. This may be said to be the capsule problem for the client in the beginning phase: to face and accept the truth that there are few packaged solutions to life-problems and to enter upon the adaptive work of problem-solving together with the agency. The purposes of this phase are to help the client to know and to experience as soon and as accurately as possible what he wants to know—that here is a place where he can have a compassionate and perceptive hearing, that here is a place that helps (or does not help) persons with problems such as his—and to provide here, in the interview, both a demonstration and an explanation of the ways and means by which he can be helped. Then the client can decide whether he will or will not choose to involve himself in using this agency's services or counsel.

The full aim of the beginning phase of the casework process, then, may be said to be this: to engage this client with his problems and his will to do something about it in a working relationship with this agency, its intentions and special means of helpfulness. The content of this process is a fairly constant one, and its method is a fairly systematic one—as constant and as systematic as a process keyed to living, feeling, changing human beings can be—while it yet remains fluid and flexible.

What follows is the effort to set down what this content or subject matter of the beginning phase in casework is; what the helping method consists of; and how content and method, both prescribed by an understanding of the forces that enable and move people, yield the particular understanding of a particular person from which help to him may be fashioned.

# 9 *CONTENT IN*

## *THE BEGINNING PHASE*

Whatever the client's problem and whatever social agency he comes to, there is a common content in the beginning phase of helping him. The particular nature of the problem, the client's particular personality, and the special function and means of the agency will all bear upon what parts of this content are given greater or lesser emphasis, which facts are pursued and elaborated and which put aside or held for future consideration. But there are certain kinds of data and understandings to be established that may be considered "constants" in all beginnings in casework.

Common sense and the logic of problem-solving decree what these data are. In any everyday, sensible effort to help another person (or one's self) to cope with some personal problem certain queries would need to be answered. What is the matter—what is it that the person needs and wants either to get rid of or to get hold of? What does the problem mean to or do to the person who has it— what is important about how it affects his physical or social or emotional welfare? What causes it or brings it about—and what, in turn, does it cause? What has the person thought and tried to do about it? What is the person trying to get or what does he expect? And are his expectations valid?

It is the answers to these same common-sense questions that make up the content to be marshaled and discussed in casework. In more formalized terms, sometimes called the data of the casework "study," the facts sought are these:

1. *The nature of the presenting problem.*—What are the circumstances of the difficulty with which the client is faced—the obstacles he wishes to get over or the ends he wishes to achieve?

2. *The significance of this problem.*—What is its import to the person (or to his family or the community) in terms of its psychological, social, and physical welfare implications? What does the problem mean and feel like to him who owns it?

3. *The cause(s), onset, and precipitants of the problem.*—How did this problem or need come up? What brought it to a head? What are the cause-effect, effect-cause forces operating here?

4. *The efforts made to cope with problem-solving.*—What has the client thought to do or actually tried to do, himself or with the help of others, to work at the problem? What are his fantasies or wishes in relation to its solution? What has been his problem-solving behavior—his protective or adaptive operations? And what resources does he have—within and outside himself?

5. *The nature of the solution or ends sought from the casework agency.*—What is the client's conscious motive in turning to this agency as a source of help? What are his ideas as to what he wants and expects from it, and what are his role and relationship to it?

6. *The actual nature of this agency and its problem-solving means in relation to the client and his problem.*—What and how can this agency do to help this person? What enabling resources does it have to give? What requirements must it make of the client? What is its proper function in relation to the problem presented?

From the two-way exploration of these data the caseworker and client come to a joined understanding of their roles and next steps in tackling the problem. It is a *joined* understanding, not an equal one. On his part, the client may have withheld, consciously or unknowingly, certain facts of significance. He may have only a glimmering recognition but a strong trust in what the experience ahead of him is likely to be; on the other hand, he may have considerable clarity about it but some misgivings and only tentative willingness to involve himself. The caseworker, on his part, able by reason of his objectivity to observe at the same time as he participates, empowered by his knowledge to appraise at the same time as he acts and responds, will draw from this perusal of the objective and subjective facts some tentative conclusions as to the nature of the problem and its possible solutions and also as to the nature of the client as a personality and his willingness and ability to engage himself in solving that problem. This partial diagnosis is the result of the evidence produced in the client's account and by his responsive behavior in the interviews. His thinking about his problems, his feelings and responses to them, his efforts to cope with them in the past and present and in the interview itself, his ideas for dealing with them—all these reveal not simply the difficulty the client has brought to the agency but, more than this, what he is like and how he may operate in adapting to and coping with difficulty and with help.

These general categories of content deserve some further elaboration.

### The Facts of the Problem

The first business of caseworker and client is to learn the facts of what the problem is as it exists, seems, and feels today. The tense is present imperative. ("Past imperfect" may enter into discussion, and always there must be considerations of "future indicative," but first we must talk about *now*.) The business which brings the client to the agency is that some problem that has recently assailed him or with which he has struggled for many years has on this day become more than he can manage alone.

How may the "facts" of the nature of a problem be known? Fact has two faces: the one of "objective reality," which is to say the one that most persons in a given society would perceive or experience as existent or "true"; the other of "subjective reality," which is the particular way something is experienced by a particular person. All objective fact is sterile unless it is endowed with meaning. Our American schooling inculcates "respect for facts," but even those statistical facts that we most "respect" have no meaning except as they are viewed in the light of some idea. Conversely, subjective fact has no communicable meaning except as it is viewed in the light of objective data, nor can its appropriateness, validity, or realism otherwise be assessed. This is why both kinds of facts are always within the caseworker's concern.

The client himself usually begins by telling the external facts of his problem. The details will not remain the same from one day to the next, because the problem is "lived" by a human being; and, while its actuality may be established both by the client and by the objective eye of the caseworker, the meaning that is imputed to it will be different for each client and for any one client from day to day. That a man is jobless is a fact. That he is jobless in a period of high employment injects different meaning into that fact than if he were jobless in a depression; that he is jobless as a single man is different from his joblessness as the father of children. One unemployed man feels ashamed, another feels angry, a third feels secretly relieved, and so on. Involved in the nature of the problem, then, are all the facts and value judgments of the social milieu and all the particular personal meanings they have for each individual. It is to both faces of this content that the caseworker must continuously be related.

The reasons for ascertaining the facts of the presenting problem both as it is and as it is experienced by the person have been dealt with earlier. Yet in practice there are circumstances in which caseworkers are deflected from doing so, and it may be worth noting what these are. Sometimes the client will present not his problem but the solution he has arrived at, asking the agency to implement this. If the caseworker without inquiry as to facts relates to whether or not he can meet the client's request, he may be both misled and misleading. Three mothers, for example, come to the family agency asking for a camp vacation for their children. To each of them camp promises the solution of some problems they face. But what are the facts? Mother A feels that she is at the breaking point because of her child's behavior problems, and she has seized the idea of camp as a temporary surcease for herself and as, perhaps, some magical cure for her child. Mother B has been told by her physician that she needs bed rest, and two weeks of having the children away seems to her to be the best way of arranging this. Mother C simply wants her children to have a country vacation which she cannot afford to give. In each of these situations the facts of the presenting problem as it is and as it is felt to be by the person would be the basic material from which any valid planning or appraisal of solutions could be made.

A second obstacle to ascertaining the facts occurs when the caseworker himself leaps to conclusions. This may happen when the problem that the client presents seems typical of many others the caseworker has known, and he begins, not by individualizing the person with his problem, but by tucking him into some taken-for-granted category. For example, a visiting teacher referred a child to a guidance clinic with the complaint that he was "troublesome and aggressive" in school. But the boy's mother said, "He's no trouble to me. He's a little mischievous, like any nine-year-old would be." So the caseworker went to see the boy in school, and, like most little boys being observed by an unknown adult, he was respectful and wary and soft-spoken. And now the caseworker was in a dilemma as to what the problem was or where to take hold of it. The problem lay, of course, in the facts of what "troublesome and aggressive" and "mischievous" were made up of, what specific behavior, attitudes, and actions combined to make up this generalized difficulty.

In another instance a young married woman came to the family agency saying she wanted help in deciding whether or not to follow her husband to a city some distance away where he had gone to a new job. She wept helplessly as she elaborated on the two-way pulls she felt—to go and to stay. The caseworker assumed that her problem was neurotic ambivalence. But the facts, had they been drawn out, might have thrown an entirely different light on this situation. That the woman was indecisive was only one fact of the problem. The caseworker needed to learn specifically, piece by piece, what the separation was about, what actually had happened, what the circumstances of the husband's move were, what she and he had thought and planned together, how she had interpreted his leaving, and so on—in short, what the facts were of this woman's problematic social and psychological reality. Furthermore, only by such facts could the real or neurotic nature of the woman's ambivalence and helplessness be judged.

One further common bypass of the essential facts of the problem stems from the frequently expressed idea that we deal, in casework, not with the problem but with the person who has the problem. The corollary is assumed to be that, therefore, the humdrum, bone-dry facts of the situation in which the person finds himself are insignificant compared to the facts of his personality patterns and dynamics. (Perhaps it is this fallacy rather than that of too ready generalization on which the caseworker operated in the paragraph above.) This deserves some exploration. Whatever the special interest of the caseworker may be, the client who comes to a social agency brings himself in relation to a social problem. Connected, all at once. When the dual aspects of this interaction are explored, the facts will reveal that the genesis of the problem is to be found in the client himself or in his social situation or in some interaction of the two. In either case he, as a person, will need to be active in such changes as must come about. It is in that sense that we deal with the person: we engage him in whatever internal or external developments must be set in motion. But it is at the same time equally true that the *problem* is what client and caseworker both hold in the center of focus; this is the business in which each is investing his powers. In this sense we do work on the problem, with all its tangled threads of physical, social, and psychological facts.

If, then, we are accurately to appraise a person's capacities or difficulties, his strengths and potentials or his helplessness and limitations, we must view them in the light of the facts of what problems in his current living situation he is contending with. Furthermore, if in order to cope with the problem there may be resources necessary which the caseworker through agency or community must provide to the client, again the objective facts of the problem itself need to be known and considered. It was important, for instance, when a mother reported that all four of her children were enuretic, to establish the tellingly simple fact that all four occupied one bed. It was important in meeting the emotional needs of a post-alcoholic woman to learn and take action in relation to the facts of her husband's poor earnings, the physically repulsive slum housing they occupied, the details of her household drudgery and their significance. These are facts of problems which cannot be separated from facts of the persons who live them and which, furthermore, need to be known by the caseworker before the facts of subjective reality can be appraised.

The other face of fact, inseparable from the first, is the subjective meaning of the objective facts for the person who is involved in them. How the person experiences his reality, how he feels about what he is experiencing, what his interpretation is of its meaning—all this the client and the caseworker need to know for several reasons. One reason is so that the client may be helped to know the difference between what exists outside himself, making him the way he is, and the inner image he projects into his situation, causing it to be or to seem to be the way it is. A second reason is so that through the expression and sharing of his feeling a bond of relationship may be drawn between him and the caseworker. Either in the beginning phase of casework process or at any later point, it is the same. As the caseworker gives active encouragement to the client to say what he feels, and as the caseworker recognizes with him the naturalness of his emotion, the client begins to feel his tensions about himself lowering. This is the first experience the client has of the caseworker's real intent to understand *him* as well as his problem, for, with all of us, to feel "understood" is the result of finding that our feelings are understood.

Of all the feelings which every human carries in him—those he has tucked out of sight or watered down, those warring in conflict, those that are transitory, and those that run long and deep—which are the concern of the caseworker? Which are the feelings the caseworker encourages the client to express? The choice is plain. It is of those feelings that are aroused or created by the situation for which the client asks for help and also by the very business of taking help. They are those feelings that infuse the facts outlined in the structure of fact-finding. They are feelings of the here and now, those excited by the current situation.

We know that such feelings may have roots in the past, that they may, indeed, be carried over whole and inappropriately from the past, and that they will be connected with other areas of feeling. Later on, the surge or splay of feelings from other parts of the client's life may need to be dealt with. When this becomes necessary, it should be related by the caseworker to the present problems for which help is being sought. But in the beginning inquiry into the nature of the problem and the engagement of the client with the agency, the feelings that are encouraged to expression are those aroused by the current situation. They consist of the client's reactions to what circumstances or people have done to him, or his surges of guilt or self-blame for his inadequacy or failures, or his shame and hostility at being in a position where another person must help him. Simple or commonplace though the problem may be, it is never felt as such by the person who has it. He feels it fresh and sharp at the point of bringing it to share with someone else, even though he may have lived with it for a long time. And even though the roots of his problem may lie in old and unresolved feelings, what he knows and is aware of in the beginning interviews with the caseworker is how today's problem in his relationships to other people or things or to the source of help moves him. Some of his feelings will make themselves known only through his body language—his tension, tears, lassitude, or whatever. Some will be expressed verbally, either spontaneously or with the caseworker's encouragement.

The reasons for focusing factual inquiry on the anxieties and conflicts of the present situation are, again, those of common sense. Like much of common sense, they hold within them deep psychological truths. These currently experienced feelings are in the client's immediate consciousness; they are readily accessible and shared, sometimes bursting to be told. The client is aware of the ostensible (not necessarily basic) reason for them, and it seems logical to him that they should be shared. They are susceptible to realistic testing as to their validity and appropriateness against the facts of current objective reality. They are "alive and kicking" today, and thus they are subject to changes in their intensity and quality by the new and different experience that is found in the casework relationship and by the efforts at modifications of situation and attitude that take place within it.

To know one's feelings is to know that they are often many-sided and mixed and that they may pull in two directions at once. Everyone has experienced this duality of wanting something strongly yet drawing back from it, making up one's mind but somehow not carrying out the planned action. This is part of what is meant by ambivalence. A person may be subject to two opposing forces within himself at the same moment—one that says, "Yes, I will," and the other that says, "No, I won't"; one that says, "I want," and the other, "Not really"; one affirming and the other negating. It is the very essence of conflict that these opposed feelings seem to be of equal strength.

So it is in recognition of this common phenomenon of two-way feelings that the caseworker needs to help the client to tell both the positive and the negative sides of those currently active feelings that bear on his problems. He will be propelled or deterred, pushed forward or pulled back, made afraid or made steady, by his emotions. If he is not to be left prey to the unacknowledged feelings and if instead he is to be helped to work through those that hamper him, both sides of his feelings must be inquired into, brought to his conscious possession, and shared in discussion.

It has become an axiom in casework that the client himself is the primary source of the facts of his problem. This is because it is his. No one can know it as he does, inside as well as out, and, if he is to be helped to work on it, he can do so only out of his conception of it. But there are situations in which his conception must be changed because it is unrealistic, inadequate, or distorted by lack of knowledge and information or because of skewed perceptions. Moreover, there are agencies in which it is required policy that certain facts bearing on the client's eligibility for service be verified or supplemented. Under all these conditions the caseworker may need to go outside the interviews with the client for the necessary objective facts. Verification of earnings or residence, substantiation of a medical or psychiatric condition, interpretation of a school problem, consultation with a family member, clarification of the client's experience with another social agency—these are the kinds of inquiries or consultations outside the interview with the client that may be necessary to know the full face of fact.

There has been some conflict among caseworkers in recent years regarding obtaining information about the client and his problem from sources other than the client himself. Perhaps it merits comment here. There was an extended era in social casework when it was assumed, tacitly or explicitly, that almost everyone who knew the client knew more about him and his problem than he did himself. The client stated his difficulty, but the caseworker turned to his family members and friends (and sometimes his enemies) as "more objective" sources of understanding of him and as more potent planners for his adjustment. The reasons for this were compounded of attitudes about people who asked for help, of the valiant reaching-out to establish a "scientific," objective base line for casework judgments and operations, of a sociological orientation (in the first two decades of this century), and of inadequate knowledge with which to understand the meaning and import of behavior.

The swing away from outside investigations about the client and the use of other sources of information was a wide one. Casework is a profession full of feeling, and the changes and growth that occur in it frequently occur less by gradual modification and more by emotion-laden, polar swings. The extreme position was to view the client as the sole source of information about himself and his problem. The reasons here, too, were compounded of many factors. They embraced a changed attitude toward clients as persons with full rights to privacy and to self-determination, as persons who were potentially capable and motivated; the rapidly developing psychological knowledge that enabled the caseworker to "read" the meanings of words and behaviors in the interview; the increased number of persons coming to agencies for help with their interpersonal problems rather than for material aids; and—perhaps?—the greater comfort for the caseworker, or greater sense of "professionalism," when he and his client and their intercommunication were contained within the four walls of an office.

Happily, the recent movement seems to be to a balanced position. It is recognized that there are some vital facts that the client cannot provide because he does not know them or has no access to them. It is recognized in certain agencies that, while a "verification" may be unnecessary with a particular man or woman, it is required because it is held to be in the general interest. Enough is known about emotional disturbance to know that it may distort the perception of reality and that the factual situation may need to be established through the eyes of someone less involved than the client. Sometimes behavior and feeling cannot even be gauged as to their appropriateness, nor can valid expectations be held until the client's social reality is ascertained in its likeness or difference from his psychological reality. For all these reasons, what are called "collateral" sources of fact or fact interpretation may need to be sought. When such sources are used, it must be certain that they are supplements to rather than substitutes for the cient's own account. The data so gathered are not "against" the client, do not grow out of essential distrust of him, but are directed toward the end of more effective help to him.

When facts must be established or clarified through the use of other informants or records, the client ought to be partner to this effort. Both his permission and his understanding ought to be enlisted. His permission will most readily be granted if he is assured by the caseworker's specific explanation and by his obvious intent to be helpful that the information being sought is intended to carry forward the help to be given. His understanding will be enhanced as the caseworker shares with him something of the reasons why the data seem necessary and what bearing they have on the problem to be solved. That something is "routinely done" has very little meaning to the person upon whom a routine is being practiced. He may submit to it with resignation or rebellion, but he will not be inclined to implement it. But, when a "routine" has real pertinence to his own individual situation, a person will almost surely be interested and co-operative. The obvious corollary here is that basic to the caseworker's being able honestly to gain permission and to explain pertinence is his own conviction that there *are* relevance and validity in the facts being sought from outside sources. Furthermore, it is a client's right to determine whether or not he will share his need and wants with anyone outside the agency or family of agencies to which he has applied, and it is the caseworker's ethical obligation not arbitrarily to wrest that right from him.

There are notable exceptions, as there are to all generalizations. There are clients so mentally, emotionally, or morally disturbed that in society's judgment they have temporarily forfeited their rights, since they cannot carry the responsibilities to which the rights of adults are bound. There are persons so disabled in any one of a number of ways that they can participate only minimally as informants or discussants or actors in their problem-solving task. In instances such as these the social agency and its caseworkers take on a protective or authoritative role, and the client becomes the "recipient" in the fullest sense. But, by and large, the client who can take part in discussion of his troubles and of ways by which to cope with them is one who can be led to understand and agree to the caseworker's proposal that facts may need to be supplemented or attested to by communication with others (see Perlman, 3).

## The Significance of the Problem

How a person perceives and feels his problem will greatly determine what he will want and be able to do about it, and this is one
reason why the caseworker must attend so closely to trying to understand the subjective meaning of the client's problem. But at the same
time the caseworker must maintain the perspective with which his
professional knowledge and values equip him and view the meaning
of the problem in the light of this difference. This is to say that the
significance of the client's problem may be interpreted by the caseworker quite differently from its interpretation by the client. This
different view or understanding is what enables the caseworker to
have some notion of ends to be aimed for and thereby to give direction to the problem-solving work.

A married woman, for example, may see her husband's philander-
ing and their resultant discord as caused by her mother-in-law's encouragement; the caseworker's view of *its* significance will be deeper, broader, more complex. Depending on the facts, he may see the
infidelity as caused by the wife's frigidity or the husband's personal
immaturity or as evidence of some personality breakdown in the
man. A delinquent boy referred to a court caseworker may see his
problem simply as an "unlucky break"; its significance to him is that
he has been "framed" and is in trouble "for no good reason." The
caseworker sees many other meanings in the boy's problem and his
attitudes. His problem has significance in its effect on the community welfare, on his gang, and on his family. It "means" (again, the
*facts* attest or suggest) that this is a boy with defective character
structure, and it suggests that there is no one in this boy's family who
can help to guide or control him. In both these examples it may be
seen that the significance or meaning of the problem as it is judged
by the caseworker bears upon what solutions may be sought, what
means utilized, what directions followed, and what the general expectations can be. Also, from the very first, it points to whether and
to what extent the client will need to be helped to see the significance of the problem in different perspectives in order that he may
grapple with it realistically and effectively.

In large part this imputing of significance to the problem by the
caseworker is what is meant by diagnosing. "Shared diagnosis," the
idea that the caseworker holds openly between him and the client

the significance of the problem they are working on, does not at all imply that he shares everything he understands or perceives. This would be hurtful at worst and useless at best. It means, rather, what has been suggested here—that the caseworker, to enable the client better to grasp the problem and to focus his work efforts, matches his and the client's separate appraisals of the significance of the problem and selects for joint consideration that which most truly relates to the client's needs and goals. To weave this back into the problem-solving process, the joined discussion by caseworker and client of the significance of the problem is in large part the consideration of "ideas about the facts," ideas that point to what must be understood and done.

### The Causes of the Problem

The special nature of a problem and the possibilities of its solution can scarcely be known by an account of its symptoms or manifestations alone, nor even by these combined with the person's psychological responses to it. Essential to the client's and caseworker's grasp of the particular character of the problem and of the individualized way to deal with it is some knowledge of what caused it to come into being.

As soon as we say "what caused it," we are confronted by the puzzle of the endless chain in every human life, the interwoven links of cause-effect and effect-cause. Whatever the ultimate or basic causes in a client's difficulty may be, the causes we are concerned to identify and understand in the beginning phase of casework are those that precipitated or brought to a head the current problem. Perhaps in the ongoing process of work on the problem underlayer after underlayer of causes will become evident, and the caseworker's understanding of the problem and its mutability may be enhanced thereby. But even then the causes that are in the front line of our concern are those operating to create or complicate the current problem. "What brought this about?" "When did this start?" "How did it get to be this way?" "Why do you suppose this happened?" —it is these explanations or identifications of the "trigger cause" that the caseworker seeks first.

The reasons for this selection suggest themselves readily. These are the causes most accessible to the client's own recognition. More-

over, recent in origin and still in ferment, they are most accessible
to being dealt with, whether they are to be halted, modified, cir-
cumvented, or the client armed against them. And, because today's
effect becomes tomorrow's cause in chain reactions, some early identification is needed of these active agents that breed the problem
and in turn are bred by it.

The situation of Mrs. Redd offers an illustration of this.* When
she was referred to the medical social worker, she was suffering an
attack of neurodermatitis, a condition that had recurred at a number
of crucial periods in her life. She was involved in another real crisis
—her baby had been hospitalized in a diabetic coma. The "cause"
of Mrs. Redd's neurodermatitis lay in her lifelong, tightly repressed
guilt and hostility to her own demanding, overwhelming mother.
Perhaps it lay even farther back in her constitutional predisposition
to express tension through her skin. But neither of these basic causes
would yield to change. The "trigger cause" of Mrs. Redd's skin erup-
tion (and all the accompanying symptoms of anxiety) was her
baby's illness and its implications. Her tension was heightened by
certain misconceptions she had about diabetes and by the pressures
she was experiencing in learning the diabetic regimen. These were
recent, relatively superficial causes; yet they were firmly linked to
basic causes, and they bid fair to forge another link in the chain of
difficulties. It was these precipitants on which the medical social
worker took hold, working both to modify causal agents (engaging hospital personnel in understanding Mrs. Redd's needs for more
time and patience) and to fortify the mother to cope with the problems (through clarifying the facts of the baby's illness and partializing
the mother's immediate tasks). The neurodermatitis cleared; Mrs.
Redd's anxiety abated; the medical routines were learned; the baby
could be taken home. Basic causation was untouched, but valid,
realistic help was given in relation to the most recent causes of the
most recent problem. For the time, at least, benign effects replaced
disastrous ones, and a deteriorating process was halted.

Whether or not it is possible to deal directly with the problem's
immediate cause, there are other purposes to be served by an inquiry as to onset, precipitants, and cause-effect interactions. The
nature of the cause immediately casts further light on the nature of

* We first saw Mrs. Redd in chapter 3, p 31.

the problem. It provides ideas as to possible solutions, as to what means and ways might best be used, and as to the expectations of the degree of change and the rate of movement that may be anticipated. It suggests these only roughly, of course, but even such sketchy foresight gives focus and direction to the caseworker's efforts. Three middle-aged women, for example, present almost identical symptoms to the family caseworker—feelings of depression, lassitude, inability to mobilize themselves. One dates the onset of her depression to the death, seven months before, of her husband, to whom she had given devoted bedside care for three years. One "has been like this" as long as she can remember and has had several periods of hospitalization for severe depressions. One believes that her sad and useless feelings started following her recent hysterectomy. The precipitating causes immediately suggest differences in diagnosis and case management. What facts the caseworker selects to explore, what resources he elects to employ (certainly the use of a psychiatrist is suggested for the second case, certainly a physician and possible physical therapy for the third, along with casework help), ideas as to what seem to be pathological and what relatively normal reactions, the implications for treatment methods and expectation—all these are highlighted by the establishment of cause-and-effect facts.

Finally, it is in the nature of human problem-solving efforts, client's and caseworker's alike, to seek to establish cause. From the small child who takes the wheels off his wagon or takes a clock apart to find out what makes them turn or tick to the philosopher who ponders the ultimate why of existence, all of us struggle to identify causation. Perhaps it is an illusion, but it has been fostered in all of us that, if "cause why" is perceived and understood, we are in some part empowered to cope with phenomena. Conversely, happenings that defy reason also defy control. Perhaps it was this illusion, believed too literally, that led caseworkers over many years to the endless pursuit of the endless causation of their clients' problems, hoping somehow that final understanding would yield the open-sesame to change! Yet this remains true: without some recognition of the connections and interrelation between causes and effects, we encounter chaos. And, conversely, when a causal connection is established between happenings and behaviors, between events, actions, and consequences, there arises in both caseworker and client some sense that the problem is at least subject to comprehension and that, when a first step has been taken toward understanding, some logical next step can be taken toward mastery.

## The Client's Problem-solving Efforts and Means

No problem remains as it was at the moment of its first being experienced as a problem. Sometimes, it is true, we try to put a knotty difficulty away from us as though to keep it in cold storage, but this in itself is a defensive action consuming psychic energy. The immediate response of the human organism at the moment of its being attacked or frustrated, whether from within or without, is to turn on its many modes of adaptation. Depending on the individual, the way he perceives the difficulty and the way he characteristically reacts, he may attack the problem head-on by trying to cope with it or manipulate it; he may retreat to rally his forces or in the hope of escape; he may think about it alone or together with others, or just worry about it fruitlessly, or escape into fantasy; he may try to take planful action or be blindly impulsive—and so on. Whatever his physical, mental, and emotional responsive behavior, by what he does or desists from doing, he affects the nature and the outcome of the problem. His success or failure at coping, in turn, affect his sense of himself as able or helpless, as adequate or inept.

When the client brings himself and his problem to the agency, he has already, consciously or unconsciously, been at work on it. What he has tried to do or what he has desisted from doing, what ideas he has turned over in his mind, what resources he has tapped or left untouched—how, in brief, he has attempted on his own to grapple and cope with his difficulty is a significant part of the content of discussion between him and the caseworker.

What the client's coping efforts are has this further import. At first, client and caseworker may be said to concentrate on what *is* and on something of what *has been*. Now it is necessary that their eyes be turned toward what *might be*. What "might be" depends on three major dynamic sources of change: the opportunities the agency can provide in the form of tangible aids and/or the caseworker's therapeutic skills; the presence and usefulness of resources in the client's social milieu, from within his family circle out into the com-

munity at large; and the motivation and capacities, dormant or operating, in the client himself. It is the latter two which are revealed
in the content of discussion about what the client has thought and
tried to do about his problem.

As the client is helped to express the ideas he has had and the
things he has done, he presents a motion picture of himself. His
imagination, initiative, judgment, flexibility, and drive; his panic,
helplessness, withdrawal, emotional or intellectual poverty; his hopes
and their realistic or wishful quality; his use of other persons and
resources; his trust or distrust of people to whom he has turned—
some of these are glimpsed as he gives an account of his behavior in
relation to his problems. And, as they are assessed by the caseworker,
these data give evidence of certain characteristic reactions and adaptive behavior that may be anticipated from the client, of his endowment, and of the bearing of these upon relationship and method.
Such discussion will reveal, too, the resources of other persons and
things that are available to him, those that he has or has not thought
to use. In brief, the presence or absence of the powers the client can
bring to problem-solving—powers of energy, intelligence, resourcefulness, and resource—become manifest if he is drawn out by the
caseworker to tell what, in relation to this particular problem, he has
already done and how he has already operated.

Yet the real test of the pudding is in the eating, and the most
telling revelation of the client's willingness and ability to engage
himself in work on his problem is his responsive behavior to his firsthand knowledge of the agency and to his experience with its caseworker. This test and the appraisal of the client's appropriate motivation and capacity are the by-products of the next vital area of
content.

### The Solution Sought by the Client and Its Relation to Agency Help

The question every client has in his mind as he goes to an agency
for help is whether he can be given (or aided to get) what he wants.
Sometimes he asks this in direct or indirect ways, but often it remains unspoken. It is, however, a most important question to bring
out into the open. His motivation to continue working with the
agency can be expected to increase or diminish in relation to wheth-

er he thinks he can gain what he is after. His ideas of what is expected of him, what he is to do, and what he can expect of the agency will strongly influence his co-operation. His free decision to go forward with the caseworker can arise only from his knowledge of what he is choosing. For all these reasons the mutual discussion of what the client wants and expects and what the agency can give and expects is of considerable importance in the content of beginnings.

Happily, in the last few years there has been a gradual change in the intake practice that had been usual among many social agencies.* This was the practice of "ending" intake at the point where the client had presented to the caseworker the nature of his problem, its recent causes, and his efforts to cope with it. It was from these data that the caseworker determined whether or not to "take the case." On the basis of his appraisal of the facts of the client's difficulty and need, the caseworker judged whether or not the agency should go forward into providing its services. Where this judgment was affirmative, the client was assured that help would be forthcoming, and this was followed by the promise that he would be gotten in touch with or that this same caseworker would undertake to see him regularly.

The client went home and waited and thought. It can be imagined what some of his thoughts were, They would not be different from those any of us would mull over if we had deposited our problem and part of our emotions on the shoulders of another person and were given to understand that it remained for that other to decide what has to be done. For the client there might be blissful relief that responsibility could be relinquished, followed, perhaps, by a sense of betrayal when subsequent contacts revealed that this did not happen; or uneasy distrust of what plans would be hatched in his absence; or rising doubts as to what possible good could come of talking to a caseworker every Tuesday morning; or the marshaling of all the client's negative feelings about changing himself or his situation and a decision to let well enough alone; and so forth. In short, there would be all the varieties of defenses roused against the fears of the unknown. What had been left unknown (in small part

* For indications of this change see Anderson and Kiesler (*1*), Coleman *et al.* (*2*), and Freudenthal (*5*) listed under chapter 8.

or in whole) was what the agency could do in relation to this problem and how it proposed to proceed, and then what the client felt, thought, and would do about this new approach in dealing with his problem. It was as caseworkers digested the full import of the nature of self-determination, its relation to volitional choice and to the dynamics of participation, that it became clear that a major part of content in the beginning phase is that of the very problem of engaging the self in this different problem-solving process.

The content of the discussion of the solutions sought and the means at hand is in the large made up of four parts.

1. The client's expression (with the worker's helping him to make it clear) of what his expectations or wishes or questions are in relation to the agency's help—what he wants of the agency at this time.

2. The caseworker's explanation of the agency's possibilities in relation to the particular problems the client presents and in relation to his hopes or fears. This should be an *individualized* explanation, not a stereotyped spiel of agency purposes and promises. No client wants to know, in the midst of his harassment, "what the agency is all about"; he wants to know only what it is about in relation to *him at this point.* Nor can he entertain the vision of the remote future as well as he can take hold of and weigh the next few steps he must look forward to. The agency's possibilities contain its limits also, that is, those things it cannot do or provide, those wishes it cannot fulfil. It contains, too, those conditions of operation that are set by policy or by general desiderata. It is here that the worker may need to articulate, simply and clearly, the difference between the chance ways the client has used to this point in his efforts at problem-solving and this professionally organized way he now undertakes to use.

This is not to say that this clarification is once and for all worked through. Actually, the problem of ends sought and means available may arise at any point in ongoing work when change becomes threatening or resistance halts progress. Again, there are times when what was originally identified by client and caseworker as the problem or its locus shifts to reveal another and more vital problem area for work together. In such instances as these it becomes necessary to rework this part of beginning: the open discussion of the means and meanings of the client's and caseworker's joint engagement in the problem to be worked.

Two common misuses of the conditions of agency help deserve some mention. One is using them as though they were hurdles over which the client must leap or climb to prove his "fitness" for help. When the caseworker sets up conditions in this way or allows the client to encounter them in this way, he is operating less as a caseworker and more as a functionary. Sometimes conditions that are immutable or held to be necessary do indeed present formidable obstacles to the client. When this is so, the job of the caseworker is not to stand by while the client takes measure of his helplessness but rather, by encouragement and discussion of the considerations involved, to help him work his way through the obstacle. A second misuse of agency conditions is using them as "routine." ("I told her that our agency charges fees for persons who can afford to pay and that she would come within the one-dollar-per-interview group. She asked if she could pay two dollars, but I said that this was not necessary." Here the worker sees fee-charging as a "routine," to be gotten over with; but the client—?) Except, perhaps, for a professional beggar, asking and taking help is no routine matter. As an intensely personal experience, with variations of meaning for each person, it calls for sensitive reception and flexible response on the helper's part. Therefore, the kind of help the agency can give and the operations which condition that help ought, with each client, to be considered freshly in relation to their fitness in his particular situation and to his reactions to them.

3. The client's reactions—his responses in feeling, thought, and action—to what the caseworker has put forth of the "what" and "how" of their work together. The responses of the client may express frank rejection of the agency's kind of help ("I thought you would have some kind of a boarding school for the children; I don't want a foster-home"), open acceptance ("Yes, this is what I'd like to try"), submission ("Anything you say"), or mixed reactions ("I'm not sure—but maybe").

Despite the differences among these responses, some degree of two-way feeling is involved in all of them. In the rejecting client the negative feeling is dominant, but it is toward the particular service and condition of the agency; his "wanting," the push in him to get help, though of a different kind, still remains. (The unmotivated or unwilling client, who has no inner sense of "wanting," presents something of a different problem, to be discussed later.) In the readily participating client the positive feeling toward the agency is dominant, but there may be lurking questions or doubts which he quashes for the moment or which he decides to hold for future testing. In the submissive client negative reactions may be strong, but he is characteristically afraid to express them. He pays the continuous, impoverishing price of relinquishing his rights for protection by another person, and therefore he cannot be a real participant in determining his fate until he can assert his feelings. In the client with ambivalent reactions the pull toward help and the pull away from it may from one moment to the next shift dominance. One feeling may in effect cancel out the other and keep him in continuous indecision, or the unspoken negative feeling may rise to ascendancy once he is alone with himself again. What all this says, then, is that there must be on the caseworker's part a fourth consideration.

4. The recognition of and assistance to the client to face up to his ambivalent feelings about engaging himself in this venture so that he can freely "make up his mind" to use the caseworker's help. A failure to bring out and work over the client's under-the-surface indecision may explain the loss of many cases by agencies after the application interview. The client may have struggled with the two sides of "wanting" alone rather than with the caseworker's help, and he may have chosen the safety of known discomforts as against the risk of the loss of himself through what he may perceive as complete acquiescence to another. To avoid this situation, then, the caseworker's help to the client must be to recognize and help him express his negative reactions so that they may be openly subject to conscious management rather than to allow the client to be unwittingly subject to them. It is the caseworker who must take the initiative in proposing to his client that they turn over together in discussion the yes-and-no feelings the client is experiencing and the reality factors that ought to be weighed in coming to a decision about getting and taking help. This "choice" in the beginning phase of casework is at best a tentative one, because the client cannot know surely what the experience of relationship and problem-solving will be to him. All he can know is this sample of helpfulness he is experiencing now, from the caseworker's attitudes and from what he feels is being given to him and is being expected of him, and what he draws

from this effort to clarify both his problem and his and the agency's ongoing relation to it. This is what he can choose to accept or reject.

The literature and practice of casework have been long concerned with the concept of self-determination. We say it is the client's "right," as, indeed, we believe it is the right of every human being who is able to take self-responsibility. The essence of self-determination is precisely this: that the individual should take cognizance of what he feels and thinks, wants and does not want, and of the possible results of both, and that, then, he should decide upon or mobilize himself to a choice of action or circumstance. This is the purpose served by the casework process of stimulating the client to consider the agency's purpose and conditions and his willingness or reluctance to embark on solving his difficulties: his decision to go forward together with the agency should be self-determined and chosen as freely and understandingly as is possible for him. This action, the result of joint consideration and discussion, constitutes the difference between making up one's own mind and having it made up by another person or a pushing circumstance, between making a conscious adaptation and falling into a happy or unhappy situation. For many clients this is the beginning of the difference they will experience between their former and their new mode of problem-solving.

For the caseworker the by-product of this process of helping the client to know and make this first decision is the further evidence produced of the client's willingness and ability to work at problem-solving.

The content of casework's beginning phase can be so neatly and logically set down when it is done on paper! But in the living encounter between caseworker and client it will rarely move in orderly progression from the statement of the problem to its psychosocial significances, to its causation, and so forward. The client may present solution first, or the problem may fan out, fold upon fold, or the caseworker may need to inject, even before the problem is fully explained, some facts about the agency of which the client seems unaware. Each of us tells the same story differently. The client's telling of his burdens or his hopes will move from one aspect to the other, to and fro, back and forth, subject to no logic but that of his own drives and communication patterns. In practice, therefore, there arise the questions as to what content shall be focused upon by client and worker, what shall be more and what less emphasized. To answer these questions, one risks the Scylla of categorical dogmatism or the Charybdis of vague uncertainty. Some few and well-known ideas may help steer this narrow course.

Three interrelated guides have already been set down (chapter 3) by which to achieve and hold focus: the selection (1) of that problem or aspect of it which the client himself feels is most important; (2) of that part of his total problem which falls within the helping function of the agency; and (3) of that problem which in the worker's judgment most needs and can yield to help.

The first of these is formulated in casework's axiom, "Start where the client is." There is more than basic courtesy (though that is not a disposable virtue) to this. It is the recognition of the client's need and right to ask that he be helped with what, to him, is most distressing. It recognizes, further, that a person will not be motivated to change or act except out of his own concern and that he with his problem can only be taken hold of where he stands. It is obvious that this is not the same as saying that the caseworker and client necessarily remain in the same area where they started. They remain together in their communication, to be sure, with the caseworker's constant attention and connection to what the client is saying or revealing. But the caseworker's professional knowledge and judgment qualify him to lead the client to some shift of perspective or emphasis.

The second guide, that of the use of the agency's function as the framework within which the content may be focused, is also readily understandable. Sometimes the worker's curiosities or interests or the client's momentary thought associations will take them off-track into accounts that have no relevance. There is little usefulness to the client in discussing matters for which the agency can give no help, unless it is to make referral elsewhere. Conversely, the caseworker's and client's clarity as to the relation between the agency's purposes and means and the kind of difficulty for which help is being sought will give direction to what is being discussed.

Related to both what the client wants to discuss and what within the agency's purpose is relevant, focus is held upon what, in the caseworker's estimation, most needs attention or can most feasibly be dealt with. It is within the use of this third guide that the case-worker may by question or direct suggestion shift discussion from one subject to another or lay stress on some particular aspect of a situation.

The situations of Mr. Rose and of Mr. Brown exemplify this. Mr. Rose comes to the family agency to ask for homemaker service for his children while his wife is temporarily hospitalized. As the case-worker observes and listens to him and appraises his reactions, he judges that Mr. Rose is responding realistically to what has happened to him. He is naturally anxious and worried, but, despite these feelings and the physical fatigue which working and attempting to handle the care of the children have caused, he is yet able to mobilize himself to seek an appropriate helping resource, to explain his situation clearly, etc. The relation of his need to the agency service is clear, and his ideas of what he expects of a housekeeper and his rights and responsibilities in relation to arrangements are in complete accord with those of the agency. He gives evidence, in short, of needing, wanting, and being able to use the agency's homemaker services.

Mr. Brown presents this same problem to the same agency—his inability to provide care for his children while his wife is temporarily hospitalized. He seeks the same solution—the agency's homemaker services. But as he speaks, first, of the effect of his wife's illness upon him (his ulcers have flared up; he cleans the house until late every night, because his wife left so many things undone) and, then, as he tells of his exacting requirements for a homemaker and of the precise supervision he intends to give her, he reveals that he, as a personality, and his ideas and feelings about his and his wife's responsibilities, his and the agency's roles, and so on, complicate both the nature of the problem and its solution. Perhaps the first problem that must be faced with Mr. Brown will be his unrealistic expectations of the agency and the homemaker. What the worker will have to lead him to talk over is the content of his problem in adapting to what the agency actually can offer.

The relation of problem to solution is considerably different in Mr. Brown's and Mr. Rose's cases, and therefore the content covered in each situation will be different. The difference will be not of the essential categories of fact but of emphasis and focus. In Mr. Rose's case the focus of content will be largely upon the facts of need and those of means. In Mr. Brown's case some centering of attention will be needed upon his unreadiness to perceive and adapt to the difference between an agency homemaker and what he seeks, which is the combination of submissive housemaid and loving mother.

After the homemaker has been in Mr. Rose's home for a week, she reports that his five-year-old daughter suffers severe behavior disturbances. When at the caseworker's request Mr. Rose comes to discuss this, he seems to prefer to avoid the subject and to want to dwell on how helpful the homemaker has proved and how relieved his wife is. Here again the caseworker must take the initiative in shifting the focus of content—away from the diversions Mr. Rose presents (out of his anxiety about his child or perhaps his fear that the agency will remove the homemaker) and squarely onto the question as to whether Mr. Rose understands that his child is disturbed and whether he would like help for her. Focus and emphasis shift as the content of discussion will be upon the facts of the child's symptoms. The caseworker will need to inquire how Mr. Rose perceives the problem; what the child acts like; what reaction he has to it; how it has affected his wife, the other children, and the homemaker; what he sees as the cause or contributing factors to the child's difficulty; what he and his wife have thought to do; what their efforts to cope with it have been; whether they would be interested in the caseworker's help for the child; and so forth.

As this new problem emerges, the content has to be shifted by the caseworker to a different area of inquiry—to the details of another story, so to speak. However, the categories of the facts sought remain constant. How this body of fact and idea is developed between client and caseworker and how it may have therapeutic value is the function of the caseworker's method, to be discussed in the next chapter.

# 10 METHOD IN

## THE BEGINNING PHASE

To separate what is done from how it is done, content from method, is possible only for purposes of analysis. In any form of communication from one human being to another, whether by words and gestures or by art forms, the "how" is itself experienced significantly, and therefore it becomes part of content. It is in full recognition of this fact that we go forward to examine casework method, separating it from the content which it both conveys and infuses with meaning.

Just as the beginning phase of casework holds within it a structure of content which is constant throughout the casework process, so it holds the major constants of methodology. In the ongoing process many of these methods will be ramified, refined, and given wider play, and some new ones may be introduced; but it may fairly be said that the alphabet of method is contained in the first interviews with the client. This must be so, else there could be no continuity between what happens first and afterward.

The methods in the beginning phase of the casework process are, in the large, these: relating to the client in such ways as to lower his anxiety and to heighten his sense of trust and hope; helping him to express and to think about his problem in its situational and emotional terms; aiding him to focus his various needs in relation both to the facts of the agency's services and to the ends he seeks; and enlisting his participation in the problem-solving work to be done. All this is done by means of the kinds of behaviors on the part of the caseworker long known and used—relationship, support, reassurance, clarification, advice, explanation, and so on.

### Relating to the Client

Because the client needs to feel in his first experience with the agency that he is received understandingly and with the intent of helpfulness, the caseworker's attitude and mien must convey this. It is an attitude of attentiveness, respect, compassion, and steadiness. It is an attitude that is joined with the caseworker's awareness and control of his own feelings, so that he can maintain his professional perspective and not become engulfed in the client's feelings or what they evoke in the hearer. It might have been written of the caseworker that "nor heaven nor hell can his soul surprise." It is this constancy of receptiveness and responsiveness fused with objectivity and therapeutic intent demonstrated by the caseworker's behavior that helps the client to lower the barriers he may have erected in protection against his fears.

To recognize a person as himself, different in his own way from all others, and to receive him understandingly transcends simple pleasantness and sympathy. "Recognition" calls for lending one's self openly to take in the particular uniqueness of this person and of what he is saying about himself and doing with himself. Behind this must be the knowledge with which to impute meaning to his words and actions. "Understanding" involves that seemingly paradoxical response that combines emotional sensitivity with objective appraisal, that joins the ability to feel with a person to that of thinking knowledgeably about him. More, it entails being able to see and hear beneath surface speech and mannerisms, in order to know what a person is meaning to convey or to cloak. The caseworker knows that words and actions may both disclose and conceal simultaneously, that half-said things may be the most important ones, and that what is and what seems to be often need to be differentiated.

There are instances, even at the beginning of contact, when the client's eyes are so turned in on himself, or so fixed on his problem or on past relationships, that he seems not to perceive the case-

worker at all or to respond appropriately. Then it may be necessary
for the caseworker to put into words some clarification of what he
is there for, what his helpful purpose is, or, by questioning (not
challenging, but drawing out) the client, to bring him to face up
to his unrealistic response. (For example: To a woman who was
transferred against her wishes from clinic psychiatrist to psychiatric
caseworker and who persisted in calling the caseworker "Doctor,"
the caseworker "explained again that I was not a doctor but her
social worker and that the reason for transfer was so that I could
help her in some different ways.") Needless to say, such "rational"
explanations need to be carried by patient, steady demonstration of
the caseworker's relationship role and intentions. It is this demonstration of sympathetic attitudes and intent that, more than words,
encourages the client to begin to tell his troubles.

### Helping the Client To Tell His Troubles

The infinitive "to tell" has several meanings. One is to put something into words for communication. Another is to recognize, know,
and distinguish something. These two senses of this infinitive are
involved when we speak of the caseworker's helping the client *to
tell* his troubles. It is enabling him to share the matter for which he
seeks help and to perceive that matter with greater clarity so that
his efforts to cope with his problems will be appropriate and effective.

To enable the client to tell his troubles and what he wants requires more than an attitude of receptivity. There are, to be sure,
some few problems so simple and some solutions so readily at hand
that skill may not even be necessary. But most of the problems
that are brought to social agencies are so interlaced and charged
with personal feelings that they are not easily or logically communicated to one's self, much less to another. This means that the
caseworker must be not only a keen listener but also an active agent
in helping his client to tell about his problem and himself with
focus and direction, to expand and clarify certain facts and put
others aside for the nonce, and to view himself and his problem as
they are related to the particular helping means and purposes of this
agency.

It has long been said in casework, reiterated against the sometime practice of subjecting the client to a barrage of ready-made questions, that the client "should be allowed to tell his story in his own way." Particularly at the beginning is this true, because the client may feel an urgency to do just that, to pour out what *he* sees and thinks and feels because it is *his* problem and because he has lived with it and mulled it within himself for days or perhaps months. Moreover, it is "his own way" that gives both caseworker and client not just the objective facts of the problem but the grasp of its significance. To the client who is ready and able to "give out" with what troubles him, the caseworker's receptivity may be invitation enough, and the caseworker's nods and murmurs of understanding—any of those non-verbal ways by which we indicate response—may be all that the client needs in this first experience of telling and being heard out.

But often to "allow" a person to talk is not enough. Often it is difficult for the client to tell his troubles, in the sense either of distinguishing or of expressing them. This is because, as one is disturbed, perceptions may be muddied. Disturbance may create blocking—the muteness that serves as a dam against an overflow of feeling, or the blankness that erases what, for the time, a person cannot bear to see. Many people do not talk easily—those who have long practiced keeping their troubles to themselves, holding themselves in, feeling that it is not safe to say what they want or feel, and others who all their lives have responded to experiences by impulsive actions rather than by turning them over in their minds or talking about them. These persons often have few words with which to give an account of their troubles, and theirs is often a fragmentary telling which reveals that they do not even communicate connectedly within themselves. In such instances the caseworker will need to help the client to express himself.

Such help consists of the ordinary ways we all know and use to stimulate a person to "go on" or to assure him that what he is telling is important, or to suggest that he explain a little more about this situation or that. Sometimes only direct questions will help. For a time, in reaction against investigating methods, the direct question was in some disrepute in casework, and even today beginning caseworkers often ponder on how they can couch a question so that it will not affront the client. But, unless a direct question is impertinent (that is, either attacking or irrelevant), there is nothing the client or the caseworker has to fear from it. Sometimes it is well for the caseworker to give some brief explanation to the client as to why certain data are sought. Questions which seem "reasonable" are likely to enlist the client's efforts to answer them. A further help to the client to release his speech and express himself lies in the caseworker's supporting comments related closely to what the client is struggling to say or in the pick-up and repetition of what the client was saying when he blocked or seemed to close off discussion.

As has been indicated, the chief cause of inability "to tell" lies in the defenses that have been erected against emotions that seem to the client to be inadmissible or intolerable. One of the chief aids to releasing the client from his emotional bondage is the caseworker's relating consistently to his feelings as well as to the circumstances or situations he sketches. Something has happened to him, and he feels about it; he has decided something, and he feels about it; he has done something to someone, someone has done something to him, an episode has occurred, a situation exists—about any and all of these the client feels. When the client cannot readily admit or express his feeling, the caseworker can still relate to it, chiefly by his reiterated recognition of the complete naturalness or usualness that feelings are involved in personal problems and by his indications that it would be expected that for anyone certain general kinds of feeling would occur ("I can imagine that you must have felt badly," or "Most people would feel cheated by that," or "It would be natural to be angry"). Even if as sometimes occurs the client must still deny that he feels at all or must reject for himself the general feeling attributed to most persons, he still retains from the caseworker's comments the awareness that to feel is allowable, even natural. This awareness, taken along with him, may begin to lessen his own intolerance or fear for his inner experiences.

We often do not know exactly what we feel until we have communicated it to someone else. We may know that a store of discomfort is gathered in us, but of what it is made and how it is confusing and complicating our efforts to deal with our problems we do not know until we put it into words. To tell it, then, to a sympathetic listener provides us with some better view of it and, from that, some better chance of managing it. Finally, as has been said, we are motivated or immobilized by our emotions. For all of these reasons the caseworker must help the client to express and thus to know his emotional interaction with his problem.

Helping the client "to tell" is continuous throughout the casework process. Even if it were desirable, it is not possible to tell the whole story of any single incident or situation in our lives, because "the whole story" is tied together with our whole selves, our past, present, and emerging future. As his situation unfolds, as each week's impact affects it, as memory pulls him back or aspiration tugs him forward, the client will need, interview by interview, to tell, to communicate, both to himself and to the caseworker, the emerging facts and their import to him and his efforts to cope with them. And the caseworker will both encourage his spontaneous or planned outpouring and aid him by the unfolding means at his command.

### Focus and Partialization

"Telling" is only the first step in problem-solving. It must be bent upon some end or goal, not to a far-off, sky-blue hope that somehow what is talked out will be worked out, but to some nearby, though perhaps temporary, point of accomplishment. We have long since learned that talking about our troubles or feelings does not in itself resolve them. It offers temporary relief, to be sure, and the sense of a shared rather than a lonely burden. But chiefly it is for the purpose of making known to ourselves and to our helper the facts of situation and feeling in order to see them more clearly, to review them in the light of new ideas, to select the more from the less important, and to assay them in relation to a possible solution. This is why any one of us tells his troubles to another—not just to "blow off steam" (which, unless ours is a one-time problem, will only accumulate again) but on the assumption that the other person's clarity of vision and perspective is in this instance better than ours and that therefore he can aid us in finding ways to overcome the obstacle or achieve the goal. This is the aid the client needs and seeks from the caseworker, too, so as an essential part of moving from difficulty to solution the caseworker gives help in focusing and partializing the problem.

When a number of problems coexist, the client may find himself lost or overwhelmed by their interlocking maze. Second, even a single problem has several levels from which it may be viewed—its surface, situational manifestations, its immediate psychological meanings, its interrelation with the individual's characteristic patterns of reaction, and so on. Third, there are persons who are readily thrown off-track in their thinking when feelings of tension arise. These are the circumstantial, tangential talkers we all know—the ramblers who never quite find a settling place in their thoughts. And, since being beset by multiple problems of mind, matter, or emotion may tend to distort or diffuse any person's capacity to focus, the caseworker must serve as an aid to this means of getting at a problem.

By "focus" is meant the selection of some center of attention or consideration. Technically, focus is described thus: "a point of meeting of a system of rays after passing through a lens or being reflected by a mirror; figuratively, any central point." It is the caseworker who acts as this lens or mirror to draw the rays of the problem or discourse to some central area. He does this in several ways. As he listens to what the client is saying, he is at the same time sorting and sifting out the major from the lesser concerns, the more from the less relevant data, trying to identify what calls for first (not necessarily most basic) consideration. Sometimes this is fairly easy, when the problem is uncomplicated or when the client himself has ordered his thinking and centered his difficulties. But often it requires that the caseworker have developed, all at once, that fine co-ordination of listening sensitively, organizing his ideas as they fly up from what he sees and hears, and responding in ways to help his client share such organization.

The help given the client toward focusing is by directive questions, comments, or suggestions. It should go without saying that "directive" does not mean "dictatorial"; it means, simply, indicative of the way to proceed or the place to pause. Such suggestions as "Let's go back for a minute to what you were saying," or such comments as "This seems like an important thing to talk about some more," or such questions as "What feels like the most important part of this is you?"—all simple, natural communications—may serve to find what, for the time, will be the center of work between the client and the worker.

Sometimes the client himself asks for this kind of direction or leadership. "Let's see," he may say helplessly in the midst of his account, "what was I getting at?" Or he may reach out for some guiding rationale: "I really don't see where this talking will get me." Or he may surrender to the complications of which he becomes acutely aware as he lays them out between himself and the caseworker: "It's all so much—I don't know where to begin." Because the caseworker's perceptions should be clearer than those of his beleaguered client and because his knowledge of the point to which they are talking is more sure, it is the caseworker's responsibility to focus and to point direction.

An example may be seen in Mrs. Oliver. A harried, disordered-looking woman, she came into the family agency to discuss her marital problem. Her speech was torrential. With scarcely a word from the caseworker she gave the chronology of her marriage, of her husband's brutalities toward her, of her illness which made her more helpless to fend for herself, of her husband's peculiarities of personality, of her child's behavior problems which she believed were due to his father's treatment of him, of her ideas about going to work (but she was sick), of leaving her husband (but she needed money), of taking her child to a psychologist (but her husband was averse to this), and so forth. From the record it is not clear whether the caseworker simply listened because he himself was hard put to discern where to hold Mrs. Oliver or whether he operated on the assumption that, when Mrs. Oliver had told her "whole" story, they could know what to tackle. Whatever the explanation, the fact was that, by the end of the first hour of Mrs. Oliver's "telling her story in her own way," the attentive caseworker was as confused as the client as to where to begin or to end in this widening whirlpool of difficulty.

It was also clear that, rather than getting relief from "telling," Mrs. Oliver's anxiety increased as the sound of her own words made her problems seem even more real to her. The caseworker might have given early help to this anxious woman, whose many problems pushed her mercilessly, if he had actively intervened to stem the torrent of speech and to hold Mrs. Oliver for a moment to identifying which among these many problems seemed most pressing to her, what "hurt" her most, what it was she was bringing to *do* together with the agency. "Perhaps we can hold that for another time; this time let's stick to talking about such-and-such," or "You have so many troubles all at once that maybe we ought to take hold of one that you first want help with." Comments such as these help the client to pause, to select, and to consider some one area and its relation to what it is he has come to ask for. The discomfort caseworkers have about interrupting the client needs to be viewed in the light of whether what the client is telling bears on and furthers the purpose for which he has come to the agency. It is actually reassuring to him to know that the person to whom he turns for help is not also foundering in confusion and that he has a clear idea of what their talk together ought to be about.

As the discussions between client and worker go forward, their focus and direction may shift. It might be found, for example, that Mrs. Oliver is so emotionally disturbed as to need psychiatric care, and for a time the establishment of the nature of this difficulty and the preparation of Mrs. Oliver to see a psychiatrist would occupy the center of attention. Or it might be learned that her discomfort in her marriage does not seem great enough to offset its satisfactions and that her child suffers severely from the impact of the neurotic equilibrium she and her husband maintain. Now the focus might move to the facts of the child's difficulties and to a consideration of what means could be used to help him. Again, it might become evident that in all the situations in which Mrs. Oliver finds herself— with husband, child, neighbors, etc.—she, by her behavior, excites their punishing responses to her. Then the focus might shift from a situation level to that of her patterned behavior in interpersonal relations. And so on.

Even with the general area of focus clarified, there are many situations in which the problem is of such complexity and magnitude as to need even further narrowing-down if it is to be workable. In the family agency the focus may be upon the marital relationship, in the child guidance clinic upon parent-child interaction, and in the public assistance agency upon management of money, but even within such foci the size and detail of the problem as it is encountered by the person having to do something about it may seem overwhelming. This calls, then, for the carving-out of some part of the identified problem for intensive or first consideration in relation to problem-solving. Such small-part focus as this has been called "partializing the problem."

Any one of us when faced with a large problem tends to try to grapple with it by breaking it up into parts. We may do this by reducing it to specific instances that are characteristic of it, or we may separate it into sections which may be dealt with in progression—this part to be taken care of first, that later, etc. It is disheartening for a woman to face up to "How can I handle my bad relationship with my child?" but it is not too frightening to face up to "What can I do about my child's refusing to go to school, or his sassy talk?" It is terrifying to the man leaving the mental hospital to think, "How shall I return to work, family demands, new neighbors, all at once?" but he will be able to countenance the thought of taking one step at a time, first to get to know his wife and children again, then other matters. All of us when faced by heavy responsibilities try to manage that problem-filled load by partializing it, that is, by breaking up what is sufficient for each day, or by selecting first things to be done first and then by getting to work on the specifics involved. When these specifics or parts are put together, they will make up the whole. Thus, when the specifics of the mother's everyday interaction with her child or the post-psychotic man's steps into the outside world are put together, they constitute the problem in the whole; but they can best be managed and worked upon in the small piece.

The reason for this need to partialize lies in the ego's functioning. If that which is perceived seems too overpowering, the ego seeks to flee from it or to defend against it or, more constructively, to attempt to cut the problem to size. To cut a problem to its manageable proportions is a first step in adaptation. It facilitates clear perception and channels the energies of the ego. Often the client cannot do this alone. In helping him to carve out some portion of the larger problem, to reduce it to some here-and-now samples for beginning work on it, the caseworker is acting as adjunct to the client's ego. What he does, in effect, is to lift out of the larger problem some portion small enough so that even the timorous ego dares to look at it and try to tackle it. When that portion seems manageable, there rises in a person some greater sense of confidence that he can "get on top of it." And, if he is able to achieve some change with this partial aspect of his problem, the client, like any one of us, may be motivated to tackle other parts.

What part is it appropriate to carve out in the beginning phase of the client's work on his problem? The criteria that suggest themselves are these: *greatest immediacy*—that is, a part which is manifestly and directly before the caseworker and client; *representativeness*—that is, a part which is intimately related to the larger problem; and *manageability*—that is, a part which the client, despite fears and defenses, can be expected to be able to cope with.

In the beginning interviews the choice of "part" is all but readymade. It is the business of forming the pact that is the basis of an ongoing productive partnership between client and agency. Its immediacy is clear. "Where do we go from here?" or "What do you do and what do I do?" are questions uppermost in the client's mind and in the forefront of the caseworker's thinking. Its representativeness is recognizable to anyone who has experienced the inevitable flow and ebb of motivation that occurs throughout a person's work on his problem—now the incentive to struggle and move forward pushes the client, now he is tempted to draw back and stand still. Resistance to what is new or threatening cannot be settled once and for all. It can be worked only piecemeal, because it is aroused piecemeal, by the special content of what is in work at a given time. The resistance to engaging one's self in a new problem-solving venture typifies what will occur now and again as the problem or focus shifts. To grapple with it in the beginning is to give the client his first of what will be a number of experiences in facing and working out his negative feelings. The manageability of this portion of beginning is aided by its being a problem in and of the relationship between the client and the agency, with the caseworker right there to work on it.

The quality of the client's ability and motivation for using help will be shown in how firmly he can take hold of considering and choosing what he will or will not do together with the agency. The caseworker's ways of helping him to make this choice are of vital importance in making the choice feel sound and workable to him.

### Helping the Client Engage Himself with the Agency

Perhaps of equal importance in determining the nature of the client's problem is determining the nature of the solution he seeks and the ideas he has as to how it may be arrived at. One client may hope for some service or look for some outcome that is realistically not possible. Another may ask for an available service but under unfeasible conditions (such as the woman who does not want her husband to know that she is applying for money to supplement his earnings; or the woman who wants the agency's help in re-establishing a home for her placed children but does not want her court worker consulted). Yet another client may be quite clear as to his need but in conflict as to what it is he wants to do or have done about it (such as the adolescent boy who feels miserable with his parents, his school, and himself but, because of this, does not trust another representative of adulthood to help him; or the father who can no longer undertake the care of his children while his wife is mentally ill and yet cannot face up to placing them). Then there is the client who needs but frankly does not want the caseworker's help (such as the delinquent boy who constitutes a problem for others, not himself, and therefore seeks no solution except release from the agency; or the person who has sought one kind of help and has been referred to another—such as the mother referred to the medical social worker to discuss her young child's skin eruptions which she judges to be the result of a food allergy but which the doctor judges to be psychogenic). And, finally, there is the client who has scarcely been able to think or imagine his way out of his problem, so hopeless has he felt, and his inclination may be to cast himself helplessly upon whatever mercies the caseworker and agency may have.

The kind of solution sought, the person's idea of his and the agency's role in striving for it, his amount of hope and confidence—all these factors will create a number of important differences in the process of help. It therefore is incumbent upon the caseworker to discuss with the client what it is he wants or expects. Because this particular area of content and method in casework beginnings has been given less attention in the practice and consideration of casework than many other aspects of interviewing, and because it is in this area that the crucial work with the client's motivations is done, it will be given some detailed discussion in what follows.

Preferably, the client's opportunity to state and discuss his ideas of solution and what relation they have to the agency should be given him within the first interview or two. It is not necessary that the caseworker know all about the problem in order to gauge whether it falls within the scope of the particular agency. As soon as it is ascertained that this type of difficulty is one for which the agency has knowledge, experience, and service, the question becomes that of whether this particular client wants and is able to tackle his problem in the ways the agency can make available to him. Therefore, although only the bare outlines of the difficulty have been sketched in and although only the surface emotions that accompany it have been expressed, the caseworker needs to inject the questions that will reveal the client's expectations of the agency. (What follows pertains to the client who is himself seeking help. The "unwilling" client, sent or brought to the agency through some agent of authority, will be discussed later.)

Now there is set in motion that to-and-fro, contrapuntal movement which typifies the conscious effort to work a problem in some systematic way. This to-and-fro, back-and-forth, in-and-out movement between client and caseworker is between feelings and facts, about his expectations and the real possibilities, his need and his desires, what he wants and what he can get. Now the focus is upon the facts of the problem, now upon the client's feelings about it, now upon the facts of the agency's means and resources, now upon the client's thinking or feeling responses to them, now upon the relation between the client's ideas of solution and the agency's, so this discussion weaves on.

The caseworker is an active participant in all this, contributing such facts as the client may not have or see, suggesting different perspectives, helping by suggestions or comments to clarify and illuminate the issues and choices and to link the client's needs and desires with the real ways and means of fulfilling them, giving hope, assurance, and encouragement whenever they can be realistically supported. Because of its fluid nature, this process defies being held still long enough to be described except as, again, one risks making it seem static and oversimplified in order to analyze its parts and describe its progression.

To the client's expression of his ideas of solution the caseworker gives attentive ear. A person tells a great deal about himself as he shares the modes and nature of his problem-solving thoughts and the quality of feeling they contain. In response to what the client proposes or seeks, the caseworker sets forth the selected facts of those parts of the agency's service that are relevant. Thus the worker lends to the client, for his consideration, the information about those parts of agency helpfulness which he may be able to use in achieving his ends or overcoming his difficulty. In so doing, the caseworker either affirms that what the client seeks may here be found or shows that there is some difference between what the client expects and what the agency can provide. Here or at some later point in the first interviews, depending on how discussion unfolds, the worker will need to make clear, too, the conditions of their working together—their joint and separate responsibilities, the time of interviews, the agency requirements as to eligibility or procedures, and so on. These conditions, also, are partialized, related only to establishing a sound beginning together.

The client will naturally have reactions to the facts of what the agency can or cannot offer him and to the conditions of help. It is to these feelings, expressed verbally or otherwise, that the caseworker now relates himself. They are the determinants of whether or not the client will go forward with the agency, and it is vital, therefore, that they be recognized and worked. They may be heavily weighted on either the positive or the negative side, or they may seesaw between those two poles. The caseworker attempts to influence the feeling so that the client takes clear cognizance and firm hold of his intent to work on his problem. In no sense does this effort consist of a persuasive attempt to inveigle the client into consent. It consists, rather, of the open, above-board consideration of both aspects of the client's reactions to what is in store for him. This is so that he can know and consciously examine his needs, the means of meeting them, the consequences of his choice, and, from this, to freely choose what he will do.

Immediately it must be said that there are many instances in which conflict about the kind and conditions of help is minimal. These are situations in which such change as must occur is to take place chiefly in the client's situation, not in the ways he himself feels or acts. This happens when the agency service sought is readily matched with the need and when the person seeking it feels the problem to be one he had no part in creating. (Mr. Rose, who sought homemaker services owing to his wife's illness, was an example of this, not alone because specific aid was present for specific need but also because he was not threatened by his need and anticipated realistically the requirements on his and the agency's part.) There are other, almost opposite, instances when the client is so depleted of physical or psychic energy and resources at the point of application that help must be given him freely and unstintingly until his panic or apathy gives way and he feels that his survival or integration is secured. That is, he must gain his footing again in order to be able to take some responsibility for decisions and choices. The discussion of what is wanted and what can be had is, in the first instance, a relatively minor part of content, fairly simple methodologically, and in the second instance it may need postponement and careful partialization.

The caseworker tends most to be misled by the client who appears to be ready to use the agency. A client's acquiescence may blind the caseworker to his own knowledge about opposing pulls in feeling. He is so pleased with the client's appearance of positive response that he may relate only to this. Yet, inexplicably, this client sometimes does not return for his next interview, or, when he does, there seems to be in him some undercurrent of doubt or of ungratified expectancy, as if he is somehow being failed. What may have happened is that he was at the first so pushed by his need that he reached for any help and that now, in his second or third contact, he finds that this is not "any help" but a particular kind of help, which is perhaps more slow or laborious or demanding than he had realized. Or, as he went home and took counsel with himself or members of his family, those doubts and fears that he had not recognized while in the warming presence of the caseworker began to creep out and assail him and made him wonder whether, after all, he should not let well enough alone. Within his first few interviews he should have been fortified against these doubts and, rather than being allowed to embrace uncritically what was being offered him, should have been led to some consideration of the limitations as well as the gratifications of the help he sought and to some open awareness of the reluctance in his feeling as well as the eagerness.

Unless the resistant and reluctant feelings are drawn into the light and air of discussion, the client is left to deal with them alone, which is the same as to say that he is left to cope with the problematic side of his feeling, the very aspect with which he needs help.

What this suggests, then, is that, particularly with the client who seems compliant to agency means and conditions of helping and who embraces unquestioningly what is offered, the caseworker must provide the opportunity for the expression of his doubts or questions.

The principle that governs the discussion with the client of his reactions to using agency help is the same as that which holds in other situations where ambivalent feelings need resolution. It may be stated thus: Give full acceptance to the expressed feeling but draw out and work over its opposite side. Thus, with the client who is indecisive and unsure as to whether he can trust or really wants the agency to help him, the caseworker recognizes and warmly encourages the "yea" of his response at the same time as he accepts the naturalness of his "nay" feelings and gives them frank consideration.

There is also the client who openly rejects what the agency can do for or with him. He may cling to some plan or formula that cannot be implemented and will not accept an alternative, or it may be that he has from the first seen no need for help. In such applicants it is less often the conscious fear of self-involvement and change that is operating and more often their inability to perceive the relation of what the agency has to offer to their idea of need. Their motivation has been not to find some way of working out a problem but to find a means (the agency) to produce a predetermined solution. In these instances the caseworker must accept the negative, rejecting feeling and attempt to explore whether there is any positive wish for help. Such a wish may exist either because of the push of present necessity or because of the fear of future consequences. What, the caseworker asks himself, has brought this person here and held him in the interview thus far? It is these fragments of motivational push that the caseworker will try to identify with the recalcitrant applicant toward bringing him to see more clearly in what areas of his need the agency may be useful to him.

The applicant who wants none of the agency or the caseworker is obviously the hardest one to reach, engage, or even tolerate. Yet tolerated he must be, and effort must be made to reach and engage him, for several reasons. One is that it is this client—he who is a thorn in the community's flesh (such as the delinquent adolescent) or who is troubling to the community's peace of spirit (such as the unwed mother)—who is considered to be the proper responsibility of the social worker. What is social work for, asks the supporting community, if not to make social beings of these unfortunate misfits or to protect society against their depredations? Where can they be helped or dealt with, if they are not to be put in places of confinement and punishment? And this is indeed a valid question to which social workers face up with greater or lesser courage. Ultimately, these persons are sent to a social agency, sometimes to those that offer their services as freely chosen by the client and at other times to those that serve a protective purpose or act as the helping arm of authoritative bodies. Of the several professions that use psychological means of influence, that of social work most consistently encounters the problem of the unwilling client. Caseworkers, then, face this unique challenge and opportunity, if it can be developed, to work out ways by which to engage the unwilling person.

Methods by which such persons may be helped at least to begin work with the caseworker can only be suggested here. Probably the minimal wish or motive of persons who are forced or badgered into coming to a social agency is to avoid the consequences of their actions—whether that consequence is the agency or worse. They may not wish to be or to act differently, but they do wish they would not be punished or frustrated by the results of what they do. In beginning with such persons, then, the caseworker must relate himself, as always, to the client's moving power, and in this instance it is the crude motive of self-protection. The help offered is never that of evading society's demands; rather, it is assistance in meeting them, if only in order to ward off further trouble. The concern that the caseworker tries to rouse and to get the client to consider is that of self-preservation from unhappy consequences. Hopefully, if relationship with the caseworker holds some gratification, the client may move from the level of self-defense to feeling some discomfort with himself and wanting to be more acceptable, first to the caseworker and then to the society that the caseworker represents. *

The caseworker must know from the start that this client does not

---

* At this writing, the Family-Centered Project in St. Paul, Minnesota, directed by Alice Overton, is working intensively on the problem of engaging the participation of "unwilling," multiple-problem families. See Alice Overton, "Casework as a Partnership," *Children,* September–October, 1956.

want to be here, that his feeling is negative—more than this, that he is often suspicious and antagonistic. This must openly be understood with him. Sometimes after this acceptance the client will listen and take in the caseworker's explanation of the difference between his distorted conception of the agency service and what it actually can be for him, though always he will reserve his trust until the worker proves to be helpful, not hurtful. But, even should he remain unconvinced, the facts of the consequences of his refusal to control or modify his behavior remain immutable. They have not been created by the caseworker; they are there. The caseworker's efforts must be to get this client to face up to these facts and to their meaning to him and his own welfare and then to lead him to consider and choose whether he wants to work on some ways of operating that may offer him more gratification than his present behavior yields. The material resources that many social agencies can provide may make agency help a tangible reality to a client who is unresponsive to attitudes of helpfulness, and these resources often provide the opening chink to his belief in the caseworker's helping intent.

One of the deterrents everyone encounters on having to make a decision to embark on a new venture is the fear of committing one's self to unknown events for an unknown period. One could become anxious indeed if the dentist after examination suggested simply a regular weekly appointment and quite wary if, for instance, a school proposed that one take a course until one had learned enough. In most of us a feeling of security and safety lies in our knowledge that we are free to quit a situation if we do not like it or that it has some time limit. The implications of these common reactions for casework beginnings are clear. To decide to form a working partnership about one's problem becomes far less threatening and far more acceptable if it is agreed upon for a trial period. This period is one of mutual exploration and testing-out. It may end at some agreed time, perhaps a number of weeks, at which point it is understood that there will be a joint stocktaking. Or it may be more congenial to worker and client to set no specific time span but rather to understand together that resistances will arise in the guise of doubts, feelings that there is no longer a reason to come, and so on, and that at any point when this is recognized by either client or worker it will be the signal for discussion and for the client's freedom to choose, again, whether or not to go on.

Perhaps this note is superflous, yet so often have general casework principles become rituals that it presses to be said: This discussion with the client of his positive and negative reactions to engaging himself with the agency, of the conditions and values of service, of the choices he may make, is no routine "song and dance" through which client and caseworker move as prelude to the main business. It may be in itself a main business, or, as has been indicated, it may involve only brief consideration. In either case it takes the client through his first steps of experience with solving a problem by casework help. It is a process that must, like others, be shaped and adapted to the particular client, his personal organization and problem and relation to the agency. Whether choice and decision are achieved in a few words in one interview or as the result of discussion over several meetings depends on all these variables.

Now, when client and caseworker are agreed that the client wants help from the agency in dealing with his identified problem, that the agency is able and ready to give such help, that certain conditions govern and enable this partnership, a working pact has been arrived at, and the ongoing phase begins. By the things he has said, in the ways he has behaved spontaneously or responsively to what the worker has conveyed to him, by his quality of thought and feeling, the client has already revealed many aspects of himself as a personality and as a participant in casework. These are diagnostic by-products of this first help he has been offered, and they will be amplified in a later chapter.

### Some Comments on Techniques

Within the broad outlines of the structure and method of the casework process are those refinements of skill called "techniques." It is no wonder that caseworkers seek avidly to learn such skills. There are so many knotty problems with which they deal, so many stubbornly closed doors that will not yield to their opening devices, that they look eagerly for some keys, be they words or actions, which will prove to be open-sesames. But the more individualized and creative a process is, the more skill eludes being captured and held in the small snares of prefabricated kinds of behavior; and the paradox is that the less susceptible skill is to being caught and mastered by ready-made formulas, the more anxiously are formulas sought. "What should I say when . . . ?" "What does one do if . . . ?" "How do you get a client to . . . ?"—these are the questions case-workers typically bring to supervisors, to psychiatric consultants, or to their peers, seeking for *the* manner, *the* word, that will break the impasse.

Within any "systematic arrangement or adaptation of means for the attainment of some end" (a dictionary definition of an art), each artist or artisan will develop and use techniques which are his own. Within the systematic structure and the psychological principles of casework's process of problem-solving, each caseworker will have his own special ways of saying and doing what his knowledge and purpose tell him will promote his ends. A technique is a particular way in which a principle of methodology is translated into action. It is the expression of an individuality, the unique manner or style by which an individual acts out his conscious purpose. In the pic-torial arts, to take an analogous situation, certain common purposes and principles may govern what a number of artists do, yet each will paint even the same subject quite differently. Van Gogh, Monet, Renoir, and Seurat, for example, were all concerned to capture light and to show its effect on color, texture, and form; yet, despite their common intent and working materials and the common principles they applied, their techniques, the ways by which they expressed their purpose, were highly individual.

Within casework method, which is the expression of basic prin-ciples of affecting human behavior benignly, there are possible many variations of technique. Certain of them seem "second nature" to some caseworkers; others seem foreign. Which are "best" often salts down to a judgment by a particular person for whom a particular technique feels most right or for whom it has worked. The tone and attitude that convey the words, the quality of relationship, the stage of work, the personalities of client and worker in interaction, and (let us be honest) the hindsight which outcome provides are but a few of the variables that may make a given technique seem good or bad. Each caseworker strives to act appropriately, that is, to speak and act toward his client out of his awareness and understanding of him and his relation to the problem, the agency, and the problem-solving process; this may be halting and awkward, at first. Then, as the caseworker's growing knowledge and understanding fuse with his "feelingfulness" and these, by usage and successful experimentation, become integrated into his very marrow and nerves, so to speak, there is a transmutation of "appropriate action" into "skill."* With this said, perhaps in the nature of protest against the substitution of synthetic devices for fresh and fitting responsiveness, it must be repeated that skill is governed by some general principles of therapeutic communication.

We are accustomed to thinking in terms of certain classifications of casework help that combine some differing methods and techniques (see Austin, *1*, and Hollis, *5*). But, whatever the treatment process or end, the caseworker's spoken communications with his client are of two main kinds. One consists of questions and comments, aiming to draw out to a maximum the client's relevant participation. The other consists of information and counsel aiming to provide the client with some necessary knowledge or guidance. The comments upon these which follow are purposely limited (lest they overrun the chapter's bounds!) to considerations that seem often to trouble practicing caseworkers.

It may fairly be said that, in general, questions direct themselves to the answer's mind rather than to his heart. They say, "Tell me what I don't know," or "Explain to me (and to yourself) what is not fully understood." To a question, the individual tries to make a rational response, that is, he turns his answer through the selective sieve of his mind. Even a question about feelings, "How do you feel about this?" or "Why do you feel that way?" may lead the individual to sifting his mind for a "logical" answer. Questions are necessary to ascertain the facts of objective reality. Moreover, they stimulate the client who is able to do so to think about something reasonably and logically. They call for conscious mental work on the client's part. In these ways they are necessary and useful to problem-solving.

Comments more readily address themselves to the person's mood

* In this connection John Dewey's comment in *Art as Experience* is pointed: "Craftsmanship to be artistic in the final sense must be 'loving'; it must care deeply for the subject matter upon which skill is exercised."

and feeling. They affirm and encourage the expansion of subjective reality and emotion. They convey the listener's empathic responsiveness, his understanding of what is being said, and his encouragement to go forward with it. This is why a client's emotional responses can usually better be encouraged to expression by comment than by questions. When we are asked to "explain" our feelings, we more often rationalize than savor them. When, on the other hand, we are assured that to feel strongly and perhaps "badly" is expected or accepted and that it is understood and supported by another person, there is more likely to be a direct flow of feeling from its source. Yet, should a person not wish to share his feeling, he would still be free to ignore or reject a neutral comment.

Comments seek to facilitate, maintain, focus, or expand the client's communication and, always, to convey the sense that the caseworker is with him in feeling. The latter is mostly conveyed by the caseworker's facial responses and bodily attitudes, which, more truly than words, reveal his reactions. The major kinds and purposes of comments are these: those that indicate that the caseworker is "with" the client appreciatively, understandingly ("I can see what you mean"—or even murmurs and nods of acceptance); those that point the direction in which the client was traveling, to help him regain focus ("You were saying such-and-such"); those that reflect his feelings, to help him perceive them and know that they are accepted ("That made you angry"); those that encourage his further consideration and churning of ideas for further understanding ("I wonder why that would be so"); those that supply a missing connection, to help him grasp the relatedness of one fact or idea to another ("This makes me think of another instance you told me about when you felt the same way" or "But now is different from then"); those that venture some interpretation to help him see the meaning of a fact ("Sometimes people act this way when they want to punish their families"); those that support him as a person, to enable him to feel secure as he continues to grapple with his problem ("You're doing all you can do, considering what you've gone through"); and so on.*

* In "The Initial Phase of Psychotherapy," Coleman (2) suggests: "There are six types of comments which are commonly used in psychotherapy, and these are sympathetic, reflective, focusing, facilitating, confronting, and connecting comments."

Questions and comments are not always distinguishable from each other, for facial expression and voice inflection often determine their nature. But both must be governed by enabling purposes, and both must relate to the tenor of what the client himself is saying. When this is not possible, when, for example, certain clarifying data must be ascertained within limits of time or when focus and direction must be established, it is helpful if the caseworker gives some explanation of why a redirection or transition is injected. If the reasons for this are in the client's welfare, they can honestly be explained in those terms, and he is likely at least to tolerate them.

Particularly in the beginning phase of casework the client may want or need facts about the agency or other helping opportunities, and certain of his decisions will depend on establishing actualities. There are also situations in which the client lacks facts or knowledge about the nature of his problem. In these and like instances the caseworker must give such information directly. The rule governing what the caseworker "puts in" of a factual, explanatory nature has already been suggested: that only such pieces of information be given as have immediate pertinence to the client's need and can be used by him.

An implicit or explicit request that the client frequently makes is for direct advice. This is what he has been accustomed to receiving from other persons to whom he has turned for help, and it is natural that he anticipates, unless he is asking for a specific service, that advice is the kind of help he will get from the caseworker. He reaches out for it, and, with the frequent perversity of human beings, he is often armed against it. Understandably so, because the advice he has been given by others or has given himself has not worked.*

Far from meeting this expectation of the client, some caseworkers today have come to give wide berth to any counsel that smacks or "advice." Because advice was once our stock-in-trade, given kindly or otherwise, and because we found that even asked-for advice could not be followed if feelings, motives, and circumstances pulled in opposing directions, we came to avoid advising clients or, at least, to viewing advice with misgivings. In so far as this avoidance

* Diogenes is credited with saying, "When Thales was asked what was difficult, he said, 'To know one's self,' and what was easy, 'To advise another.' "

has been accompanied by efforts to help the client work through to his own solutions, it has been to the good. Yet two tempering considerations are here proposed.

To a request from a client that the worker offer him a panacea, the caseworker tends, often, to turn away and to suggest instead that in the process of work together the answer will be found. Valid enough, this is. But what may be overlooked is that considerable anxiety underlies many such requests and that what the client's question begs is not for an explicit piece of advice but for recognizing and dealing with the anxiety that underlies his query. Thus when the mother asks, "Shall I stop spanking my child?" she actually anticipates that the advice will be to stop, but what she is really asking is that the caseworker attend to the fact that she feels acutely uncomfortable about what she has been doing. When a man asks, "Do you think I should break up my home?" he is ready to defend himself against a flat "Yes" or "No" answer. What he really is asking is, "Do you see what a terrible conflict I'm in?" Thus, rather than passing over a request for advice or postponing its resolution to the future, the caseworker would do well to listen for the underlying anxiety that prompts it. If the client's voice and face and body tensions say that a charge of feeling lies within the question, the caseworker must relate himself to that feeling rather than to its defensive disguise. If, on the other hand, the query or request for advice is clearly promoted by needing or wanting to "know," and where there is evidence that the client is able to carry out what is advised, the caseworker need not fear saying what, in his professional opinion, is desirable or valid.

There are occasional situations in which harm may ensue unless direct advice is given either to desist from or to carry out some action. Advice may not be asked for or, if requested, may not be followed; but the knowledge or foresight that the caseworker may have in a given situation greater than the client's places upon him the responsibility to share it. For example, an unhappy woman who hated her job and thought she would quit it was advised ("I suggested," says the caseworker's record) not to leave it until they had had the chance to talk through the causes of her dissatisfactions. And a frightened man who reported that his wife had threatened the day before to kill herself and the children was advised (in no tentative terms) and hastened into getting immediate psychiatric attention for her. Sometimes neither doing nor undoing can wait on the client's achievement of willingness and ability, and, when this is judged to be the case, direct advice, and sometimes direct action, is clearly warranted.

The methods by which the caseworker involves his client in the work of the beginning phase of casework are those which, with variations of emphasis and detail, will characterize the ongoing phases of the casework process too. The consistent therapeutic attitude of the caseworker, the repeated grappling with facts of circumstance, happenings, and feelings, the aids to keeping focus and direction, the queries and comments that communicate compassion and understanding and serve to ascertain, amplify, clarify, illuminate, and share problems and plans, the fusion of support and stimulus toward working through conflicting emotions and toward making decisions and taking constructive action—all these are casework's basic enabling means. Each client will respond to them differently, and his individual ways of reacting to and making use of them will reveal to the caseworker what his motives and capacities for adaptation and problem-solving are.

Diagnosis and the implications it holds for ongoing work with the client are drawn in large part from the caseworker's assessment of the client's responses to help. Effective methodology not only is inseparable from sound content in casework problem-solving, it not only is experienced by the client as part of what the agency does with and for him, but it also provides the most reliable testing conditions for what the client can and will do about his problem, given systematic and skilful aid. Thus, at the same time as the caseworker shapes his interviewing content and method to promote his client's maximal adaptation, he observes and appraises the effects of his actions. From the diagnostic conclusions he draws, his ensuing methods and goals are fashioned.

# 11 DIAGNOSIS: THE THINKING
## IN PROBLEM-SOLVING

In each case the caseworker has his own problem-solving task: to determine how best to help his client. To be guided by forethought rather than impulse or habit, by plan rather than trial-and-error experiments, he must go through his own professional problem-solving work of marshaling the facts of person, problem, and place; of analyzing and organizing those facts within the particular context of the casework situation; of reflecting upon them and of coming to some judgment of their meaning for what he is to do and how he is to do it. This mental work of examining the parts of a problem for the import of their particular nature and organization, for the interrelationships among them, for the relation between them and the means to their solution—this is the *diagnostic process*. The conclusions this process leads to, stating what the trouble seems to be, how it is related to the client's goals, what means the agency, the caseworker, and the client himself can bring to bear upon the trouble—these conclusions are the *diagnostic product*. Diagnosis, if it is to be anything more than an intellectual exercise, must result in a "design for action."* It is the reflective thinking which shapes the problem-solving work.

* Dr. Cameron, from whom this phrase is taken, goes further in his essay, "A Theory of Diagnosis," to say: " 'What is it' is always bound up with 'What am

Probably no process in casework has been as troubling to case-workers as this one of diagnosis. The symptoms of its problematic character express the range of the caseworker's defensive-adaptive responses—from a relentless pursuit of "complete" diagnostic understanding as though it would magically yield a cure to a reluctance to come to any conclusion beyond an "impression"; from blocking at case recording to grasping at ready-made labels; from viewing the concept of diagnosis as a credo to holding it to be anathema.

The causes of these attitudes and this behavior about diagnosis are multiple and tempting to explore (and the reader may well find and ponder them in himself and others!), but the temptation will not be yielded to here. Instead, our effort will be to seek and point to the reasonableness and usefulness of diagnosis and, in the course of this, to try to dispel some of the misconceptions that often becloud it, whether as process or product.

The fact is that whether we are "for" diagnosis or "against" it, whether we believe in its usefulness or not, whether we feel adept or inept at it, every one of us is diagnosing as he relates to another person in a purposeful, problem-solving activity. Every one of us in such a situation makes mental note of what he is observing and experiencing, draws inferences from what his senses convey to him, and anticipates next moves on the basis of the meaning that has been read into or drawn out of the signals. Consciously or not, we seek to clarify the nature and configurations of the material (person-problem-place-process) that we are attempting to influence. And, consciously or not, we try to organize our half-felt, half-thought impressions into some conclusions, temporary though they may be, that will give direction for what to expect and do next. This holds true in any kind of problem-solving work that is not blind hit-or-miss, whether it involves fixing a radio, painting a picture, arranging a party, or influencing the feelings and actions of another person.

The argument for diagnosis in casework, then, to be precise, is

---

I going to do about it'; diagnosis is thus a declaration of intentions" (4). In the same vein Dr. Ackerman, in his article, "The Diagnosis of Neurotic Marital Interaction," writes: "Diagnosis has meaning only in the context of devising a plan of action" (1). Some writers on social casework diagnosis, notably Hamilton, prefer to separate diagnosis from evaluative conclusions (8).

simply an argument for making conscious and systematic that which already is operating in us half-consciously and loosely. It is nothing more or less than bringing into conscious recognition that veritable swarm of intuitions, hunches, insights, and half-formed ideas that we call "impressions"; then scrutinizing them in the light of what knowledge we hold, selecting some as important, casting off others or placing them in our mental filing system for future scrutiny; then putting the pieces together into some pattern that seems to make sense (at least for the nonce) in explaining the nature of what we are dealing with and relating it to what should and can be done. What makes sense to the caseworker himself comes thus into his full possession: it is subject to his conscious appraisal and use. Moreover, it is communicable to others who may share the responsibility for what is to be done. "To diagnose," as a process of thought, and "to make a diagnosis," as the product of that process, mean, then, to take the simple but important responsibility for consciously thinking about what we feel, sense, know, or half-know in order to have it in hand and head as a guide for what further needs to be known, understood, or done; and to say, "This is what I think, at this point, to be the nature of the problem as it relates to the nature of the person who wants help with it, as they both relate to the help I (or others) can give."*

At times the fear has been voiced that if the caseworker becomes too systematic, too intellectual about diagnosis, he will lose in his relation to his client that finely attuned responsiveness, that empathic, intuitive understanding more spontaneous and sometimes more acute than intellectual grasp, or he may even be pushed to turn his interview into the kind of interrogation that is directed at a diagnostic rather than a therapeutic outcome. But, as Dr. Maurice

* The evident assumption in all this discussion is that understanding the nature of the material with which we work leads, inevitably, to more economical and skilful work with it. For me, a meaningful definition of skill has been this one: "Skill is the capacity to set in motion and control a process of change in specific material in such a way that the change that takes place in the material is effected with *the greatest degree of consideration for and utilization of the quality and capacity of the material.*" The definition is Virginia Robinson's, from her essay, "The Meaning of Skill," in *Training for Skill in Social Case Work* (Philadelphia: University of Pennsylvania Press, 1942). The italics are mine, to call attention to an implication that can scarcely be avoided: "consideration for and utilization of the quality and capacity of the material" involves a process of diagnostic thought and appraisal.

Levine has pointed out, the attempt to understand is both "intellectual and empathic" (*13*). Empathic understanding rises out of and permeates the direct experience with the client; intellectual understanding is the result of conscious thought about the significance of what is known and has been discerned. In the skilled caseworker the intuitive and the intellectual combine rather than conflict, each in the service of the other. (There are, to be sure, persons who are helpful therapeutically and who have never submitted themselves to the guidance of conscious diagnosis, but it is doubtful that this omission is the explanation of their skill!)

Perhaps a major obstacle to the caseworker's pursuit of problem-solving in the systematic way that diagnostic thinking demands is that there has not always been clarity in the diagnostic literature or teaching as to the "what" of diagnosis.* The essential content of the diagnostic design and the considerations that give it boundary and focus need more careful delineation. Faced in every case with a crowding array of facts and impressions, the caseworker must have some structured idea of how to find the center of his diagnostic concerns. What follows is another effort to say what social casework diagnosis is concerned with and how its range or limits are determined.

If, for the moment, we could pretend that the term "diagnosis" did not exist, it might be possible to think about it afresh. It would probably be agreed that, at the point of engaging himself with his specific object matter, any worker, be he craftsman, artist, healer, or educator, faces this same problem: to understand and appraise the makeup of the material with which he is to work in relation (and always thus) to what he proposes to do with it. A block of stone, as object matter, will be viewed, understood, and appraised by a builder or a sculptor in terms of its strength, its malleable quality, its color, and so on; but builder and sculptor will understand and appraise it differently in relation to what each plans for its use. A rabbit will be viewed, understood, and appraised differently by a trapper, a cook, and an experimental pathologist.

* An examination of recent writings in casework reveals some diversity of ideas as to the essential subject matter of diagnosis. See, e.g., related to diagnosis in problems of marital discord: Ackerman (*1*) and *Diagnosis and Treatment of Marital Problems* (*21*); related to casework diagnosis in general: Hamilton (*8*), Hollis (*9* and *10*), and Rawley (*14*).

A human being is the most complex among all the "object matters" worked upon or with. Those who work with people need some understanding of human makeup and human operations in general and a realization of the specific differences each individual presents. The "worker" who seeks this understanding and appraisal might be a teacher, a doctor, a salesman, or a social worker. Immediately, as the kind of worker is named, it becomes apparent that his working function and purpose with a human being will differ from those of another kind of worker.

Not only, then, will a skilled artist, scientist, or artisan seek to understand the nature of his "object matter" in general and to appraise the specific nature of the individual instance but, for precision and economy of skill, he will view and evaluate this material in the light of the relationship between it and his specific goals and then between this and his available working means. In other words, in any endeavor where a worker undertakes responsibility to change the nature of some material or to influence it, he must try to arrive at some conclusion as to three things. They are: (1) the character of the problem to be worked out, whether it is to achieve some goal or overcome some difficulty, and the relation of this to (2) the qualities and attributes (of the material, the person, the thing, or the circumstance) to be influenced, and the relation of this dynamic combination to (3) the ends sought and the means available. This tripartite interrelation, when it is identified and formulated, may be labeled a diagnostic appraisal. This holds for the practice of medicine, engineering, education—and social casework.

Diagnosis in social casework practice begins when a person with a problem comes to the agency. The person and the problem as units and the dynamic interplay between the two might be studied endlessly were there not some binding limits. These limits are set by what the person wants to do or to get in relation to his problem and what help the agency is able and willing to give him through its own or other resources. Thus the content of the casework diagnosis falls into the same triangular pattern as that of other professional designs for action. It consists of: (1) the nature of the problem brought and the goals sought by the client, in their relationship to (2) the nature of the person who bears the problem (his social and psychological situation and functioning) and who seeks (or needs) help with his problem, in relation to (3) the nature and purpose of the agency and the kind of help it can offer and/or make available.

The content of casework diagnosis, then, is focused, weighted, and bounded by the *purpose* and *means* of the client and the agency. Therefore, those facts and data that take central place in the caseworker's thinking and those that are put aside as secondary or even irrelevant will in any one case differ from one kind of agency to another and will also be changed for any one case within the same agency as new problems or needs emerge. The latter case is exemplified in the situation of Mr. Rose (chapter 9, p. 138), where the need for a temporary homemaker suddenly opens to reveal the need for parental and child guidance.

The former case may be exemplified in the situation of Mr. Grey, an elderly man, perhaps beginning senility, who comes to the attention of three different social agencies: he applies to the Department of Public Welfare for old age assistance; in the clinic, where he is a patient because of acute gastric symptoms, he is referred to the medical social worker for help in diet management; and he is brought to the admission desk of a psychiatric hospital one day by a policeman who has found him wandering about in a disoriented state. The caseworkers at each of these agencies will see this same man, withered, weary, uneasy, somewhat distraught and foggy in his thinking, and each will relate to him in terms of what they grasp of the meaning of his behavior in relation to his circumstances. But for each there will be a different problem in the center of attention, and this problem in relation to the particular agency function will determine the data each seeks and appraises. The public assistance caseworker will focus on the man's need and eligibility for money and then on discerning whether he is physically and mentally able to maintain independent living. The medical social worker will focus on the problem of why Mr. Grey does not follow his diet, whether it is lack of money, of understanding, of conviction, of capacity—or all four—that keeps him obdurate to the doctor's orders. The psychiatric social worker's focus will be on working along with the psychiatrist to clarify the nature of the man's mental confusion and to determine whether he needs, wants, and can get outpatient or custodial care. At some point early in the fact-finding it is to be hoped that these three social caseworkers will be in communication with one another, for in this whole man the relation of need for money to get food and proper diet to pain and physical energy to a clear or confused sensorium may be closely interlaced. When they talk and plan together for Mr. Grey, each caseworker might appraise him as a person in the same way, yet each will bring an appraisal of Mr. Grey in relation to a different aspect of his life-problem, because each diagnosis is cast by a different presenting problem in relation to the particular agency's purposes and means.

Within this frame of reference there are several characteristic kinds of understanding that caseworkers strive for in order to give effective help. First and clearly essential in all casework practice is an understanding of the current problem the client is experiencing and the many factors that affect its existence, its nature, and its solution. This may be called a *dynamic diagnosis*—that is, a diagnosis of the forces in active play in the person-problem-situation complex. It embraces what is commonly called the *psychosocial diagnosis* (see Hollis, *10*) as well as that diagnosis of the client's current functioning that I call his "workability" (see chapter 12). When the examination of these factors reveals that the client's personality makeup or operations create or vitally affect the problem and/or its solution, then the nature of his personality maladaptation or dysfunction must be identified and assessed. This may be called a *clinical diagnosis*—that is, a classification and appraisal of what is the matter with the person himself. Whether the dynamic diagnosis stands as sufficient or the clinical diagnosis is deemed to be necessary, it is often useful to understand the causes and development of the presenting difficulty. (Cause may be as recent as yesterday in some instances, as old as the person himself in others.) The effort to ascertain the birth of a problem and its cause-effect-cause development is called an *etiological* or *genetic diagnosis*.

The specific content and conditions of usefulness are different for each of these types of diagnoses, but there is frequent overlapping among them. A dynamic diagnosis always contains some etiology, at least of the problem's recent causation, and it may, depending on the nature of the problem and on the caseworker's perceptiveness, contain some rough clinical appraisal of the client's personality. An etiological diagnosis would be all but useless were it not geared into the caseworker's idea of the current problematic situation; and a classification of the client's personality makeup and functioning would be only a feat of the intellect and no part of a design for action except as it was firmly combined with the dynamics of the problem presented and the client's and agency's purposes. Because of some of the confusions that still cluster about these diagnostic contents, each of these aspects of understanding toward treatment merits some separate discussion.

### Dynamic Diagnosis

The dynamic diagnosis is a kind of cross-sectional view of the forces interacting in the client's problem situation. These forces are currently operating within the client himself, within his social situation, and between him and his situation. The dynamic diagnosis seeks to establish what the trouble is, what psychological, physical, or social factors contribute to (or cause) it, what effect it has on the individual's well-being (and that of others), what solution is sought, and what means exist within the client, his situation, and organized services and resources by which the problem may be affected. The formulation of a dynamic diagnosis would, in effect, be a judgment based on a configuration of the data already listed and discussed in chapter 9. Clearly such a judgment would not evolve from the simple addition of one item to another but rather from the combination of these data in relevant ways, from viewing their relationships to one another, and from the assessment of their single and combined significance in the light of possible action.

Depending upon the factors of problem, person, place, and purpose, the dynamic diagnosis may be a simple or a complex formulation.* Psychological factors may be dominant in one instance, social in another (and one might consider that a dynamic diagnosis may sometimes be sociopsychological, not always psychosocial!). The particular focus of the diagnostic fact-finding in the beginning phase of casework (to be discussed later in this chapter) will inevitably be subject to changes. It is not that the dynamic diagnosis will necessarily undergo a "complete switch," as one caseworker put

---

* The renewed awareness in casework of the family as an interacting social situation and of the individual client as an inseparable part of this dynamic situation thrusts an added dimension of diagnosis into caseworkers' considerations. See Ackerman (1), Gomberg (6), and especially Pollak *et al.* (12) listed under chapter 2.

it in explaining his fear of committing a diagnostic *faux pas,* but it will broaden, deepen, or shift in emphasis as the client and his situation come to be better known and understood. Moreover, the problem-solving process itself injects change-producing stimuli into the client's situation and is in itself a "dynamic" to be accounted for and understood.

The test of the dynamic diagnosis in any case is its usefulness to the caseworker himself in providing guide lines for his inevitable problem: What is necessary and possible in this case, and how can it best be done? John Dewey once suggested: "A first-rate test of the value of any philosophy which is offered is this: Does it end in conclusions which, when they are referred back to ordinary life-experiences and their predicaments, render them more significant, more luminous to us, and make our dealings with them more fruitful?" I suggest this is also a first-rate test of the value of the dynamic diagnosis.

### Clinical Diagnosis

A clinical diagnosis, strictly speaking, is an attempt to classify a person by the nature of his sickness. It identifies certain forms and qualities of his personality maladaptation and certain needs and forms of behavior that characterize his malfunctioning. These, in turn, point to the patterns of operation and response that may be anticipated from the person and how, roughly, they may be expected to affect his social and interpersonal relationships, including those with the social caseworker.

The person who wants help with his personality disorder usually seeks a psychiatrist and is then a "patient" rather than a "client." When this is the case, the clinical diagnosis describes both the nature of the problem *and* its relation to the person and the helping means and goal. When, however, a client sees some aspect of his social maladjustment as the problem for which he asks help (and this may include problems of interpersonal relationships as well as person-circumstance relationships) and takes himself and his problem to a social agency, the clinical diagnosis may or may not be useful. It has usefulness when it becomes apparent that a disorder of personality accompanies the social disorder, creating or complicating it. Then the clinical diagnosis says, in general, what that personality problem is and, in broad and sketchy ways, what needs and behavior of the client may be anticipated as help is offered. But because the clinical diagnosis does not say what the nature of the psychosocial situation is or what its relation is to the particular resources and aims of the client himself or of the agency, it can be considered only a partial diagnosis in the practice of social casework. It remains necessary that a dynamic social casework diagnosis be made—a diagnosis that says what problem is to be centered on for work, what factors in addition to the client's personality bear upon its nature and solution, and what the relationship is of these to the client's and agency's aims.

The idea of making a clinical diagnosis has troubled many caseworkers. This is understandable, because it is an assessment that requires knowledge gained not from perceptive everyday living or even from omnivorous reading in psychiatry but from the repeated, firsthand experience of observing, studying, and working with people with personality pathology. This is an experience to which the student of psychiatry is repeatedly exposed, but the student of social work is not, although some social caseworkers—who practice in certain settings in both tutelage and working relationship with psychiatrists—gain this firsthand knowledge. Recent writings in casework reveal differences of opinion about whether or not caseworkers should have this experience and should make a clinical diagnosis.*

My own position is that the precise classification and delineation of the clinical syndrome of the client belong in psychiatry, not in social casework, but that the floor of casework competence requires the knowledge to identify gross kinds of malfunctioning of the personality. This is to say that, whether the caseworker is working in medical social work, child welfare, family welfare, old age assistance, or elsewhere, he should be able to recognize the signs and indicators of psychosis, of neurosis, and of disorders of character and behavior. The large, general categories of personal malfunctioning carry diagnostic implications about how the client may be expected to undertake his problem-solving (whether it is to take medicine,

---

* See Hollis (9) and compare the statement therein with that by the editor of *Social Casework* on p. 139 of the March, 1956, issue (Vol. XXXVII, No. 3); compare also with Gomberg (6) and with pp. 230–32 in Hamilton (8).

place his child, become a better spouse, or qualify for relief) and how, therefore, the caseworker may need to trim and adjust his own methods and aims. Perhaps the term "clinical diagnosis" is a misnomer for the rough classification I suggest. I use it not only for want of some better term but because it suggests that the caseworker's recognition of a client's sickness, even though he may have only a general idea of its implications, may be a vital part of the dynamic diagnosis. Not least among the ways in which it may influence what the caseworker will or will not do is that it may point to the possible need for psychiatric consultation or referral.

In many agencies where caseworkers deal with clients whose problems in carrying their social roles effectively are interlocked with their personality problems, there has been a considerable stress recently upon the necessity for the precisely differentiated clinical diagnosis, usually developed in consultation with a psychiatrist. The actual working value of such diagnoses merits our careful thought. It is not unusual for case records to show great diagnostic effort and incisiveness followed by a course of treatment that scarcely seems to be organically related to the diagnostic conclusions. This may be because the caseworker has not grasped the full import of his diagnostic tour de force or because dynamic factors other than the client's dis-ease seem to have taken precedence in affecting treatment, or perhaps it is because clinical classification is as yet only rough-hewn. Psychiatrists themselves have been the first to point out this latter fact, and there is evidence that even at one moment in time there may be considerable difference of opinion among psychiatrists as to to the nature, significance, and treatment implications of a single individual's emotional problem.* Nor are treatment method and technique highly differentiated as yet, though they are often talked about as though they were, and more is known about the characteristic dynamics and etiology of mental and emotional disorders than has been, to date, translated into precision of treatment method.

This is not to suggest that the ongoing study and experimentation

* Two recent studies bear important testimony to the uncertainties in clinical classifications—see Ash (3) and Hunt *et al* (11). In Rawley (14) Dr. Karl Menninger is quoted as follows: "To say that the patient has 'schizophrenia' is unscientific because we are being precise about something that is wholly amorphous."

being made in psychiatry and medicine to achieve diagnostic and treatment precision are unproductive. It is rather to say that present-day clinical diagnosis and its implications for treatment must be viewed by social caseworkers not as fully definitive or as a "prescription" for treatment but with the recognition that it is rough and that, moreover, it is but one of a number of important guides to what may or may not be done with a person in his problem situation. Each man, we must remember, is more than his disease or malformation. Within the classification "schizophrenia," for example, are persons who are bright and those who are dull, the physically sound and the debilitated, those whose environments will cushion or undermine them, those whose talents are such as to make sublimations possible or who are empty of expressive means, those who want help or who shun it. These individual differences can never be uncovered by a classification system; they account for how this man is different from that one, though both may be suffering from the same type of the same disease. Not only is each man who has a personal or social problem more than his problem but he is different by his capacities, by what he wants, and by his resources from anyone else who has the same problem. So it is that the diagnosis of each man must be more than the rough sorting-out of emotional and mental malfunctioning that clinical classification provides.

In the triangular diagnostic configuration set forth earlier the clinical diagnosis contributes to understanding the nature of the person who is to be dealt with; in social casework practice there remains the necessity to gauge the relevance of this understanding to the problem to be worked on, the ends sought, and the means available.

### Etiological Diagnosis

In the caseworker's reflective thinking about a client's problem, about what part of it might be grappled with, first or later, the question of its cause and development may often need to be answered. The purposes of establishing recent or precipitating causation have already been discussed in chapter 9 (pp. 126–29) mainly as these: to clarify whether the problem lies chiefly in the client himself or in his life-situation; to deal directly with causal factors so as to nullify them or modify their impact; or, conversely, to take into account such causal factors as are immutable.

The term "etiological diagnosis," as commonly used, relates less often to immediate causation and more often to the beginnings and life-history of a problem, usually to the problem that lies in the client's personality makeup or functioning. The usefulness of understanding such a chain of causation may be several fold.

The duration, consistency, and pervasiveness of internal disturbance or overt malfunctioning in a person contribute vital evidence to expectations of change and movement in his problem-solving efforts. While his problem to be solved may not be that of his psychic difficulties at all—more likely it will be perceived and formulated by the client as some problem in his relationship to other persons or social situations—yet the ways he operates or can be expected to cope depend on how deep and long and widespread his emotional and behavior problems are. The history of the adverse experiences he has encountered, but particularly the history of his successful or unsuccessful adaptations to them—his "solution" of his difficulties, for example, by retreat, by intrenchment, by blind fighting, or by compromise, detour, and constructive substitutions—*this history of his development as a problem-encountering, problem-solving human being* may provide the caseworker with an understanding of what his client suffers from and what the extent of his coping ability is likely to be.

Yet—and this caution cannot be repeated too often—the evidence in the history must not, in our action or in our thinking, substitute for the evidence revealed in the client's current behavior and reactions outside and within the casework situation. Full-grown adults, it is true, react in patterned ways, and a history may quickly reveal such patterns; but it is also true that the patterns are subject to modifications of kind and intensity depending upon how different and regenerative a new experience is and upon what present but unexercised capacities may be aroused and stimulated by the caseworker. The temptation is great among us all to believe that an account of the past is more "true" than our observations of what is dynamically in operation before us; certainly it is more easily comprehended because it has attained a static quality. But against this temptation we must pose our recognition that living is never static and our intent to make of the casework situation an experience of difference and change.

Especially as it focuses on the beginnings and development of some one aspect of the client's functioning, an etiological diagnosis may have considerable usefulness in explaining the persistence of inappropriate behavior or rigid reactions. This understanding may be sought by the caseworker when, despite the fact that the client's present problems are in the center of attention, the client's responses seem to rise out of some earlier, fixed reaction pattern as though some past experience intruded upon his clear perception of the present one. At such a time the caseworker himself may need to see and test and thence to help his client to see whether the recognition and discussion of this early cause in its inappropriate effect upon the present may release the client from the grip of the dead hand of the past. When this occurs, it may be seen that the past history and its appraisal in the light of the client's current capacities, goals, and problems are used for therapeutic purposes.* This is a situation in which diagnostic understanding by the client, along with that of the caseworker, may have spontaneous or potential treatment value. It is possible, of course, that a client may never see the connection between the history he recounts and his present actions; he may lack this insight capacity. Then this, too, has diagnostic and therefore treatment significance to the caseworker.

In work with the problems of children, etiological material has particular pertinence. The reason is obvious: the "causes" in the lives of children are still in large part of fairly recent origin or in current operation, and they are often readily accessible to influence or dissolution. Moreover, the child is in a process of more radical change and growth than the adult can be, and new "causes" provided by casework services may serve to counteract the forces that warp or retard his growth. Add to these considerations the fact that the young child does not and cannot take responsibility for articulating his problem in any measure comparable to the adult, and the reason becomes apparent for understanding how his difficulties came about as a guide to how he may be helped.

In some settings, notably in psychiatric clinics for adult and

* A nice illustration and exposition of this usage may be found in the case presented by Gomberg (6).

child guidance, the "taking" of a background history of the patient is almost routine. This practice arose at a time when it was assumed that certain causes inevitably led to certain effects and that, therefore, if causes could be identified, effects could be predicted with fair certainty. But there has been general recognition in recent years that such a mechanistic conception does not hold for phenomena as complex as human lives, and, as anyone who has studied life-histories quickly discerns, there are many inexplicable discrepancies between people's past experiences and their present adjustments. For these reasons, among others, the routine scrutiny of the client's or patient's past life for the key to his present behavior is now used with more discrimination than it once was.*

It must be said that, in the business of learning about how in general people get to be the way they are and how the human being knits his life-experience into himself, there is probably no substitute for the repeated experience of taking and analyzing life-histories. As a means of learning it is rich in content for the developing professional helper, and perhaps this is the rationale for the practice in so many clinics where psychiatric interns and residents and psychiatric social workers meet the client or patient first by seeking etiological material. This usefulness for the learner in casework or psychiatry and the security it gives to the diagnostician, valid or not, ought frankly to be recognized for what it is and differentiated from the assumption that it always is helpful in treatment planning or action.

The etiological diagnosis in the sense of the life-history of a person or a problem may contribute to understanding the nature of the problem to be dealt with, the person who has that problem, and the ways and means that can be anticipated as helpful. Such a contribution is made largely through its revelation of fixed or malleable behavior or circumstance patterns. As such, it may supplement or change the caseworker's ideas of what he can expect his client to be and do. But, like the clinical diagnosis, it is only one facet of knowledge by which casework thinking and doing may be guided. Because it does not tell "all," even about the past, it cannot explain

---

* See *The Functioning of Psychiatric Clinics in New York City* (22) for a study that bears on the effects of "history-taking" upon the patients' continuing contacts.

"all." Because man may be as strongly driven and drawn by "what is" and "what is to be" as by "what was," the portents of his past must be viewed as contributing to, never as substituting for, the many dynamic factors at play in his current problem-solving efforts.*

The method of the diagnostic process will not be discussed here. It has been given clear exposition elsewhere.† It is the method of logical thinking we use every day. As we make any effort to solve a problem in daily living, we move from what we observe to what we infer or deduce (based on our sum of knowledge and experience) to some conclusive explanation of what we make of it, and from that to anticipation of what will or can be made to happen next. Our acting upon that expectation tests and confirms the validity or exposes the invalidity of our conclusion. This phenomenon of the human thought process has been identified by logicians, but it was not invented by them. As Alfred North Whitehead has said, "Science is rooted in . . . the whole apparatus of commonsense thought."‡ The use of conscious, logical modes of thinking in casework is implicit in its responsible problem-solving activity. Actually this is all that is meant when casework is credited with being "scientific."

In sum, the purpose of the diagnostic process and product in social casework is to give boundary, relevance, and direction to the caseworker's helpful intents and skills. As process, it seeks to identify and appraise the nature of the problem in relation to the kind of person the client is, his inner and outer functioning and resources, in relation to the agency's helping means. As product, it gives focus and direction to the ongoing transactions between caseworker and client, and caseworker and such other persons as are involved either as parts of the problem or as participants in its solution. It attempts to

---

* Perhaps the final social casework word on the use of the etiological diagnosis was said more than a quarter of a century ago by Mary Richmond. She quoted Jung as follows (in part): "A person is only half understood when one knows how everything in him came about. Only a dead man can be explained in terms of the past." And she added: "Our examination of the yesterdays and the todays should be with special reference to our client's tomorrows" ("Some Next Steps in Social Treatment," a paper read at the National Conference of Social Work in 1920 and published in *The Long View* [New York: Russell Sage Foundation, 1930]).

† See Dewey (5), Lehrman (12), and Richmond (16).

‡ "The Organization of Thought," in *The Aims of Education* (Mentor Books, 1949).

identify cause-effect connections so that some intervention may be injected to halt or change the course of a problem. It does not write a treatment prescription, but it points to some general expectations and thus gives guidance to the caseworker's operations. It demands some structure of thought, which is the condition of planned action. In the caseworker it substitutes conscious, responsible appraisal and anticipation for diffused impressions and chance responsiveness. These purposes of diagnosis hold throughout the life of a case.

### Diagnosis in the Beginning Phase

As has been said, at any given time the data that are brought under diagnostic examination will be different as the situation requires, related to the immediate or long-term client-worker purposes. Thus, if one accepts what has been proposed here, that the purpose of the beginning phase in casework is "to engage this client with his problem and his will to do something about it in a working relationship with this agency, its intentions, and special means of helpfulness," it follows that understanding the nature and the relationships of the data that bear on this special purpose will be the diagnostic focus in that phase.

Once the caseworker has obtained enough information to establish that in its general nature the problem brought and the solution sought by the client lie within the realm of agency function and means, the immediate question to be answered is the nature and extent of the client's ability and willingness to work on it. This is to say that in the beginning the client's "workability" becomes the center of diagnostic attention. Whatever the nature of the client's problem or malfunctioning and however it came about, any change depends primarily upon what the client wants to do about it and what he can put into such doing. If the client from the first is to be an active agent in his own behalf, his resources of motive and performance powers must be known and used. It is the evidence of such powers that from the first must be observed, assessed, and responded to in order that the caseworker's operations be finely attuned to the client's use of those powers. Whether the caseworker needs to sustain, challenge, intensify, or clarify the client's motivation depends upon his understanding of its quality and quantity and directedness.

How he will conduct his interviewing—what he will say or leave unsaid, how he will put it—depends, again, less upon the classification of his client's personal or situational problem and more upon his diagnostic scrutiny and appraisal of the client's demonstration of functioning capacity. To understand the problem of a human being suggests what needs to be done or what might be done, but it is necessary to understand the powers of drive and ability he is able to muster in order to know what *can* be done.

The evidence for this diagnosis of the client's motivation and capacity to use agency help is chiefly that of the client's spontaneous behavior and responsiveness within the interview situation and outside it. The content of the first interviews, as set forth in chapter 9, involves the client in discussing his trouble, his feeling, thinking, acting relationship to it, his ideas of causation and solution and so on. All this results in much more than information about the kind of trouble he is wrestling with. It provides a three-dimensional motion picture of a person not only telling about himself but acting himself out, responding both to what he brings with him and to the new stimuli he encounters in the caseworker's attitude, queries, empathy, reactions, and information. Then, as the caseworker injects both some explanation and a demonstration of how social casework may attempt to give aid with the difficulty, the client's reactions to this, his positive, negative, or mixed responses, his taking-hold or relinquishment—these and other kinds of behavior give further evidence of his willingness and ability to engage himself. This has been put rather nicely by Sanford Sherman, when he says that by this evidence "a diagnosis is converted from diagnosis of a *person* to diagnosis of a *client*" (17), that is, of a person seeking a particular kind of professional help.

The diagnosis of a client's "workability," then, is a by-product of the work in which he is engaged from the start. The caseworker arrives at this diagnosis through the evolving evidence of the client's functioning in his first steps of problem-solving. It is the beginning treatment (treatment used here to mean "dealing with" or "subjecting to some action") that produces this category of evidence and by which it can most reliably be tested.

As with other forms of diagnosis, the validity of the diagnosis of "workability" depends upon the perceptiveness and special knowledge the diagnostician brings to bear upon what he observes and also upon the skill with which he can evoke significant responses that have relevance. The evidences by which the client's attributes of willingness and ability to cope and to use casework help with his problem are signs that have long been perceived but not always identified or classified by caseworkers. Because these indicators have been given less attention in our practice and literature than have those signs that bespeak malfunctioning, and, because they point to the client's working powers—what we so frequently subsume under "ego strengths"—they merit discussion in a chapter of their own.

# 12  THE CLIENT'S WORKABILITY

## AND THE CASEWORK GOAL*

Some explanation is due the reader for the use of this coined and perhaps irritating word, "workability." It is chosen in some effort to identify that combination of motivation and capacity that enables a person to engage himself (with greater or lesser degrees of effort and effectiveness) with the persons and means of solving his problem. It accounts only for the client's dynamic relationship to his problem and the agency at a single point in time. As used here, it means both "ability to work" and "responsiveness to therapeutic influence." It makes no pretense of predicting outcome or degree of success, nor does it take into account such resources or opportunities as may be enlisted in the client's behalf. Its purpose is to prime the caseworker's effort to name and appraise the client's spontaneous responsiveness to casework help, in order that such a diagnostic appraisal may enhance the appropriateness and flexibility of what the caseworker puts into the interview.

Some gauge of the client's probable responsiveness provides the caseworker with forehandedness. Reports and accounts of the client

* This chapter is an expansion of a paper read at Boston University School of Social Work in March, 1956, and published in *Social Work*, Vol. I, No. 4 (October, 1956).

from other sources or from earlier experiences all provide some rough framework of anticipation as to how the client will react. Yet his actual responsiveness has no better testing ground than in the casework interview itself and in its resultant effects. The client's modes of defense and adaptation are in constantly shifting relationship and emphasis, subject to changes of kind and degree as stimuli change or as his perceptions change. Were this not so, if behavior were iron-bound by the past, there would be no point in casework or in any other therapeutic effort. Against any foreknowledge of the client, his spontaneous, immediate responsiveness in the present-day interview and his post-interview reactions must be viewed for their new meanings. How the client's drive and ability show themselves in grappling with the task that today's interview or today's living situation sets is the major evidence in gauging and promoting workability. The little ways in which he fails or succeeds in appropriate response and adaptation must be the guides to the ways in which the caseworker will have to act. "Probable responsiveness," then, must be viewed as prediction in the rough only; actual responsiveness, workability, must be tested afresh in each beginning situation.

What we seek to appraise of a client's working ability is not the total sum of his strong and healthy parts. When this has been done, as when caseworkers have attempted to list "assets" in balance against "liabilities" in any given case, it has resulted in a static itemization. It is like describing the appearance of a man of whom it could be said that he was fat and nearsighted and toothless but, on the other hand, was tall and had a ruddy skin and a good nose. But what did he look like? And in the context of what ideas was his appearance being dissected? For it would make a difference if it were as suitor, movie actor, or truck-driver. In any appraisal that is diagnostic rather than impressionistic, the data must be selected in relation to their bearing upon some purpose and for their connection with one another. Relatedness is again the key: the relation of the asset to the problem and to the sought purposes and means. Thus, when we want to understand what ego strengths and what problem-solving assets the client has, we do well to cull out and examine selectively those that relate closely to the problem he wants help with and to the help that is available. What follows here, then, is not an effort to name all the qualities that constitute a client's ego strengths or assets (indeed, I could not if I would) but instead to identify what seem to be the major attributes by which a client's willingness and ability to use agency help may be recognized and then enhanced.*

### The Client's Motivation for Casework Help

"Willingness" is used here in the limited sense of the client's conscious, mobilized intent to involve himself in using help. Without this, no armamentarium of understanding and skills is of any avail. No matter what the nature of the client's problem is, he must want some help or change and must reach out with some part of himself to use it. In social casework practice perhaps more than in other helping professions, the caseworker's skills and energies may often have to be put into grappling first with just this problem: to help the person to want and then to will to be a client. Because of this, and because this necessity may arise at any point in a case when the client's doubts or resistances draw him away from the agency, the caseworker must be aware of what elements combine to make up "willingness," in order that their presence or absence may be recognized, and so that the caseworker may act in such ways as to awaken and call forth what dormant motivation the client may have.

There are several progressive stages through which a person moves in order to be "willing." Sometimes this has been achieved by the client before he arrives at the agency, but often the caseworker must help him to achieve willingness. "Wanting" usually precedes "willing." A person feels the need of something and is pushed by that feeling, or he perceives something that he believes will increase his well-being and is pulled by that image. He *wants* to get rid of some difficulty or to achieve some goal. But "wanting" may remain like "wishing," simply a yearning for change, a desire or hope that something will happen outside one's self—that circumstances or other persons will provide the longed-for goal. Thus the client may come to the agency *wanting* change but wanting it to happen to him largely through the efforts of others. This is not un-

* For impetus and contribution to my thinking about this matter I am indebted to my students in our post-Master's casework seminar and to my faculty colleagues, particularly to Lilian Ripple, director of the Research Center of the Social Service Administration of the University of Chicago, for the stimulation afforded by her current study of motivation and capacity in relation to beginning use of casework services (see Ripple, 8).

common in persons who are physically debilitated or in persons whose life-experience has made them psychologically dependent upon others or on chance to determine their fates.

"Willing" involves taking several steps beyond "wanting," one at a time or all in one leap. They consist of seeing one's self as a potential force in shaping one's ends; of charging one's self with taking some active part in making whatever changes must come about; and of mobilizing one's self to act. Within this movement from wanting to willing, one may see the typical adaptive functioning of the ego from perception of need and goal to organization and mobilization of energies directed toward achievement.

As a person encounters obstacles along the way, however, whether those obstacles are in the outer reality or in counterpulls within himself, his mobilization and drive may be dissipated or blocked, and he may retire from willing to the easier role of wanting or even just wishing. This may happen to a client many times in the course of ongoing treatment, and he will need to be helped by the caseworker again and again to perceive his need and/or his goal, to see himself in relation to it, to choose to carry his part of solving his problem or promoting change. The client who has voluntarily brought himself to the agency has surely mobilized himself to come. But his willingness may be dissipated when he finds that the solution he proposes is not readily at hand or that the kind of help that is proffered him involves demands as well as rewards.

Two conditions must hold for the sustainment of responsible willingness to work at problem-solving: discomfort and hope. Even the imperceptible shifts of body positions that occur in us a thousand times a day are responses to felt discomforts; certainly, a shift of psychological equilibrium must be occasioned by some sense of discomfort and the attendant push to gain greater comfort or a steadier sense of balance. Thus a person must feel more uncomfortable than comfortable with his problem in order to want to do something about it, and this malaise will serve to push him. Accompanying this push from within (or some push from without that results in discomfort) must be some promise of greater ease or satisfaction, and this promise pulls the person to bend his effort toward some goal. The promise is inherent in hope—hope that is carried in the personality itself as the product of gratifications in his past experience combined with that which is inherent in the situation or is given by the caseworker if he can offer valid assurances of help. The existence of either element without the other, or of an excessive degree of either, will deplete motivation. Discomfort without hope spells resignation, apathy, fixation; it means that the person feels so depleted of energies, so disabled and bereft, as to have no future orientation, no sense of "becoming." Hopefulness without discomfort (that is to say, without any inner sense of wanting to strive) is th mark of the immature, wishful person, he who depends on others or on circumstances to work for his interests. Such future "becoming" orientation as he may have is unfounded in reality, and he sees himself as the potential victim or preferably the darling of happenstance. Using his best perception of reality as his gauge, the caseworker may appraise his client's combination of discomfort and hope in order to judge what he should try to diminish, to modify, or to encourage, in order to rouse in his client that push or pull which mobilizes him for change.

Willingness to engage in change involves another consideration: the client's drive should be directed toward a valid, realizable solution or goal. Motivation may be strong for unattainable ends, or it may be dissipated because of aimlessness. The caseworker must ascertain what it is that the client is mobilized to do and whether he has a realistic idea of what ends are feasible and available for his working efforts. The answer to this will suggest how the caseworker must clarify or modify the client's ideas.

What are the signs by which the caseworker may know the client's "willingness"? The first, of course, is the client's presentation of himself with a problem, something that has made him uncomfortable enough to seek the agency's help. Accompanying what he says will be his behavior—body or facial tensions, emotional expressions, or the use of defenses against showing or feeling these—which bespeaks some stress. He shows that he is more uncomfortable than comfortable about his problem situation, more distressed than satisfied.

In the interview the client says what it is he wants, what solution he seeks. He is after something. As the caseworker explores his ideas of what he wants, their realistic or unrealistic quality becomes clear. If his goals are valid in the light of the problem and the available coping means, his willingness may be seen as well directed. His participation will give another important clue to his willingness. The client should see himself as an active agent in relation to his problem, either as contributing to it in the past or as working on it in the present. The caseworker needs to both test and promote the person's readiness to recognize that his behavior is an actual or potential dynamic in his problem situation or in its solution—that he is a working member of the caseworker-client team.

The client's efforts to engage in the interview work are indications of his willingness. Whether he can communicate, respond, or think appropriately depends, of course, upon his capacity and also upon the worker's skill in freeing him to operate; but his *trying* to participate bespeaks his positive motivation. Thus, in response to the worker's questions or comments, the motivated client invests himself with some intensity; he "puts himself into" explaining his situation, making himself clear. When motivation is positive, he tries to operate in mutuality—that is, he tries to follow what the worker is saying, he answers questions, ponders a point; in short, he demonstrates his intention and efforts to co-operate.

Perhaps the most telling test of motivation or willingness occurs when the worker injects into discussion the realities of the kind of help that is available and its conditions. Sometimes this meets the client's expectations, and he is pleased to find that the agency can promise a better resolution than he had thought possible, but often the reality of available help is disappointing because it contains no ready-made solution, or it falls short of fulfilling his wishes, or the way to the solution remains to be explored and holds many uncertainties. The client's willingness at this point may be seen in his effort to bear the frustration of waiting and working and in his expression of hope and trust in some later solution. He is willing to postpone gratification because his hope and confidence sustain him and also because he is trying to trust what he has perceived as a trustworthy person and place. So he tries to accept, tentatively at least, the fact that the agency has a valid basis in its experience for its procedures or policies or differing perspectives, and he agrees (again spontaneously or in response to the proposal and encouragement of the caseworker) that he will go forward with the agency for at least a trial period.

## The Client's Capacity To Use Casework Help

Capacity or ability, as used here, refers to such qualities of emotional and personality makeup, of intellectual and physical endowment, as the individual has and can use in the task of problem-solving. "Can use" is the chief consideration because of the frequency with which potential capacities in human beings are blocked or held in abeyance by conflict. An important part of the caseworker's help to a given client, of course, may be that of bringing potential capacities to fruition. The phrase "in the task of problem-solving" sets further boundaries upon what capacities the caseworker seeks to discern in this, the beginning stage. Within these boundaries the capacities we try to ascertain are those of emotion, intelligence, and health.°

### EMOTIONAL CAPACITY

Perhaps the primary capacity in being able to use the help of another is that of being able to relate to another. Without this, things can be done to, for, and about a person but never *with* him. A capacity for relationship is a many-nuanced, finely graded thing. It includes the tenuous, veiled sense of proximity or distance one may encounter in a schizoid personality, the challenging wariness of the distrustful person, the hungry clinging of a dependent person, and the responsive give-and-take of an ordinarily adaptive person in communication. A capacity for relationship may be validly assessed only when the worker demonstrates himself to be a receptive, responsive, empathic, helpful "relater."

Of the many ways by which relationship capacity may be discerned and known, an essay in itself could be written. The whole person relates, and so his body positions, his facial expressions, his emotional tone, and his verbal responses—all these and more—give evidence of whether his essential movement is toward people, away from them, or against them. In briefest outline the indicators of good relationship capacity follow. A client who relates realistically to the caseworker at first meeting relates with some reserve—that is,

° What follows identifies and discusses many of the same capacities named by Green (3). He lists as a guide "to the most important ego functions" the following: object relationships, reality testing, judgment, motility patterns, tolerance for frustration, affectivity, defense mechanisms, and basic intellective capacities. See also Murray and Kluckhohn (6).

he restrains the full play of his communication. This is not because he is necessarily wary or afraid but because he wishes to "take in" or to "feel out" the nature of the other person in order to respond appropriately. He acts in relation to the other rather than to his own momentary needs or impulses. The person who at first meeting either seems closed off or pours himself out is at the moment relating chiefly to himself. The relating person hears at least the overt content of what is being said to him. He perceives with his eyes and other sensing organs what the other seems like, and he responds appropriately to what his senses convey to him.

As the client discerns that the interest in him and queries of him are for helping purposes and that he is being accepted for the person he is, some greater ease permeates him, and he opens himself and his problem a little further. Trustfulness deepens with the caseworker's demonstration of responsible understanding and helping intents. The client who relates well and appropriately sees and accepts the caseworker's professional identity (though his vision may have to be corrected now and again as feelings distort his sight). Thus his responses to the worker as a helping partner are relevant. As discussion together goes forward over a number of interviews, he shows that he is able to deposit something of himself (that is, that he can share his feelings, hopes, and confidences) in the caseworker and can take in from the caseworker such attitudes, ideas, and understandings as are proffered for his use. He maintains (often with considerable help from the caseworker) his sense of adult identity at the same time as he feels togetherness with the caseworker in their mutual but different tasks (see Towle, 9).

Relationship capacity may also be seen in the client's accounts of his relationships with other persons in his current life and in the concerns and feelings he shows in speaking of others. Good capacity for relationship may be seen in a client's ability to understand the feelings of other people involved in his problem, to hold some sympathy for others even though for the most part he may feel against them or be self-absorbed. It is indicated, further, by a client's differentiated reactions to different relationships, which means that he brings perception and pliability to interpersonal encounters rather than a fixed pattern of response (see Mitchell *et al.*, 5).

Intimately tied in with the ability to form and sustain relationships is the ability to "feel"—that is, to experience, to know, and to bear one's emotions. Stated flatly thus, "ability to feel" sounds like an absurdity, because all human beings feel and have emotions. But not all human beings retain the capacity to experience and know their emotions in the sense of tasting and savoring them or allowing them to wash over both the heart and the mind in order that full, knowing possession may be taken of them. The experience of many people has led them to coat their feelings with enamel, so to speak, or to imprison them in darkness for so long as to dwarf them. Such persons have had cause to fear their feelings, to be afraid of being overwhelmed by them. These persons' motive powers may often be curtailed or cut off from the purposes of the mind.

There are other persons who are literally creatures of their own emotions who are continuously ravaged and buffeted by the internal anarchy of their feelings. These persons experience their feelings intensely, but they do not "know" them in the sense of recognizing them for what they mean or from whence they stem, nor can they tolerate them or bring them into harmony with their purposes. Such persons are in a sense owned by their emotions, and they are literally spent by the emotional energy that, rather than empowering their purposes, runs amuck in them.

In both of these kinds of persons the mind and the heart may be said to have poor communication with each other. To experience is not necessarily to know, and to know is not necessarily to experience; both must take place and fuse for the person to be able to feel whole and capable. One of the kinds of change that the casework process repeatedly aims for and that often seems to unfold out of the experience of a meaningful relationship is this very change of feeling within the person that helps him know, experience, and tolerate himself as a feeling as well as a thinking and acting person. But, in order for this to come about, the ability to experience feeling must be present at least in the seed.

A person with good emotional capacity is one who dares to experience his feelings and can express them, and yet can contain them when necessary, as when he is asked to recount certain facts with which much feeling may be associated. The signs of such capacity may be seen sometimes singly, sometimes together, but they are more validly appraised in the whole than in fragments. The client with good emotional capacity, as he talks about himself and his problems, shows by his facial and bodily responses not only that feeling is invested in what he is saying but that the feeling is appropriate both in intensity and in kind to the content he is discussing. He is able to admit to having feelings rather than having consistently to deny or to project them. He can say, perhaps with some struggling, what he feels like—that is, he can explain and communicate his feelings to another person. Not only can he talk about them but he can dare to act them or live them out in the safe presence of the worker. Yet they are subject to his efforts at control—he is not overwhelmed by them. And, finally, he shows that he can respond to the caseworker's demonstrated compassion, concern, and strength and can utilize these qualities to affect his own feeling.

The ways by which the person tells and explains his dilemma and need, his part in it, his reaction to it, and the ways in which he responds to the new stimuli of the agency or the worker's operations tell much not only about the nature of his anxieties but about his efforts at defense and adaptation. That his defenses may be named and seen in operation does not produce an appraisal. The material for appraisal is the flexibility or rigidity of the client's efforts to cope with his problem and of his efforts to deal with it, the free responsiveness or stubborn chronicity of his behavior, and the inappropriate or constructive nature of his responses. These signs may be seen in the interview interaction; they may also be discerned in the client's (or others') accounts of his typical behavior in the near past when he encountered difficulty or conflict; they will be seen in his ability to carry out what he consciously wants to do. That the client has and uses defenses is to say only that he has ways of maintaining his integration and steadiness. That his defenses of protection can give way to maneuvers of adaptation and coping as he experiences support and enabling help is to say that he possesses his emotions (rather than that he is possessed by them) and that his ways of achieving dynamic stability may be judged to be efficient and economical.

### INTELLIGENCE CAPACITY

A person's intelligence quotient offers no gauge of his ability to solve problems that are of intimate concern to him. Just as motivation and emotional freedom empower the intellect, the lack or crippling of either debilitate it. Nevertheless, intellectual adequacy is certainly not a handicap, and surely the part of our communications that is verbal is facilitated by a grasp of word meanings and association to ideas. Perhaps what the caseworker needs to assess is less the client's intellectual and more his "social intelligence" capacity. "Social intelligence" defies even the psychologist's exact definition, but a few of its major components can perhaps be described.

The first essential feature of intelligence is perceptiveness. The person who may be called perceptive sees with more than his two eyes. He "sees" as if by some combined use of all his senses at once, and also connectedly, as if a spontaneous contact occurred between sensing and ideation. He sees what is outside him and also what is within him, and he sees both the connection and the difference between the two. (Thus, popularly, we say a baby's first indication of "intelligence" is when he gives indication that he perceives his mother as a related but separate being.)

The range of perceptivity, like that of capacity for relationship and feeling, is wide and varied, from the person whose mental receiving set seems blunted or blurred to him whose sensitivity registers every degree of differentiation. Such a range may be found within any one person at different times, because at times of intense emotion our perceptions are affected. Depending on the situation, we may be blinded (as with rage or with love) or we may experience heightened awareness with a concentration and narrowing of perception on one object (as when one "smells danger" or "senses" another person's feeling). Perceptivity may be considered good when a person observes clearly and precisely and, beyond this, sees into things. Perhaps it may be said he sees three-dimensionally, in breadth, depth, and relatedness. He reads valid meaning into what happens and thereby is able to make connections and differentiations. This capacity is obviously a primary condition for good ego functioning. The client who may be accounted perceptive is he who sees—or can readily be brought to see—not only his problem in relation to himself but also his relationship to the agency and to casework help.

A second attribute of social intelligence is the ability to communicate, both within one's self and to another. Communication, we know, may occur at many levels. One is through the language of the body; gestures, bodily attitudes, and facial expressions often say deeper things than can be conveyed in words. Any of us at moments when we are sensitively open to experience knows the kind of whole understanding that may come to us as if through our pores rather than through our minds. So it is that with young children, or with adults who momentarily or typically are childlike, the caseworker's words may have only minimal meaning, and what they will receive and respond to will be via what is "sensed." Another level of communication, usually accompanying body language, is that of subverbal sounds—the assents, the negations, the small noises of pleasure or pain that are unshaped communications. These are part of our everyday communication, and, like body language, they convey general rather than finely differentiated responses.

However, in order for a person to become "self-possessed," that is, in order to be able to know, understand, consciously take hold, and manage what one experiences, there must be words. Words identify parts of experience; they name differences. But, more than this, the groping to give something a word-name represents the forging of a link between sensing and thinking. To be able to put something felt or experienced into words means that some inner communication system exists between the heart and the mind. Until a human being's experience is transferable to his mind, it is unavailable to his conscious management. In the last analysis, this is why talking, using words to give names to amorphous masses of feeling, is the major tool of psychotherapeutic methods. Social relationships depend heavily on one's ability consciously to appraise and manage one's self in relation to others. This, in turn, depends upon the ability to communicate accurately what one senses, feels, thinks, and does. And this is why social intelligence may in part be gauged by the client's ability to convey meaning in words and why, too, the caseworker attempts to reinforce this capacity in clients by encouraging the verbal expression of feeling and thought.

Of course, words may also be used as defenses and misleaders, so that one must guard against banking upon this ability to communicate verbally except as it appears together with signs of appropriate affect and behavior. When it appears in such combination or emerges thus as a result of the client's growing sense of freedom, it represents the adaptive and integrative functioning of the ego.

Another important element in social intelligence is a capacity for attention. To "stick to a subject," to hold something in the center of one's considerations as one recognizes but does not pursue tangents, is essential to any working-over of a problem. The ability to pay attention to an idea or a problem probably involves both motivation and at least the partial deposit of interest in something outside the self. There are instances, to be sure, when attention becomes too fixed, when the center of interest begins to absorb all the person's interests and energies. This, clearly, is indicative of loss of both perception and adaptability. Capacity for attention in problem-solving may be said, then, to require both focusing and pivoting. Attention is for the purpose of coming to some understanding grasp of an idea or situation which, in turn, is for the purpose of making some judgment or conclusion about it.

Good judgment is a major asset in social intelligence. It follows upon realistic perception, upon the connections made between cause and effects, between past and present and present and future acts and consequences, upon the ability to remember and from this to anticipate and plan. It depends, too, upon the person's emotional ability to sustain the tension that considering, weighing, and choosing involves. It can be seen, then, that judgment will always be strongly influenced by the person's emotional capacities and state. Because, as has been said before, the client comes to the agency at a point where ego integration is low, it cannot be expected that his capacity for good judgment will show itself in free-flowing decision-making. It may be seen, rather, in his readiness to exercise this capacity as the caseworker helps him to deliberate, weigh, and consider facts and ideas before he takes action.

Social intelligence in any situation is probably heavily dependent, too, upon know-how. In order to operate "intelligently," a person must have some idea how to go about coping with a situation and what his role is supposed to involve. While he may not know the details, he must have some general conception of what is required of him and of the situation. The extent of a client's know-how may be seen in his efforts to solve his problem prior to coming to the agency, in the ways he presents his problem, in his grasp of the caseworker's explanation of the mutual but distinct roles they will take in working together, and so on. The client who "has no idea" of what to expect or what to do may need considerably more direct suggestion and information from the caseworker than he who is in possession of some working knowledge.

Know-how is tested in appropriate action in a given social situation. Such action is manifestly subject to distortion or vitation as a result of emotional conflict. The extent or spread of conflict, indeed, may be known by the differing kinds of situations in which, while the person may understand his proper role, he cannot function. Conversely, it is a good sign when, despite internal disturbance or external difficulties, a person is still able to act in accordance with the social demands upon him. The coherence of know-how with overt action gives an indication that the ego's executive functions are fairly intact despite such internal disturbances as the person may be experiencing. Perhaps, in sum, social intelligence may be said to be the person's capacity to change or modify his behavior as a result of what he perceives, knows, or experiences in reality.

### PHYSICAL CAPACITY

The client's physical capacity is probably easiest to assess, certainly the easiest on which to get specific expert opinion. Except as the problem brought by the client is that of his physical condition, what needs appraisal is chiefly whether or not the client has physical energies free to invest in work on his problem or whether his energies are being consumed by sickness or by the debility and exhaustion that are the toll of physical or emotional deprivations. The spirit may be willing but the flesh weak, not alone by ambivalence, as the ancient saying suggests, but also because long hardship may have drained out a man's hardiness.

## Appraising Motivation and Capacity

What has been implied needs, perhaps, to be made explicit: no check list of these above-named or other attributes of motivation and capacity will reveal the client's workability. Rather, it will be necessary to view them in their dynamic combinations. It is often not possible to determine where capacity leaves off and motivation begins. Moreover, neither motivation nor capacity can be judged simply by observation of how the client spontaneously presents himself and his problem. As has been said earlier, these abilities and drives of the client can best be seen, tested, and brought out in the planned interaction of interviewing, where the caseworker provides both stimulus and support to the client's use of his present powers. When the client gives evidence of disablement, the caseworker will need to examine and assess what factors in interaction between the client and his current life-situation (the psychosocial evidence) or what in his personality makeup (the clinical evidence) or what in his past life-experience (the etiological evidence) explain and affect his functioning. Whichever diagnostic data are used, the purpose is to give guidance to the caseworker's ongoing work of promoting and rewarding the client's adaptive efforts.

The particular purpose served by the diagnosis of the client's immediate workability calls for some separate discussion. More than any other, this diagnostic evidence, unwinding before the caseworker's very eyes, responsive to the caseworker's touch, so to speak, tells of the here-and-now functioning of the client. It tells, first of all, what remains working well in him despite the disease he may carry or the problems that bedevil him. It is this relatively unimpaired functioning that the caseworker wants to know, to support, and to exercise. We have often tended to say rather glibly that we "support the ego strengths," but it may be ventured that, unless we have identified what those strengths consist of in the particular client, we have very little idea of what it is we are supporting.

In many instances, moreover, it is the client's lack of motivation or his incapacities that are the very essence of his problem or are at least the first obstacles to be overcome. Here, as when dealing with the unmotivated client, the caseworker's first treatment efforts must be directed less to the problem that makes the person a client and more to such reluctances as interfere with his being one. "Enabling" means helping a person to mobilize his own drives and abilities for use in a desired direction, and such help can be given only as the caseworker identifies and discerns what those drives and abilities are.

Inevitably, as the caseworker sees himself responsible for creating a situation in which he reinforces as well as appraises the evidence of a client's workability, he will give the client a vital experience from the first. The beginning interviews will be more than a telling-listening, questioning-answering, explaining-understanding experience. As the caseworker lends himself to testing and giving impetus to the client's motivation and ability to begin work on his problem, he will find himself keenly alerted to the client as a functioning person, not just as a needful one. As the client takes part in such interviews, he will find himself involved with (not just related to) a person who supports and encourages him by acceptance and understanding and who also helps him to say what he wants, to know whether and how he can get it, to experience something of what work with the agency is like. His responses to this beginning treatment provide diagnostic evidence and guidance of major significance.

This assessment of the client's willingness and capacity is, as we have said, the product rather than the primary purpose of the caseworker's work with him in this beginning phase. For the client, the beginning phase should have yielded not only the verbal answers to his questions but also the vital experience of being and feeling helped. This comes about when the casework process not only has a helping end but when its helping means contain that end. This means that throughout the several interviews that bring the client and the caseworker to their joint agreement as to where, with what, and how they will go on together the caseworker offers the sustainment and stimulation, the acceptance and expectation, the focus and purposiveness, that characterize the whole helping process.

### Casework Goals

Finally, the diagnosis and the appraisal of the client's current functioning abilities are important for our thinking about casework goals. Like the concept of "diagnosis," the concept of "goal" in casework has been much used and variously interpreted. At times it has been spoken of in terms of ideals and absolutes, at others in terms of specific practical limits; frequently it is defined in terms of what it is *not*—"personality reorganization is not the goal of social casework"—from which one would infer that at least some caseworkers averred that it was. In discussions among caseworkers there is evident some underlying feeling that their goal ought to be the complete resolution of the client's problem.* The necessity of clarifying the idea of goal in our practice is dictated by several considerations: the caseworker's self-esteem and working effectiveness hinges on it; the content, methods, and duration of treatment relate to it; and the availability of agency service to a widening clientele depends upon it.

When casework goals are conceived as complete resolution of problems, including those of personality, caseworkers repeatedly find themselves frustrated and defeated. It is this experience that contributes to their self-doubt, to skepticism about their profession, and to assumptions that other professions—notably psychiatry—do achieve "cures" or permanent, basic "adjustments." When such conceptions are held, treatment of the client may become both inappropriate and endless—inappropriate by virtue of its being propelled by what the caseworker, not the client, desires to achieve, and endless by virtue of the pursuit of that will-o'-the-wisp image of an "adjusted" client who experiences no anxiety (or hope?), feels no fear (or courage?), but lives (come what may?) in complete harmony with himself and his environment. When cases are carried over long periods in some faith (rather than evidence) that changes will emerge that will more closely approximate the hoped-for goal, or because only the ends sought have been considered rather than also the means available, then agency case loads remain stationary and client waiting lists grow long. In brief, the economy of energy, time, and money, the openness of agency service, the provision of the greatest good to the greatest number—all demand that casework goals, particularly as they are viewed in the individual case, be given realistic examination.

Even in medicine, "cure" is a concept hedged about with many limits. A specific attack of disease upon the human organism may be eradicated; a person's vulnerability to certain diseases may be lessened; certain other diseases may be arrested. But there remains always the possibility of recurrences unless certain conditions of

---

* Recent writings in both psychiatry and social casework that have dealt with the problem of therapeutic goals have attempted to counteract the tendency to strive for goals unattainable by the patient or client or unrealistic for the therapist. Among these, Pollak and Neumann (7) and Wolberg (10) offer useful guidance; see also *Scope and Method of the Family Service Agency* (7) listed under chapter 5.

life are assured the individual, certain community health-sustaining measures are enforced, and the maintenance of prescribed regimens of diet, rest, aid, and so on is assured. Moreover, medicine remains plagued with the inventiveness of nature, which seems to breed new forms of disease as new drugs attack the old ones, as if to shake defiance in the face of those who presume to "cure."

How much more limited, then, must be the idea of cure in relation to life-processes more whole and more complex than the physical! In casework, too, some specific "diseases" may be eradicated (a good home may be found for a child to replace a bad one); vulnerability to vicissitudes may be decreased (changes in attitudes about one's self and others may be brought about); deterioration may be arrested (through supplementation and support of current functioning); and so on. But the individual's personal and social stability depends heavily upon the security of the larger community of which he is a part (this is why caseworkers maintain their social welfare concerns) and depends, too, upon the particular life-circumstances he encounters. What we seek, then, is no static goal called "cure." We seek, rather, to set and keep in motion such capacities for adaptation and to provide such material means and opportunities as will enable a person, at best, to master his ordeals or, at least, to make some balanced compromise with them.

In recent years the idea of "adaptation" has happily come to take the place of "adjustment." The latter too much implies resignation or capitulation to circumstance, comfortable though it may be. The former, "adaptation," takes cognizance of the continuous flux and change in human beings and of their powers and creative capacities as they consciously use themselves to mold and affect the course and circumstances of their living. Thus, in casework, the problem-solving means contain the ends; the process and the goal become fused. Within each phase of problem-solving work there is the exercise of the client's adaptation capacities, whether to an idea, a relationship, or a situation, and whether about some small or some large part of the problem. The caseworker acts so that adaptation is promoted and sustained by his stable relationship, his communication, and the tangible opportunities he may provide.

Specifically, then, the goal in each case must be limited to the attainment or the approximation of the solution sought for the particular problems identified between the client and caseworker as their business at hand. Within the boundaries of what the client's wants, his capacities, and the resources of skill and material means of the agency (and community), the specific goal is to help him achieve his previous level of functioning and/or to promote the most effective functioning of which he is capable at this time. This goal, then, must be as individualized as is the person and his problem and what he wants and is able to do about it (see Wolberg, 10). Desirable goals must be balanced against feasible ones. The clinical and etiological diagnoses point chiefly to problems, causes, and needs. The psychosocial diagnosis points to personality-social-circumstance configurations in their problematic or benign interactions with the problem to be solved. The part of this diagnosis that focuses on the client's workability, when it is combined with appraisal of helping means, points to what powers may be brought to the problem-solving task.

Thus, while the goals of the profession of social work (and of casework as one of its processes) may be thought of in terms of our highest aspirations for human well-being, the goal with each single client must evolve out of a realistic diagnosis of his problem and his internal and external solution means. "Evolve" is a significant word here, for the anticipated destination with a client cannot be concluded in advance as a finish line may be drawn for a race course. Rather, such estimation of goal must be considered by a kind of slide measure, susceptible to extension or contraction, scaled on the one edge for what is desirable and on the other for what is possible. What is desirable may be projected early from the client's need and want; but what is possible can come to be known only as it unfolds and is revealed in the responses of client and situation to the best help that can be given.

For example, the "ideal goal" for what we call a "rejecting mother" would be that she should come to feel tenderly toward her child. The caseworker, in attempting to influence (and at the same time to test) her feelings, concludes that the rigidities apparent in this woman narrow the possibility of much emotional change. The goal contracts. Now it becomes that of helping the compulsive, repressed mother to act in certain ways toward the child so that the child will not be so badly hurt by her and so that the child's consequent responsiveness will gratify the mother. Discussions with the mother as to the ways she puts advice into practice, her consequent reactions, and so on reveal that she is more disturbed and more damaging to her offspring than was originally perceived. The goal contracts further or actually changes. It now becomes that of helping this mother relinquish her child to placement.

Or one may see the reverse movement. Mr. Rose, whom we last saw in chapter 9, was applying for homemaker service. After this service was given, the caseworker became aware of the father's need for help with his daughter. The first goal was to maintain the Rose family's adaptive efficiency; then it expanded to include modification of the adaptive patterns of at least one family member. On the way to these long-term goals, a sequence of lesser aims would need to be carried out. Mr. Rose would first have to be helped to see the reasons for the homemaker's and caseworker's concerns about his child's maladjustment; then he would need to be stimulated to want help with it; then he would need to be involved in discussing and thinking about the problem together with the caseworker. His capacities to perceive, to relate, to judge, and so on would be revealed in their sturdiness or feebleness as he worked on trying to explain, understand, and act in relation to the problem. Whatever the nature of the little girl's trouble and whatever the caseworker came to see as her needs, the realistic goal would emerge from the evidence of Mr. Rose's wanting, willingness, and ability.

The eventual goal can be only a beckoning point. Our first concern with every client is that we reach the most immediate goal: that he engage himself as feelingly and as understandingly as he can in wanting to take and use our help. Unless this goal is achieved in some measure, any ideas as to eventual aims will remain in the realm of ideas only and will serve to plague and frustrate the caseworker that he cannot seem to bridge the yawning gap between what the client seems to need and what he seems to want. If the immediate goal is to be reached, it requires that the caseworker couple his thinking and action with the client's volition and adaptive responses, his goal-directed powers. Then the goal for each client becomes an unfolding prospect, not a fixed end so ideal or remote that both client and caseworker soon despair of ever reaching it.

It may be seen rather to be a series of small way stations such as are found along a mountain path. "The summit may not be achievable," the climber thinks, "what with my age, my legs, my other interests, and the flight of time. But I have come to the marker that says I have advanced, from which I can look back with some sense of accomplishment, and now I can pause and decide again whether this is my goal for today or whether I can and want to go further." So with the caseworker and his client: on setting forth in their work together, the caseworker may share with his client what the hoped-for goal might be and what the general direction is. But he should know that he must first traverse with his client the ground which yields a nearby subgoal. Here they may pause to take measure of the problem again and of their labors on it, of the client's now demonstrated push and capacity to go forward or of his wish and need to call a halt, and of the relation of the decision to the case-worker's professional appraisal of available means and desirable ends.

It is in the light of this thinking that the goal of the beginning phase of casework is conceived as that of bringing the client into a problem-solving relationship with the agency. When this is achieved (even though it may have to be regained at later stages of treatment), the client and caseworker both know as they could not have known otherwise where and how they go from here. In striving for this goal, the problem-solving means and the problem-solving ends are as one.

 *TWO CASES*

# 13 TWO CASES:

## MR. GRAYSON AND MRS. WHITMAN*

In the search for case material to illustrate the problem-solving process of casework, I have not sought the "perfect case." When such a case is found, it often lies so sleek upon paper as either to elude analysis or to rouse uneasy envy in him who studies it. One wants, rather, a "typical" case—typical in the sense that it presents the kinds of people and problems commonly encountered in casework practice, that it takes place in a characteristic social work setting, and that what the caseworker does, while it may have faults, is by its combination of logical thinking and sensitive guidance for the most part helpful to the client. In these terms the Grayson and the Whitman cases may be considered typical.

* The Grayson case may already be known to the reader, since, until recently, it was used (as "Mr. H.") in casework classes in a number of schools of social work. Originally submitted to the Case Records Committee of the American Association of Psychiatric Social Workers, it was turned over for classroom use to the then American Association of Schools of Social Work. Its caseworker remained anonymous until the second printing of this book when I learned that it is the work of Mrs. Ethel Wannemacher, administrator of social work, Friends Hospital, Philadelphia. I thank both the A.A.P.S.W. and Mrs. Wannemacher for the use of this case. The Whitman case is used with the kind consent of the Family Service Bureau of the United Charities of Chicago. Miss Frances Martin was the caseworker. Some editing liberties, in no way changing the essential facts or meanings but only to abbreviate and clarify, have been taken with both cases. Paragraphs in the interviews have been numbered to facilitate their discussion.

Only the first interviews have been taken from these cases for analysis here. The same considerations that dictated limiting the scope of this book applied to limiting the case material: the first interview is a small cross-section of the casework process; because it is small, it permits thorough examination; because it is cross-sectional, it contains some part of all the essential elements of problem-solving.

As they are seen at the agency threshold, there are already innumerable differences to be noted between these two cases. One difference is that of setting. Mr. Grayson is seen in a psychiatric clinic where social casework offers an enabling arm to the major function of the agency—psychotherapy. Mrs. Whitman is seen in a family agency where social work is the primary profession, social casework the major process, and family welfare the major purpose. A second salient difference lies in the kind of problem brought for help and in the persons who bring it. Mr. Grayson finds himself the victim of internalized conflicts over which he has little understanding or control. Mrs. Whitman's conflict is between herself and her husband, and her personal functioning is unimpaired, though her vital roles as wife and mother are disintegrating. Of particular importance for the caseworker's beginning is the difference that is readily perceived in the willingness and readiness of the two clients to take help. Mr. Grayson not only is confused as to the agency's purpose, the caseworker's identity, and his relation to this place but is manifestly an "unwilling" client, repeatedly throwing up walls of defense between himself and the agency's service. Mrs. Whitman, on the other hand, perceives clearly the agency and its relatedness to her, and, while she is ambivalent about whether or not she wants to work on her marriage, she reaches out to the caseworker freely and gives evidence that she is motivated at least to talk and think over her troubles.

In Mr. Grayson's case, then, the problem the caseworker must work upon first is that of helping Mr. Grayson move from needing help to actively wanting it. With Mrs. Whitman, the focus can be directed upon the presented maladjustment. With all these differences complicating the myriad unnamed differences within the persons, social situations, problems, and agencies involved in these two brief cases, the question to be pursued is whether the constant components of the problem-solving process can be found within each of these highly individual situations and whether this process operates with the constancy claimed for it.

### Mr. Grayson

*Setting.*—This is a privately supported psychiatric clinic for adults which by contract with the Veterans Administration takes some of the patients it refers for treatment. In this clinic the social case-worker sees each new patient to help him determine whether or not he thinks he needs or wants psychiatric treatment and to acquaint him in a beginning way with what he will experience if he decides to take treatment. In one or several interviews with the psychiatric social worker the client decides whether or not he wishes to continue with the clinic, and, if the decision is in the affirmative, he is referred to the psychiatrist whose patient he will be. When the client undertakes psychiatric treatment, the caseworker works with such family members or such circumstances as influence his well-being.

*Client.*—Mr. Grayson, a twenty-three-year-old, married veteran.

*Problem.*—Mr. Grayson's need for psychiatric treatment as recommended by a diagnostic study at the Veterans Administration Mental Hygiene Clinic. Mr. Grayson was referred to the present clinic (record does not indicate whether or not this referral was merely a notification, but this seems probable) with the diagnosis "Psychoneurosis, mixed type." A summary letter was to be forwarded. An appointment time was given him.

#### The First Interview

1. Our receptionist notified me that Mr. G. had arrived. He was early. As I was coming down the stairs to meet him, he was sitting on the edge of the chair in the reception hall, with his head lowered. I greeted him, and he looked startled and tense.

2. I told him that I was a social worker, not a doctor, and that I see all new veterans first who are referred by the VA Mental Hygiene Clinic, because we have found that most veterans like to know something about the clinic before they see the doctor. I asked whether he would like to come to my office, where we would have privacy, instead of standing in the reception hall.

3. Mr. G. began to walk in the direction of the stairs, and I pointed to my office, which was directly above. He paused and said softly, "Did you walk down the stairs to see me?" I said that I had, because, since this was his first visit, I wanted to escort him to my office.

4. Mr. G. looked at me intently. He was a lean young man, looking older than his twenty-three years. His straight dark hair, brushed close to his head, seemed to emphasize his tenseness. His dark eyes were deep-set, frightened-looking, and shifted a good deal. At my invitation Mr. G. seated himself, but it was evidently difficult for him to face me, although he was sitting directly opposite me.

5. I repeated that I was a social worker in our outpatient neuropsychiatric clinic. It was my responsibility to meet all new veterans who were referred to us by the VA Mental Hygiene Clinic, to tell them about our clinic and how it operates, and to determine with the veteran whether or not he is interested in using our clinic. I should be glad to have him ask me any questions about his having been referred to us. That was why I was seeing him first, because we do not assume that every veteran who is referred to us wants to see a psychiatrist at once.

6. Mr. G.'s eyes widened and his tension increased. He asked whether this was a psychiatric clinic, and I replied that it was. It is designed to help veteran patients with either nervous or mental problems to get well. Mr. G. said that he was in the wrong place and proceeded to get up from his chair. He pulled out of his pocket the letter he had received from the VA Mental Hygiene Clinic referring him to us. "I knew they had made a mistake when they sent me that letter—I am not crazy."

7. I expressed my keen interest in his statement. I agreed that an organization as large as the VA might make an error, and it appears from what he had told me that he thinks the VA had erred in referring him to our neuropsychiatric clinic. I asked how the VA had come to send him this letter in the first place. How did they get his name, since the VA Mental Hygiene Clinic only saw veterans who had a neuropsychiatric disability?

8. Mr. G. sat down again and, although he looked very troubled, became a little calmer. I said lightly that perhaps he feels that he had been "trapped" into coming to us and that that was the reason for my wanting to talk with him. Mr. G. remained quiet, but he looked agitated. I asked whether he had any idea what the VA had in mind in referring him to us. I got no response from the patient, so I asked him whether he would like me to tell him more about this clinic. Mr. G. pushed back his chair and then said that "they" (the VA) had done him a "dirty trick" when they sent him here. "Where did they get the idea that I am crazy?"

9. I said that he certainly had a right to his feeling about his referral, if the VA had not discussed it with him. But I would like him to know that the patients who are referred to us are not "crazy," if by that he means they are entirely out of their minds and need hospital care. Our patients are nervous, have emotional problems, that is, their feelings have gotten out of hand. They often have trouble getting along with other people, sometimes even with their best friends; some patients have trouble in their jobs because of it and do not do as well as they could otherwise. On the whole, our patients themselves feel pretty unhappy about their prob-

lems and want help to straighten themselves out. A few of our patients do have various forms of mental disorders, but these patients, too, want to function more adequately. Our patients are seen by our psychiatrists, have a definite appointment time for their interviews, and go home after each appointment. We have no arrangement with the VA for treating patients who need hospitalization.

10. Mr. G. eyed me steadily as I was talking. I thought that he had been listening intently. I paused when I was finished, and, since he made no move to say anything, I asked him whether he would like me to call the VA and ask them why they had referred him to us. Mr. G. looked serious and replied that this was not necessary. He thought we could "dope" this matter out ourselves. I said that I would be willing to try and asked how he would suggest that we proceed.

11. He cleared his throat and told me that his trouble is with his spine and feet; he can't stand the pain any longer. He stopped talking. I asked whether he had received treatment for this condition, since the pain must be pretty bad. He replied that he had. For one and one-half years he had been treated by a private medical doctor. The doctor gave him injections and pills. While he was taking the injections and pills, he felt better, but, when the "needles wore off," his pain returned. However, he continued at his work (as a machinist), but he noticed that he was becoming "more and more . . ."—the patient paused and then half-jokingly added, "nervous, irritable, and jittery." Mr. G. became noticeably agitated as he referred to his nervousness. He extended his hands to show me that they were covered with perspiration. He began to mop his forehead, ran his fingers through his hair, and then dramatically said, "I have always been nervous. I can't stand people; I can't stand noise, and, when I am in the company of people, I get a terrible pain in the stomach and vomit."

12. I said that I had a pretty good idea of what he meant. Coming here has certainly affected him this way. I am sorry that he is feeling so uncomfortable. Mr. G. was trembling, but for the first time he looked at me, and his eyes looked sad and appealing. I asked whether he thought the pain in his spine and feet was largely responsible for the nervousness which he had so vividly described to me.

13. Mr. G. was visibly taken aback by my question. He whispered that he doesn't believe that is the case. He was nervous to begin with, but the pain in his spine and feet is real too. I agreed that that might well be the case; both might be true. Since he had received medical treatment for his spine and feet, what had his doctor suggested? Mr. G. spoke very quietly and confided that his doctor had intimated that these pains might be caused or aggravated by his nervousness. He had given the patient all the treatment he could and suggested that Mr. G. seek the help of a psychiatrist.

14. I asked Mr. G. whether the doctor's opinion had come as a complete blow. He said that it had not, but he had hoped that the doctor

could cure his pain, and then he might have gotten over his nervousness. I wondered whether he had any desire to consult another medical doctor. Mr. G. shook his head in the negative. I asked what he would like to do now. He murmured that he guessed he had better see one of those "nerve" doctors—he had tried the other doctor without success; maybe he had better see "one of those psychiatrists."

15. Mr. G. began to perspire profusely again and was obviously agitated. I remarked about his upset state and asked whether there was something special troubling him now. Slowly he told me that he lives in a small town and that he is afraid that, if anyone found out he was coming to a neuropsychiatric clinic, the neighbors would think he was crazy. I agreed that this was a legitimate concern and not easy to handle. I asked whether his neighbors had noticed his difficulty in mingling with people, for certainly in a small town news travels very quickly. Mr. G. presented a number of instances when he had had to leave the room with neighbor callers in his home because he couldn't bear their small talk. We agreed that, however he looked at it, the neighbors might come to the conclusion that his behavior with people was extraordinary. He agreed that at this time it was important for him to think of himself and his health. With a wave of the hand, as if he were trying to wipe out an unpleasant thought, he decided that he had better come to the clinic for help with his problems regardless of what the neighbors might think. It is true, he has always been a "bit" nervous, but never like he is today, and he dated his condition to when he was inducted into the army. Immediately, however, he said vehemently, "I don't want to talk about that. I want to forget it and settle down and be a civilian." He then asked me to tell him more about the clinic.

16. I explained that our medical service is psychotherapy and that he would be seeing the same psychiatrist regularly and by appointment for at least a four-to-six-week period, our "exploratory" period. During this time our psychiatrist would have a chance to get to know him and to arrive at an understanding of his condition and would then be in a better position to know whether he could be of assistance to him. Mr. G. would also have an opportunity to get to know the doctor and to see whether he felt free enough to tell him about his worries and his problems and whether he had enough confidence in the doctor to let him help him. At the end of this period the psychiatrist and he would talk together about his condition, and would decide whether Mr. G. should continue with treatment or not.

17. Mr. G. literally looked amazed. "You mean that the psychiatrist will ask me what I think?" I said that he would, because our psychiatrist is eager to help him. No matter how skilled the psychiatrist is, if Mr. G. feels that he is not getting any help, there is no point in continuing. "You mean that the psychiatrist won't feel hurt if I don't want to come?" I said that he would feel sorry if Mr. G. breaks off treatment if, in the doctor's opinion, Mr. G. could benefit from it. The psychiatrist knows, however, that no good will come of it unless Mr. G. feels that he wants the doctor's help. Mr. G. looked

more relieved, and the sad look seemed to leave his eyes. He began to talk quickly about how and when he could see the doctor, and, as is our practice, I had arranged for an appointment today. This interview with the psychiatrist was to be an introductory visit. He could take this opportunity to talk about his problems with the doctor and then decide whether he wants to return. Mr. G. responded quickly, "Then it's set."

18. After the first gush of enthusiasm to see the psychiatrist, Mr. G. looked apprehensive. After all, maybe he will get over his nervousness, "What will 'they' think?" he murmured. I referred to his previous statement concerning the onset of his nervousness and then asked when he had been discharged from service. He told me. Has his condition been improving? He replied that he was getting progressively worse. Shortly after he returned home, he married a girl he had known for five years. She is now pregnant. He began to work as a machinist. Because he was anxious to earn as much money as possible, he bought old cars, put them in good shape, and sold them for a good profit. He managed to save $1,400, which he used to buy a house. He worked at top speed and then found that he couldn't stand the pace. He had to take days at a time off from work. He became more and more jittery and quarreled with his boss, his wife, and her parents, with whom they were living until they bought their house. He wanted to do everything himself and was irritated when anyone offered to help him, even when they wanted to lend him money when he was in a "tight spot." His wife told him to go to the VA for his medical care, and that is how he got there.

19. I asked whether he had received a compensation rating, and he said that he thought he would for his neuropsychiatric condition. I asked him whether he knew that the rating for disability was not a permanent thing, that our government was primarily interested in rehabilitation and therefore was referring veterans for medical care. Mr. G. looked up at me. I added that the purpose of our clinic was to help him get well. I explained more fully our connection with the VA, emphasizing the fact that we had no direct connection with the VA Rating Board and had no authority in recommending that a veteran's rating be either increased or decreased. However, the VA expects us to submit monthly reports of our contact with the patient indicating his progress. We send these reports to the Rating Board or any other department in the VA that is interested in the patient. Mr. G. looked troubled. I said that he might want to think about this matter a little more. It is very possible, should Mr. G. decide to come for treatment and his condition improve, that the VA might reduce his compensation or withdraw it entirely. The fact is that most of our patients who have been coming here are getting better.

20. It was quite apparent that Mr. G. was weighing what I had told him very carefully. He asked me to repeat what I had said about our connection with the VA, and I did. Slowly he said that he wants to get well. There is no use in getting a pension, if he will get worse. He tossed his

head and added that he is too young to live on a "hand-out." He wants to be independent. I referred to his desire to get ahead and his zeal to work and support himself and his wife. He knows that his wife wouldn't like him to be a poacher either.

21. He dropped this subject and said his wife is worried about him. She says that she hardly knows him since he has returned from the service. He tries hard to be nice to her because he loves her, but sometimes his temper is so great that he can't control himself. He "lights" into her for no good reason, and she bursts into tears. He knows that he shouldn't upset her now, because she is pregnant, but what can he do about it? It is bad enough that he is feeling so miserable, but he doesn't see why he should make her feel unhappy when she is dearer to him than anyone else.

22. I said that very often a person who is upset, as he is, finds himself in this predicament. I asked whether his wife is fearful about his condition, and he said with a good deal of feeling that she is. She has never been with a nervous person before, and he thinks that actually she has the same attitude toward him that the other small-town people have. She has tried to be patient with him, but he doesn't give her a chance because he is so irritable most of the time.

23. I told him that the picture he has drawn for me is not unusual. It is part of his present condition. We have found that it is helpful to the patient and his wife if we have an opportunity to talk with her about this double problem. Often the wife is worried to death about her husband's illness, his need to attend a neuropsychiatric clinic, and the problems that his illness creates for her. We are often able to assist her with this. Mr. G. thought that his wife would like to see me, because she doesn't talk to anyone about it. Her parents are kind but ignorant, and they must think him impossible.

24. I said that we could be thinking about that. But what does he want to do about seeing the psychiatrist today? Mr. G. said he would see him now. I told him the psychiatrist's name and said that I would escort him to his office to introduce him. I asked him to return to my office after his interview, if the doctor and Mr. G. decided that he should return for treatment, and I would give him a clinic appointment card. We could also decide whether I should invite Mrs. G. to come to see me.

25. Mr. G. met Dr. K. very warmly, and I left them. He returned after the interview to my office looking obviously relieved, smiling for the first time, and said that he is coming in for treatment. He asked me when his wife should come in. I discussed with him what he would tell her as the purpose of her coming, and he quickly understood the desirability of her wanting to come. He asked for an appointment for Mrs. G. for next week when he came, but, if for some reason his wife were not coming, he would let me know. Mr. G. shook my hand and thanked me for my kindness and consideration. I escorted him downstairs.

### The Casework Process in the Beginning Phase

In this setting the caseworker's first function is clearly delineated: to enable the person in need of the clinic's service to recognize that need and to want help. This "willingness" is a kind of eligibility requirement for going on. The caseworker readies herself, then, not merely to find out whether the client sees his problem and wants to do something about it but actively to promote the client's perceptions, to lower his defenses against change or the source of help, to clarify misconceptions, and to guide him from immersion in his problem to the choice of constructive action. This is what the caseworker here is ready to do.

Before Mr. Grayson is seen, this caseworker knows something about him diagnostically: the clinical classification of his problem is "Psychoneurosis, mixed type." This is a category so broad as to say only that Mr. G.'s emotional disturbances are severe enough to affect most of the vital aspects of his functioning. It can be anticipated that his anxieties will be high, clouding some of his perceptions, blocking his adaptiveness, distorting some of his actions, at times taking disguised forms, as in physical symptoms. The diagnosis does not tell, however, anything of what Mr. G. is or has beyond his sickness, nor does it say what relation he as a man has to his illness, or what he wants or is able to do about it. This the caseworker will have to diagnose from the ways he acts and reacts in the interview. This diagnosis will emerge as a by-product of the caseworker's effort to engage Mr. G. in wanting and using help.

Because the caseworker understands the natural uncertainty and general expectations of a person referred to a psychiatric clinic and understands that anxiety affects perception, she comes to meet and escort Mr. G. to her office and explains her identity. She is sensitively observant of all the fine body-language signs by which this applicant first communicates, unwittingly, how he feels and even something of what his problem is (paragraphs 3, 4). His tension, fearfulness, inward absorption—all show in the way he sits, looks, and responds. His comment on the caseworker's taking some trouble in relation to him may indicate his low self-esteem and perhaps his low expectation of others in relation to him. All his actions have meaning to the caseworker (else she would not have recorded them), and, in general, they convey that here is a man who is afraid—possibly of her and this place, possibly of people generally, possibly of what goes on inside him—and he is trying to cope with his fear by withdrawing. And this, in turn, means that the caseworker's first aid must be that of helping him to see that there is nothing to fear from her person or intent.

The caseworker's careful repetition of her identity is her verbal effort to help Mr. G. to perceive her accurately as different from the doctor whom most patients assume they will see immediately on entering a clinic and to see her possible usefulness to him (5). There is the thoughtful recognition here that, even though a client may bring himself to an agency, he still may not know what it is, for him. Certainly this holds true for the client who is referred by someone else. For this latter client, to "start where he is" may be to start with his unspoken questions.

Mr. G.'s response, which follows (6), indicates that he has just now taken in the reality of this place and that he wishes to flee it, to deny his need for it. There is an indication, too, that he has a misconception, as well as poor perception, of the problems psychiatric clinics deal with.

The caseworker expresses interest (not surprise or argument) in the client's statement that a mistake has been made (7). She accepts this as a possibility. But she goes further and attempts by her question to get him to look at the situation rationally (and, incidentally, to test that capacity in him). Apparently, her questions are conveyed sympathetically and gently enough not to threaten Mr. G., because, by his action, he is ready to resume discussion.

The caseworker first offers Mr. G. a guess at the basis of his disturbed feelings and indicates that it is out of this clinic's anticipation of this feeling that she is there (8). There is conveyed the idea that negative feelings are acceptable and not unusual. The next step is an effort to get the client to express how *he* conceives of this situation. When this fails to elicit a response, the offer is made to supply the information by which misconceptions may be clarified. But Mr. G., like many disturbed persons, hears more of the monologue within himself than the dialogue between himself and another.

Again, to Mr. G.'s feelings the caseworker responds feelingly—that is, again the naturalness of his feelings is readily accepted (9). She then gives facts that bear on correcting the distortions in the way he sees or understands this place and its function. The information seems to be selected; it is a partial explanation of what this place is for and how it works, shaped to what seems to be troubling this client. When there is no response to this, visibly or audibly, the caseworker asks Mr. G.'s permission for a test of the reality outside his and her conception of it (10). There may, it is true, be some threat to the client in this, not in the worker's manner or attitude, it is to be hoped, but in the ultimate necessity to face up to reality. The client does not appear to be threatened here, however. Instead, he takes hold of the fact that half-consciously he knew but tried to deny. When he affirms at least a temporary partnership with the caseworker "to dope out" his trouble, the caseworker gives him the opportunity to take the lead.

Mr. G. does so. What one sees in his presentation (11, 12, 13) is the fairly typical reaction of a person who equates emotional disturbance with insanity, who fears that others will stigmatize him, and who is victim of the layman's common conception that, if something is "all in the mind," it should be subject to will power and control. All of us, both consciously and in our unconscious, tend to find physical illness more acceptable than illness of the emotions. Small wonder, then, that Mr. G., like so many others, not only has physical symptoms as defenses against his conflicts but must cling to them and emphasize their reality. Sometimes even caseworkers half-wonder if physical symptoms that are psychogenic "really hurt." But not Mr. G.'s caseworker.

What is seen in the discussion with Mr. G. in this section of the interview is a partial but characteristic operation of problem-solving. The worker asks for the facts of treatment of his physical condition. What help has he had for it? At the same time she expresses her sympathetic feeling for the ordeal it has been for him. As his telling brings forth suppressed anxiety, she shows further relation to and sympathy for his feelings, which, she recognizes, are not only about the problem within him but the problem he is beginning to feel in giving himself over to the clinic. There is no way she can fully reassure him about this, but she gives him her understanding of his feelings and her sincere sorriness. The responsive way in which Mr. G. looks at the worker shows that, for the first time in the interview, he feels trustingly related to her.

Now the worker tries to draw out Mr. G.'s idea of his problem. Now that he has described it, what perception does he have of it? His answer will reveal something of his capacity for insight, that is, for looking beyond what is manifest. Mr. G.'s response is a frightened admission of a possibility he has not before wanted to consider. Responsively, again, the caseworker accepts his partial recognition of the nature of his problem, allowing him to cling to part of his defense. She relates to his feelings again (14). How did he feel about the fact with which he was faced by his doctor? She proposes, further, the possibility that he may still wish to deal with his physical problem in the old way—that is, by seeing another medical expert. By so doing, she is again attempting to give Mr. G. full freedom and at the same time to gauge how he sees his situation, whether his perception or idea of it is still clouded over or whether it is clear. More than this, she is saying out loud what a part of Mr. G. is surely wanting to say, and, as she can do this acceptingly, she demonstrates again her understanding alliance with him in his ambivalence. And, finally, since the client rejects this old solution, the worker places before him the question of what he proposes to do. What, then, seems to be the way to go or the thing to do—what is the step in the direction of a new solution? The client faces up to his need for psychiatric help.

But he does this only momentarily (15), because each new decision, as for every one of us, brings with it a new galaxy of problems, new things to do, to consider, to fear, and to overcome. Taking a step toward the psychiatrist has frightened Mr. G. Again he shows this, both by his body language and by what he communicates verbally. Psychiatry spells "danger" to him; his physiological response is readiness to flee or fight, and his psychological response is defense against the threatening solution. The defense is a mixture of projection and rationalization. Just as a minute ago he placed his difficulty in his feet and spine, he now places the difficulty onto what other people will think and its effect upon his self-esteem.

The caseworker, because she understands that when the problem is chiefly emotional in nature the facts of feeling are of primary importance, relates, as before, to Mr. G.'s feelings (15). She does not undervalue or brush aside the fact that what neighbors think causes Mr. G. valid concern. Rather, she attempts to affect those feelings, not by facile reassurance (how tempted one might be to suggest that what others think doesn't really matter!) or by pulling Mr. G. in persuasively, but by asking him to review the objective facts: Had his neighbors noticed his difficulties? Facing those facts (perhaps made more possible by the caseworker's sympathetic steadiness) brings Mr. G. to abandon the defensive screen of "the neighbors" and to step forward again toward coping with his problem. "I am ready to hear what you propose," he says, in effect. Now the caseworker presents, in small piece again, something of the way the agency and client will operate together (16).

Perhaps the most notable aspect of the facts of this agency's operation is that its procedures are consonant with an understanding of human psychology—indeed, they seem to have been dictated by this understanding. The clear time limit of an exploration period lowers the irrational but real fears of an indefinite commitment of one's self, of being "sucked in." Moreover, that this is to be a mutual exploration and decision, as much dependent upon the client's as the agency's judgment, restores to the client his sense of himself as self-determining. To be sure, except in custodial situations, a client is always free to say whether he will or will not continue with an agency, but he is not always psychologically free to know this or to be sure of it. The caseworker's recognition with him of this natural right and of the agency's respect for his ability to exercise this right both reassures him and bulwarks his sense of self-responsibility.

Mr. G.'s surprise (17) illustrates vividly how a person who has already lost his feeling of self-mastery assumes or fears that he will be taken over by others. The caseworker makes clear, too, reflecting the agency's clarity, that, while a person may be brought to a psychiatrist, he cannot be made to "take treatment." Caseworkers must sometimes make forced psychiatric referrals when outright psychosis calls for protective measures, but for purposes of psychotherapy the client must be motivated himself or with casework help. One further note here: In the recognition that such motivation may ebb and die, this clinic picks it up and ties it into action at once. The appointment with the psychiatrist, should Mr. G. decide to see him, is available at the very moment the client is readied for it. Unhappily, it is not always possible for an agency to arrange it so, but its value is manifest.

To this point, Mr. G. has been helped by the worker's warmth and sensitive understanding, by her drawing out and relating to the facts of his feelings, by her leading him to face up to the objective facts of his problem, and by the presentation of the facts of the agency's nature and ways of work which, in themselves, are fashioned by helpful intent and insights. He has moved from fear, distrust, and denial to at least momentary trust, perception, and readiness to take some new action in relation to his problem. But, just as physical movement cannot take place without friction, so psychological movement from one position to an opposing one does not occur without some pull-back, some unconscious effort to avoid headlong imbalance. Thus Mr. G. draws back again (18).

The ordinary temptation would be to persuade Mr. G. to resume his position to take psychiatric help, to present him with all his own arguments. This the caseworker is able to resist. Patiently, she goes back to leading him to look at the facts as a means of influencing his feelings. He has been out of the service for a long time; his condition has been growing worse; his wife has recognized his need for help. Because he still cannot take the step toward solution of his problem, even though he perceives the facts, the caseworker brings out what may be a possible stumbling block (19).

It is probable that the matter of compensation has not been the consideration that has created Mr. G.'s reluctance to get psychiatric help; it is the fear, rather, of the implication of his illness against which he seems to be defending himself. But should he yield himself to treatment and find suddenly that he has to give up economic compensation for his sickness along with neurotic compensations, he might feel betrayed or, at the very least, let down. The caseworker therefore injects this issue. It could be argued that it is too risky to pose this difficulty when it seems so important to get Mr. G. to venture into taking help and that he might better make this choice when he had begun to taste some of the gratification of treatment. On the other hand, the loss of compensation is a possibility that might now be deterring Mr. G. from making a decision, or it might occur to him after he has left the caseworker, when he will face it alone. Apparently these considerations move the worker in this instance. In any case, this principle of casework holds: if there appears to be some obstacle to the client's coming to want help, whether that obstacle lies in the client's or the agency's situation, it is better brought out and laid on the table between client and caseworker than allowed to exert its unknown influence by being unspoken and unworked. Risk is there, to be sure, but open, known risk allows for conscious management, while a problem denied does not.

Mr. G.'s response (20) is a gathering-together of his wanting and willing to get well. He has not had to pit himself against the pressures of persuasion. Rather, he has experienced once again the worker's acceptance that there are real, negative factors for him in taking help. At the same time the worker has made clear that she supports and "stands for" this new, if difficult, way of solving his problem. Diagnostically, one sees in Mr. G. strong motivation to be adequate and a striving to maintain his self-image as an independent man.

Another "good sign" is revealed by Mr. G.'s discussion here (21, 22): the ability to look out from himself to see and sympathize with what his problems do to another person, his wife. He is aware of her as a person whom he both loves and hurts; this awareness reveals something not only of his relationship and perceptive capacities but also of motivational source.

As far as the caseworker's responsibility is concerned, what Mr. G. says suggests another dimension to the problem in its relation to agency help—the probable need to aid Mrs. G. both to bear her husband's illness and to ally herself with his efforts to get well. The caseworker then expresses her understanding recognition of this need and of its naturalness (22). Again the caseworker offers the reassurance of understanding and the service of influencing benignly a vital part of the client's problem situation, his wife.

But the major decision must yet be made by the client: Will he or will he not, can he or can he not, decide to act on the basis of what he has been helped to see and think through? The question is posed directly (23, 24), and the client makes what must for him have been a courageous answer. He dares to say "Yes," because he has experienced the caseworker as an understanding, unattacking, honest, accepting person. His fears against "this place" and its intents have subsided, and he has been led by the caseworker's compassionate knowledge and skill from withdrawal to indecision to decision. He will not necessarily remain thus mobilized and ready for help. He may withdraw again, as the next interview with the psychiatrist forces him to experience all his conflicts again, or, should he continue, there will be many times of resistance and ambivalence about treatment. These problems cannot be dissolved once and for all. Within this one interview the problem the caseworker faced and worked on was the major problem of all beginnings in casework: to help the client to take the first volitional step in using agency help.

### Mrs. Whitman

*Setting.*—A private non-sectarian family welfare agency in a large urban community.

*Clients.*—Mr. Whitman, forty, and Mrs. Whitman, thirty-five, after fifteen years of marriage; Junior, fourteen; Martha, twelve; and Terry, ten.

*Problem.*—It had been Mr. Whitman, not his wife, who first applied to the family agency for help. He had been bustled into the office by a close friend of the family, a woman who understood something of the agency's function and whose concern for the family seemed to embrace the husband, the wife, and the children. Five or six years of discontent and the last year of active marital discord had preceded the crisis. Then, the previous day, following a quarrel, Mrs. Whitman had left the home, taking Martha with her and announcing that she was "through with him and the marriage." Mr. Whitman, leaning heavily upon his friend to help him, wept as he related his problem.

Mr. Whitman's plea was that the agency draw Mrs. Whitman back to him. He would be willing to do whatever he was advised in order to effect a reunion. Because the first necessity seemed to be to ascertain whether Mrs. Whitman had any interest in salvaging the marriage, the caseworker used the first interview with Mr. Whitman to help him tell his side of the story of the marriage and its deterioration, to get some necessary facts of the family situation, and to agree that following the interview with Mrs. Whitman some joint planning for ongoing service would be arranged.

Mr. Whitman's account of the problem placed the blame largely upon his wife, although there were glimmers of self-reproach in him. It was clearly evident that he was deeply attached to his wife, whether by love or dependency, and felt helpless without her. The family had moved from a small farm in a remote area to the crowded city some six years earlier, and it was as his wife was exposed to the life of the city, Mr. Whitman felt, that she "began to grow away from me." The previous year she had disclosed she was tired of housework and had taken a job, although there was no real economic need for her to do so. She had begun to find companionship after hours with her co-workers, women and men, in bowling, stopping to drink in taverns, etc. Tension between them had more and more frequently burst into quarrels, when Mrs. Whitman had told her husband she did not need him or his support. Mr. Whitman was also concerned about the children's reactions and said that the boys had urged him to get Mrs. Whitman home again and "start things all over."

The family was of the lower middle class. Both Mr. and Mrs. Whitman had unskilled but well-paying jobs. Mr. Whitman had completed the fourth grade, and Mrs. Whitman had had a year or so of trade school following the eighth grade. Consciously, both had sought, though in differing ways, for "good family life."

Because Mr. Whitman's interview was complicated by the chaperonage of the family friend and because first decisions seemed to hinge on whether Mrs. Whitman would be a party to working on the problem, it is the first interview with Mrs. Whitman rather than the one with her husband that is presented here.

### The First Interview

1. The day after Mr. W.'s interview, Mrs. W. phoned, saying that her husband had gotten in touch with her at work and told her that he had been to this agency and that we would like to talk with her. She was pleasant over the phone and did not seem too anxious about the situation or about our wanting to see her. I interpreted briefly my interest in talking with her, saying that I realized this was a difficult situation and that I thought we might be able to help her explore what her thinking was about her marital situation. An appointment was made for the following day.

2. Mrs. W. kept her appointment. She was a very unattractive woman at first glance, her features raw, her skin rough and lined. She was spotlessly clean. She related easily and comfortably. She wept at points of her account of her unhappiness throughout the interview, but, despite her quiet tears, she was able to discuss her situation in an orderly fashion and to talk about her feelings.

3. She began immediately by saying that she wished to apologize for

bringing me such a "tough case to solve." She extended this to say that she realized it must be very difficult for a worker to try to help a husband and wife who have been married such a long time and who have come to such a definite decision to separate. I nodded, and she continued to say that, despite the unpleasant features of their situation, she was glad that her husband had finally come to a social agency, as she had tried to talk him into doing this five or six years ago, but he had minimized the value of such a step, saying that he was "able to take care of myself."

4. I expressed recognition of her earlier desire to have help in her marital situation. I also expressed interest in what she saw as the situation between them now and how she saw us as helping.

5. She readily said that she saw us as being able to help her understand what she might contribute to the marriage. But, generally, she saw her husband as needing help from someone who could reinforce what she had been trying to tell him for a number of years, namely, that she has not been happy with his daily behavior. At this time she said, and repeated several times during the interview, that it was not "the big things that we have quarreled about but the thousands of little things." I drew from her that the little things were his exceeding nervousness and his tendency to nag each member of the family constantly. For example, she said that he expected their adolescent daughter to do the same housework he might expect a mature woman to do. This girl does the baking and the family ironing and makes the beds, and the boys contribute by doing the dishes and sweeping the house. This work of the children, however, does not satisfy her husband, and he is inclined to nag at them, to deny them the privileges of spending money and of having friends in the home on the basis that they haven't done their jobs well. She gave several examples of what she considered his unreasonable demands on the children and his refusal of their special holiday pleasures on the grounds of their foolishness or expense. She feels that childhood is the time for some fun and preparation for adulthood. As she discussed this, she individualized each of the children, discussing their outstanding traits and interests.

6. I recognized her desire to furnish a satisfactory childhood to her children, and she responded positively to this by extending the conversation to tell of her own lonely childhood in an orphanage. Her mother died when she was ten, and her father placed her in an orphanage and her two brothers with relatives. When she was eighteen, she left the orphanage and went to one brother's home. He was married, and he and his wife worked on a farm. They had a number of small children, so Mrs. W. cared for them and did the housework. She had known Mr. W. slightly throughout her life, and at this time he began courting her. She thought he loved her but has since concluded that actually he saw in her a husky woman who would bear children and "work like a slave" for him.

7. I wondered what Mrs. W. saw as a desirable marriage, and I asked what her ideas had been about it when she married Mr. W.

8. She said she realized now that she had entered marriage without adequate preparation, including information as to the sex act and what was involved in bearing and raising children. She soon realized she could not look to her husband for direction, so she quickly developed her own attitude about what a family should be. Despite the fact that Mr. W. "did not ever show much affection" for the children and as a matter of fact seemed annoyed by them, he always seemed pleased when she was pregnant. She said that in the area in which they grew up large families were common, and it was also understood that a woman should be constantly pregnant and "tied" to the home. She had the three children who were now living and had had a miscarriage. Since Mr. W. was cold and unfeeling toward the three children, she was determined not to have a larger family, and for this reason she used contraceptives, despite the fact that her husband expressed dislike for this.

9. I wondered how Mrs. W. felt about their marital relationship. She responded that she had never been "satisfied" in the sex act since their marriage. Following marriage, there was some excitement and satisfaction, which she thinks was because she was young, but soon after this brief period she became aware that she was dissatisfied. Her husband has always been inclined to begin the sex act without affectionate preparation. About ten years ago, a friend with whom she discussed this gave her a book to read. She read two or three others and tried to "sell" her husband on the idea of reading such books, but he refused. I drew from her that the books were *Married Love* and others of a pseudo-professional nature. Despite Mr. W.'s disinterest in improving their sexual relationship, he did not lose interest in continuing it, and she felt that he had been increasingly more demanding during the last five years while at the same time she had become increasingly less interested and discouraged. I wondered if she had ever been able to talk with Mr. W. about her feelings, other than in recommending that he read books, and she said that she had tried but that he was unreceptive to any discussion or consideration of his part.

10. As Mrs. W. discussed their marital relationship, she wept copiously. When I wondered if she thought this was the basis of most of the trouble, she nodded that she did, and then said that she had talked with some of her lady friends who also felt that sexual maladjustment was the basis of their problems. She added, however, that in addition to sexual maladjustment his general behavior, his narrow-mindedness, and so on were heavily contributory to their marital dissatisfactions. She went on, at my encouragement, to say that he disapproves of participating in activities such as the Parent-Teachers Club and that he does not approve of going to church or of any other social life. She described herself as a person who had always liked to have many friends, to dance and sing, and to move with a group of other people of her own age. He had never tried to join her in any such activities, and during the years when the children were growing up she felt "trapped." She then said that during

these years he bought and sold horses and that he made trips to small towns for trading purposes; he would leave on an overnight trip and would taunt her, saying, "I'll bet you wish you could get away." She said that during these years she consistently wished she could get away but stayed for the sake of the children and "because I've always felt sorry for him." I wondered why she felt sorry, but she could not explain except to say that he seemed "so dependent on me."

11. I wondered whether Mrs. W. felt there was anything in her husband that was positive enough to make her want to continue the marriage. She readily said that he was a steady worker, that he did not misuse his money and was not particularly stingy as to necessities such as food, but that he was very penurious as to clothing, entertainment, etc. She would not consider returning to him under any circumstances were it not for the children. As a matter of fact, she considers that even keeping the home intact is not worth the personal struggle she recognizes within herself.

12. One of the "little things" that has made her increasingly less happy is his sour and bitter attitude toward everyone and his need to lie about unimportant things. As Mrs. W. discussed examples of his trivial lying, I tried and was able to draw from her what seemed to be operating and to suggest that much of his lying seemed on the surface to be his need to seem adequate. She readily accepted this and extended it to say that she "thinks there must be some truth in this." Then she revealed, as if thinking aloud, that she feels he is greatly upset not because of his fondness for her but because it will make people think he is not adequate as a provider.

13. Now Mrs. W. abruptly mentioned her husband's suggestion that they come to see me together. She said she would prefer not to do this for the next few weeks, as she felt they both needed a "cooling-off period." Earlier, when she had stated her idea of our function, I had affirmed our help as that of aiding people to work through their trouble to happier family life. I now returned to this in more detail. I explained about casework's helpfulness to her, saying that often talking with an interested, objective person about one's feelings of anger, disappointment, or frustration could make one feel better. I added that this could also help one take a clearer look at what had happened in the marriage and to the other persons in the family and might help one decide not only whether or not to remain in the marriage but how to improve one's feelings and attitudes about one's self and others. I applied this directly to her, saying that, while she had started out by saying she wanted to end the marriage right now, she had later implied that there were some values in remaining in it. She agreed and again referred to feeling sorry for Mr. W. and to wanting the children to have both parents.

14. I recognized these feelings and said that she was unsure as to whether to stay in the marriage or not. She agreed and admitted not only

that she had been married so long that it was hard to think of not having a home but also that she was anxious about the welfare of the children should she leave Mr. W. She again expressed feelings of compassion for Mr. W. but countered these with strong feelings of irritation at him. I suggested that talking with me over a period of time, in regular interviews, might help her think further regarding the pros and cons of salvaging the marriage, perhaps help her understand how to handle Mr. W. better, and understand and bear her own feelings. Mrs. W. nodded understandingly and thoughtfully.

15. I then discussed in general terms the contributions that partners make to a marriage. This brought from Mrs. W. some discussion of her need to work, not because she really must have the money, but because of her general dissatisfaction with the home situation. She discussed the incident of the previous week that led to her leaving and said, matter-of-factly, that she did visit taverns with her work friends. She brought out that she realized it was difficult for the children for her not to return home but that she felt so upset by disagreements with her husband that she frequently preferred to stay out of the house. She expressed concern about the happiness of the children and said that they have learned to leave the home themselves in preference to remaining, because of Mr. W.'s constant nagging. She commented that she recognized she must contribute to the discord and she regretted it but felt it was based upon her husband's neglect of her and his long-standing unwillingness to approach their problems thoughtfully. I reinforced her statements that she contributed to this. At the same time I gave recognition to her frustrations and disappointments in the marriage. I stated directly that I felt that the marriage could be salvaged only by work on the part of both persons. She said that she recognized that she needed someone to help her understand why she has been dissatisfied and to help her make "a stab at decent living."

16. I suggested that we follow her own feeling as to a joint interview. I wondered how she would feel about my explaining to Mr. W. that each should be seen separately. She thought this would be acceptable to her. At first she wished that I would tell him it was *my* feeling that this should be done, but, when I said that this would not be exactly truthful, she recognized my point and returned to her suggestion of individual interviews. It was planned that I would see her the following week and that I would talk further with Mr. W. as to whether he wished to work with me toward seeing his part in the marriage. She expressed complete co-operation in terms of getting time off to see me. She had talked with her boss, who had given support to her coming here.

17. Four days later Mr. and Mrs. W. each phoned me to say that they had gotten together over the week end to plan Martha's visit to an aunt. They had been able to talk together much more reasonably and quietly

and had decided that Mrs. W. would come home "temporarily" while they sounded out with me their chances of saving the marriage.

18. It was noted that Mr. W. was greatly relieved by Mrs. W.'s return, but nonetheless he wished to go on with our interviews. I had the impression that this was planned with her in order to effect the reconciliation. However, with Mrs. W. my impression was that she saw us as going on in order to define what might be happening to her marriage. Her attitude toward Mr. W. was one of less irritation, as she explained that "for the first time in our life he's listened to my criticisms of him." She added that she felt "very sorry" for him, and we recognized together that his dependency upon her had been satisfying as well as irritating. We thought we might be able to look at the possible ways she could handle his needs as well as her own feelings to help her be more comfortable in the marriage.

### The Casework Process in the Beginning Phase

In a sense Mrs. Whitman comes, too, as an "unwilling" client, pushed or persuaded to see the worker by her husband's prior action. But it is quickly apparent, and she testifies to this, that she has seen the agency in the past as a helping resource for her marital problem and that in the contest of wills between her and her husband she held the upper hand and could have refused his request. She is here, and by her telephone conversation and her ready participation from the first she gives evidence that she is not threatened by the agency. With her it is possible, then, to focus immediately on the nature of the problem of marital maladjustment.

From Mr. W.'s version of the problem the caseworker has garnered some facts (if they are facts) about Mrs. W.'s behavior and some idea that she is seeking satisfactions that her role as wife does not provide, encouraged, perhaps, by finding herself in a social milieu that supports and excites "freedom." It remains to get from Mrs. W. herself what she thinks the problem is and how she feels about it, but chiefly, in this first contact, what she wants to do about it and whether she sees herself and her marital problem related to this agency's help. Out of these considerations and from the caseworker's observations of Mrs. W.'s responsive behavior—what she says, how she feels and acts—will come an expanded diagnostic understanding of the psychosocial factors operating in the situation and a firsthand knowledge of Mrs. W.'s workability and goals.

Mrs. W. begins (paragraph 3) by a partial denial of the possibility of help. Added to this defense is the projection of blame onto her husband, a typical response in beginning discussions of interpersonal conflict. The significance of such defenses (of denial and projection) lies in whether they are maintained stubbornly or whether they give way as the individual is given greater security and different perspectives. The caseworker accepts Mrs. W.'s presentation and then relates to her positive motivation as the stronger side of her feeling. She asks for Mrs. W.'s view of the present problem and her idea of the agency in relation to it (4).

As Mrs. W. presents her problem (5, 6), the caseworker operates in two ways: to recognize and accredit her constructive motivations —for help, for being a good mother—and to draw out the facts of the problem as Mrs. W. sees and feels them. It is from these "thousands of little things," to use Mrs. W.'s words, that the pattern and nature of the problem come to be discerned, and the client and worker do well to lay them out for sorting. As yet Mrs. W. projects the blame. Whether she has a capacity to see herself as playing some part in creating the problem or to move from blaming to trying to understand her husband remains to be tested. What the diagnosing caseworker can see already, however, is a mother who individualizes her children (she is not so immersed in her own miseries as to think of them simply as "the kids"); who sympathizes with them (perhaps identifies with being child more than with being wife?—yet to be tested); who wants more for her children than she has had. These signs point to her being able to live beyond herself.

The bits of background history Mrs. W. offers (6) do not yet illuminate the situation. It might be speculated that she was unprepared for homemaking, but whence came her capacity for feeling for and with her children? The caseworker would do well to file these miscellaneous details for future reference. At present, however, she is validly concerned less with how Mrs. W. got to be the wife and mother she is and more with what Mrs. W. wants out of her marriage. This question (7) tests whether Mrs. W.'s expectations were realistic or not and what she aspires to have.

Mrs. W.'s response (8, 9, 10) is to give further data bearing on her frustrations and disappointment in marriage, drawn out by some directed inquiries from the caseworker. This discussion yields a number of facts—facts of the couple's sexual incompatibility, of

Mrs. W.'s emotional reaction to it, of her unsuccessful attempts to deal with it, and then further facts of a different nature but part of this conflict, facts of her husband's frustration of her outgoing social impulses.

Despite this amplification of the problem, its exact nature is not yet clear. Mrs. W. places the sexual relationship in the center of difficulty, but, as every experienced caseworker knows, sexual adjustment is intimately interlocked with and responsive to all other aspects of marital life, sometimes as cause and sometimes as effect of other interpersonal adjustments. For Mrs. W. it is an emotionally freighted area, but how it affects or is affected by the other frustrations and dissatisfactions of her life is yet to be known. One thing is probable. If, because of loss of objectivity or for lack of knowledge about the complexities of marriage, the caseworker pounced upon sex or upon Mr. W.'s narrow-mindedness as *the* problem, the client's perception of *her* problem would be markedly influenced. But this is a seasoned caseworker who knows that "what is the problem," when it is many-faceted, is not told in one interview, and she knows, too, that, whatever the problem, there must first be determined Mrs. W.'s interest, willingness, and ability to commit herself to work on it.

In the course of her telling some of the facts of her difficulty and of her emotional responses certain diagnostic signs may be observed. Mrs. W. is seen as a changing person, subject to influences outside herself. She has varied interests, seeks relationships, and shows a developing awareness of her "rights" and of the opportunities (good and bad) for self-fulfilment in the permissive city culture. For marital counseling purposes the most important signs are her investment of feeling in her marriage—her weeping shows she has not made peace with the sexual maladjustment, for instance—and her persisting compassion for her husband, which tempers her hate. She feels for him, if only pityingly, and her wish has been to keep from hurting him.

With this as clue, and also in the attempt to ascertain Mrs. W.'s motivations to maintain the marriage, the caseworker poses the question whether Mrs. W. sees anything positive in her husband (11). The response is two-sided. Mrs. W. finds some objective good in him, but she balances some irritants against this. She is drawn back to the marriage by consideration of the children but is drawn away by self-preservation.

The worker's attempt (12) to interpret the husband's behavior and to draw from Mrs. W. some understanding of him when she herself still feels needful might be questioned. Yet, whatever this caseworker's reason, at some early point this important diagnostic purpose must be served: to test the client's capacity and willingness to see into her husband's (or another's) behavior, to perceive it, as in this instance, as expressing an inner need rather than a malicious intent. Had Mrs. W.'s response been a negative one—had she, for example, been quite unresponsive to the worker's asking her to think about why Mr. W. lied or had she brushed aside the worker's suggested interpretation—it would have been the signal to return to where Mrs. W. stood and to relate further to her own bruises and wounds. Mrs. W.'s responsive ideas about her husband's needfulness bespeak her relative feeling of security with the worker and some readiness to expand her perceptions and to adapt her thinking.

Mrs. W. has been helped to tell some of the problems that make up the total problem of marital discord; her feelings have been received sympathetically and understandingly. She has, by her presence and by fragmentary responses, shown herself at least partially motivated to work on her marriage. Her capacities to feel *with* her children and *for* her husband, to relate comfortably and appropriately to the worker, to talk to the point, and to move to a different perception of a small piece of the problem all augur well for her participation. Nevertheless (and not surprisingly), when she is faced with the expectation of change (she has tasted a bit of it in the worker's asking her to understand Mr. W., and she senses, now that she has told her story, that she must choose some way of coping with it), she feels the reluctance to involve herself. So she proposes that things be allowed to take their course for a few weeks (13). To this proposal the caseworker presents the different mode of solution that casework help offers (13, 14). Mrs. W.'s ambivalent feelings are recognized, but recognized, too, is the greater weighting of her positive motivation to take and her ability to use help.

What the caseworker presents, then, is not a routine statement as to the general nature of agency services as it relates to a type of problem but the specific things Mrs. W. can expect from the ways this agency will help her to tackle her problem; not a neutral take-it-or-leave-it offer of help but a demonstration of concern for Mrs. W. and of conviction that help can here be found. The caseworker is firm in her commitment to family welfare and to the maintenance of family solidarity if it warrants support, but she is also related with warmth and understanding to the opposing pulls in Mrs. W. herself and to the feelings that range in her. It is this firmness combined with compassion that infuses the relationship with promise for a client and may make him lean toward taking help despite his ambivalent feelings about the problem itself.

The caseworker focuses discussion on the marriage as a partnership (15). It is clear that she views the problem not as one in which one or another person is disturbed and needs such personal help as will, hopefully, bring him to be a better spouse but rather as a problem of interaction between two persons in marriage and then, in turn, between them as parents and their children. The problem to be solved, then, is that of achieving a happier marital balance. The content for discussion, it follows, must deal with Mrs. W. as wife and as mother, with her in a reciprocal role, with the satisfactions she may validly expect to give and to receive, and so on. With Mr. W. it will be the same. This is begun with Mrs. W. as the caseworker affirms Mrs. W.'s comment that she is a contributor to the difficulty (15), that both persons must be involved in salvaging a marriage, etc. Here, again (15), Mrs. W. is seen in ferment. Torn by feelings of self-defense and self-condemnation, righteousness and guiltiness, anger and compassion, she vacillates between pushing the problem from her and taking it on as her own. The caseworker is not swept from what must always be her firm position: that of helping the client to carry his valid responsibilities at the same time as she expresses by attitude and action her understanding of his all-too-human temptation to relinquish them. With still some reservations, Mrs. W. accepts the task.

The caseworker then plans with Mrs. W. the next practical steps (16). The telephone conversation that follows (17, 18) indicates a mobilization of Mrs. W.'s positive feeling for her husband and an affirmation of her "pact" with the caseworker.

In the course of this beginning interview, the caseworker has helped Mrs. W. to come to a decision to work on her marital problem with the help of the agency. Ambivalent though Mrs. W. is about wanting a reconciliation with her husband, she repeatedly shows that she wants a good marriage, wants to be a good mother, wants to punish but not to hurt her husband, and, finally, she believes that someone can help her to do and to be better. At the interview's end she is a "willing" client. Resistances may rise again, influence of her friends or clashes with Mr. W. may cause this willingness to fluctuate, and the caseworker will need again to work on Mrs. W.'s motivation and goal directions.

At the moment, however, she is mobilized and constructively focused. Her capacities are many and essentially unimpaired. She relates easily, appropriately, and with increasing trust. She has an emotional investment in her problem, her husband, and her children, and she is able both to express and to contain her feelings. Her defenses are flexible and realistic, and, as she finds the caseworker supporting and understanding, she relinquishes her protective armor. Along with this she demonstrates receptivity to the new ideas or perspectives that the caseworker introduces, lending herself briefly to viewing her husband objectively, to weighing the pros and cons of treatment, etc. Her expanded perceptions result in some change of feeling and some shift of her position in relation to the problem, followed by her taking adaptive action that is harmonious with her considered decision. In short, Mrs. W. shows a number of qualities that mark her as workable, qualities that were present in her but that have been led out and enhanced by the caseworker's problem-solving help.

In both these beginning transactions the caseworkers have helped their clients to move from confusion and indecision to partial clarification and choice, from being irresolute carriers of problems to becoming goal-directed participants in problem-solving. In both, for all the differences at play, the caseworkers have operated in ways that may be seen as characteristic of the casework process of problem-solving.

In both cases the caseworkers are clear as to their agencies' purpose and program. In each they lend themselves with confidence, intentness, and sensitive warmth to the needs of their clients. In each they seem knowledgeable about people and their problems.

and this knowledge infuses their observations to produce under-standing and insight. These essential qualities determine the ways in which the caseworkers enable their clients to relate to them and to communicate their troubles of situation and feeling. But these are not enough. For accompanying them there is the necessity to shape and to steer the course that will involve the client in move-ment toward some change and will enhance his capacities to func-tion effectively. This the problem-solving work provides.

If the reader will view both the Grayson and the Whitman inter-views within the framework of the preceding chapters (especially chapters 7, 8, 9, and 10), he will identify for himself both the con-stancy of means and the guidance these two caseworkers have of-fered their clients. He will see that both caseworkers relate them-selves from the first with sensitive understanding and professional purposiveness. Mr. Grayson's caseworker, acutely aware of his fear, gives generously of her patience and acceptance, staying with him always in his feelings at the same time as she leads him to look at the differences between reality and his interpretation of it. Mrs. Whitman's caseworker, recognizing the realism and appropriateness of the way her client relates, moves more readily into the business of the presenting problem, yet she, too, responds repeatedly to the emotional overtones in Mrs. Whitman's account. By the sharing and the reception of their reactions, both Mr. Grayson and Mrs. Whit-man deposit something of themselves in their helpers and in turn draw from them some part of their imperturbability and hopeful-ness. It may be see, too, that the fabric of relationship, even within one interview, is made firm by the weaving of discussion about such content as holds vital meaning to the clients.

As one views either Mr. Grayson or Mrs. Whitman responding to the caseworker's attitudes, questions, assertions, or comments, one may see their perceptions growing deeper and broader in span. Per-haps this is because they have put into spoken, and heard, words what was before experienced amorphously, perhaps because the caseworker conveys a sense of safety that makes defensiveness less necessary, perhaps because the caseworker's focused queries intro-duce a more orderly and thus more manageable way of getting at the problem, or perhaps by a combination of all of these. Even in this first interview both caseworkers seek to stimulate (and to observe and appraise) the adaptive movements, minuscule though they might be, that should follow on changed perceptions. Here and there, one may see them injecting some small challenge to their clients to think about what they are telling, to play the light of ideas across the facts they recount. Thus, for example, Mrs. Whitman's caseworker asks how she interprets her husband's behavior, and Mr. Grayson's caseworker asks if he believes his nervousness is due to his foot trouble.

Begun by the client's laying-out and sorting-over of some of the top-layer details of his difficulty, problem-solving efforts are sustained as the client's excess anxiety is lessened and his hope and confidence increased. The stimulus that the caseworker provides to pursue and consider feelings as they affect facts and ideas, and facts and ideas as they affect feelings, and all these in relation to goals, may be said to spark and charge the process. In these single interviews with Mr. Grayson and Mrs. Whitman, the caseworkers focus most intensively on arriving at the agreements and decisions involved in taking help. Thus in both cases there is a working-over between caseworker and client of the ends sought in relation to the conceptions of the agency's ways and means, so that, by making a conscious and considered choice, the client undertakes an active partnership. The caseworkers' contribution to this end in both cases is vital. It consists of an attitude that affirms their belief in the values of agency help at the same time as they take cognizance of and attempt to affect the client's doubts or reluctances. It consists also of giving information about what may be expected, drawing from the client his reactions and thinking, and encouraging him, out of the motivations he himself has expressed, to choose to tackle his problem.

Viewed in relation to diagnosis, these two interviews illustrate these points: In both cases the caseworkers seek first to ascertain and assess in rough outline the compatibility between the client and his problem and the agency's purpose and service, and, having done this, they seek to set off a dynamic interaction among these elements. The purpose of the interview is to treat—to help Mr. Grayson and Mrs. Whitman to *do* several things—to tell, to consider, to choose. Diagnosis evolves from this treatment and in the next moment affects it. Two kinds of evidence emerge in these interviews, both of which contribute to the design for action. One is of the problem as it is seen and experienced by the client, supplemented by fragments of data contributed by others. The other is of the person in his relation to his problem and to the means of solution. The first, a beginning psychosocial diagnosis, is derived largely from the client's account and spontaneous behavior. The second, a beginning diagnosis of workability, is derived from the client's responses to the ways the worker treats him during the interview. In both the Grayson and the Whitman cases, with all the variations rising out of the differences of personality and emotional state, the caseworker treats each of them as a person who is respected and understandingly received, as one who is able to set forth his situation, as one who is affected by his problem, as one who has given thought and effort to trying to do something about it, as one who has the power and the right to be "captain of his soul," as one who can exercise consideration and judgment. The degree and quality of Mr. Grayson's and Mrs. Whitman's responses tell of their motivations and capacities for using service, and the moment-by-moment assessment of these by the caseworkers guide their direction, timing, discussion matter, and immediate ends.

Ongoing treatment will deepen and broaden this stream of diagnostic understanding. The psychiatrist may need to ascertain the facts of the genesis and course of Mr. Grayson's neurosis, and from Mrs. Whitman the caseworker may possibly need to learn what in her personality makeup makes wifehood difficult for her. But, at first, the caseworkers tried only to help a man and a woman with their presenting problems and to draw out of their accounts and responses a beginning understanding of their powers and needs in relation to their problems. In both the Grayson and the Whitman interviews, the caseworkers gain only a general idea of the problem's makeup, dynamics, or causes. They gather, however, some clear and specific ideas as to what Mr. Grayson and Mrs. Whitman want and how much they want it and what they are able and ready to invest in seeking it. This is the result not of merely noting behavior for future treatment planning but of dealing with it so as to increase the client's working powers.

At the end of these first interviews, both Mr. Grayson and Mrs. Whitman have experienced a sustaining and dynamic relationship, have been aided to begin to to share their problems in ways that seem reasonable and feel reassuring, have learned something of what the agency is like and how it can help them, and have been led to move from resistance and uncertainty to choice and action. As Mr. Grayson leaves his interview, he is a man released from his top-layer surges of fear, buoyed up by some hopefulness, unlocked from the bonds of indecision and able to take a step toward change. Mrs. Whitman leaves her interview, too, with changed feelings and ideas. She feels supported and understood by another human being, temporarily released of tensions, more free, then, to look into and around her situation, to tolerate it for consideration, and to be willing, at last, to pick up and shoulder some of the burden of thrashing it out. If one looks closely, one may see that the egos of both Mr. Grayson and Mrs. Whitman have been working and worked and that their powers, puny or vital, have been drawn upon, braced, exercised, and strengthend by the beginning of the casework process of problem-solving.

*BIBLIOGRAPHY*

## BIBLIOGRAPHY

A bibliography for a book such as this should, I believe, serve two purposes. It should be useful to the reader and it should document the author's indebtedness to those who by their writings have contributed to his fund of knowledge. Those two purposes have guided my selection of the readings that follow. Therefore, the reader will not find this a "complete" reference list. He will find only such readings as bear directly upon the book's content. Some of these have been specifically called to his attention in the text; others are listed for their general value in offering extensions or enrichments of the text material. Annotations point to the particular relevance of each suggested reading, because in this day of too many books and too little time the search for knowledge may become a formidable and therefore an abandoned undertaking.

To make choices from among the many single articles in the literature of social casework and from the varied writings of allied fields has not been easy, and the reader may find that some reference he would consider to be most pertinent has been omitted. I can only say that many were left out regretfully, put aside by my criteria of present usefulness and indebtedness and by consideration of the fact that the reader will find additional references included in these professional writings.

One assumption about the reader—whether he is a neophyte or a matured social caseworker—underlies this reading list. It is that he already is acquainted with the basic sources of knowledge and thought within the general context of which this book is written. It is this assumption that would make listing the writings of Sigmund Freud all but gratuitous. Yet should Freud be known to the reader only through his interpreters and should a firsthand reading be sought, *The Basic Writings of Sigmund Freud* (translated and edited by Dr. A. A. Brill and published by the "Modern Library" [New York, 1938]) offers ready access to the world of understanding that he discovered and explored. By the same token, should Mary Richmond be known only as some revered ancestor to whose memory a respectful nod is given now and then, the reader is encouraged to skim the pages of *Social Diagnosis* (New York: Russell Sage Foundation, 1917) and *The Long View* (New York: Russell Sage Foundation, 1930). He will find in them a model of coherent thought and compassionate understanding. Virginia Robinson's *A Changing Psychology of Social Casework* (Chapel Hill: University of North Carolina Press, 1930), for all that it is now a quarter of a century old, still holds much that is fresh and provocative of thought and provides, in addition, an excellent history of casework. Gordon Hamilton's *Social Casework Theory and Practice* (New York: Columbia University Press, 1940, 1951) is to this date the one general textbook on casework—probably the first book to be known to students of casework. Equally well known as the trusty handbook for beginners and their teachers is Charlotte Towle's *Common Human Needs* (New York: American Association of Social Workers, 1952). Perhaps we least know firsthand those thinkers by whose philosophy we order our lives, knowingly or not. Because I—and therefore this book—have been most influenced by John Dewey's thinking, I commend him to the reader who has some quiet hours. Again the "Modern Library" edition, *Intelligence in the Modern World—John Dewey's Philosophy* (New York, 1939) offers excerpts from the best of his writings.

### Chapter 1. The Components of the Casework Situation

1. BOWERS, SWITHUN. "The Nature and Definition of Social Casework," *Journal of Social Casework*, Vol. XXX, Nos. 8, 9, and 10 (October, November, and December, 1949). Reprinted in *Principles and Tech-*

*niques of Social Casework.* New York: Family Service Association of America, 1950. This work of Rev. Swithun Bowers compiles and discusses the major definitions of casework from 1915 to 1947. A few of these are selected for the reader's special notice:

2. REGENSBURG, JEANETTE. "An Attempt To See Casework Apart from the Related Professions," *American Association of Psychiatric Social Workers Newsletter,* VII, No. 2 (1938), 4. Miss Regensburg's definition of casework involves diagnosis, focus upon a given problem, and treatment as a problem-solving process.
3. RICHMOND, MARY. *What Is Social Case Work?* New York: Russell Sage Foundation, 1922. One of the earliest attempts to describe and define the "what" and "why" of social casework, Miss Richmond's definition is still frequently used and is still clarifying, though limited.
4. *Social Casework—Generic and Specific: An Outline.* (A Report of the Milford Conference.) New York: American Association of Social Workers, 1929. A vital document in which, among other things, the common elements of the content of social casework are sought out.
5. TOWLE, CHARLOTTE. "Social Case Work," in *Social Work Year Book, 1947.* New York: Russell Sage Foundation, 1947. A sound definition and description.

See also:

6. PERLMAN, HELEN HARRIS. "Casework Services in Public Welfare," in *Proceedings of the National Conference of Social Work, 1947.* New York: Columbia University Press, 1948. Less a definition than an attempt to explain what casework is in a setting where it has often been challenged.
7. REYNOLDS, BERTHA. *Social Work and Social Living.* New York: Citadel Press, 1951. On page 131 is offered a useful "working definition" of casework.

## Chapter 2. The Person

Perhaps the most difficult selection of readings to make has been that for this chapter, since the recorded knowledge of "the person" defies all bounds. What I have settled on are those articles, specific chapters, and a few whole books that seem to me to hold in most readable and highly condensed form the essential range of useful knowledge about the person. If the references seem heavily weighted on the side of environmental and cultural determinants, it is because these have been less attended to and perhaps less well known by caseworkers than those of the person's intrapsychic experiences; they are proffered to broaden the scope of understanding.

1. ALEXANDER, FRANZ, M.D. "The Basic Principles of Psychodynamics," *Fundamentals of Psychoanalysis.* New York: W. W. Norton & Co., 1948. A highly condensed and helpful presentation of the fundamental balancing and adaptive operations of the personality, followed by a full bibliography.

2. ——. "Development of Ego-Psychology," in *Psychoanalysis Today,* ed. Sandor Lorand. New York: International Universities Press, 1944. A clear exposition of the functions of the ego, as is the following:

3. ——. "The Function of the Ego and Its Failures," *Fundamentals of Psychoanalysis.* New York: W. W. Norton & Co., 1948.

4. BENEDEK, THERESE, M.D. "Personality Development," in *Dynamic Psychiatry,* ed. FRANZ ALEXANDER, M.D., and HELEN ROSS. Chicago: University of Chicago Press, 1952. A condensed, trenchant, life-history of the individual, within the Freudian psychoanalytic framework, with a supporting bibliography.

5. COTTRELL, LEONARD S., JR. "The Adjustment of the Individual to His Age and Sex Roles," *American Sociological Review,* Vol. VII, No. 5 (October, 1942). The discussion of "adjustment" within the framework of "roles" provides caseworkers with an interesting means of viewing their clients' personal-social problems.

6. FREUD, ANNA. *The Ego and the Mechanisms of Defense.* London: Hogarth Press, 1937. Stemming from and developing Sigmund Freud's evolving conception of the ego and its functions, this book presents the first concentrated exposition of the ego concept. Like many "source" materials, its richness is best savored after the reader has first digested some of the later distilled interpretations of the ego.

7. FREUD, SIGMUND. "The Anatomy of the Mental Personality," *New Introductory Lectures on Psychoanalysis.* New York: W. W. Norton & Co., 1933. One of Freud's later formulations, this is a compact and engaging presentation of his theories of the functions of the personality.

8. GINSBURG, SOL WIENER, M.D. "The Impact of the Social Worker's Cultural Structure on Social Therapy," *Social Casework,* Vol. XXXII, No. 8 (October, 1951). Social workers are also "culture carriers" and need to be aware of this in appraising their clients.

9. KLUCKHOHN, CLYDE, MURRAY, HENRY A., and SCHNEIDER, DAVID M. (eds.). *Personality in Nature, Society, and Culture.* 2d ed. rev. New York: Alfred A. Knopf, 1953. See especially the following chapters:

   ALEXANDER, FRANZ, M.D. "Educative Influence of Personality Factors in the Environment." A brief, pointed discussion of the factors involved in the development of personality.

   ERIKSON, ERIK H. "Growth and Crises of the Healthy Personality." An expansion, yet admirably concise, of some of the author's ideas on the healthy personality set forth in his stimulating book, *Child-hood and Society.*

KLUCKHOHN, CLYDE, and MURRAY, HENRY A. "Personality Formation: The Determinants." A succinct, compact chapter on the constitutional, cultural, role, and situational factors which shape personality development.

——. "Outline of a Conception of Personality." A highly condensed explanation of the personality and of its functions, combining social science and psychoanalytic theories in a commendable and successful effort to present the whole man.

PARSONS, TALCOTT. "Age and Sex in the Social Structure of the United States." How social structure and values affect the development of attitudes and behavior.

10. KLUCKHOHN, FLORENCE R. "Dominant and Variant Cultural Value Orientations," in *The Social Welfare Forum, 1951.* New York: Columbia University Press, 1951. A presentation of some organizing ideas on cultural differences as combined within man's relation to time, nature, other men, values. A fresh way by which to view one's own and one's clients' cultures.

11. LINTON, RALPH. "Concepts of Role and Status," *The Cultural Background of Personality.* New York: D. Appleton–Century Co., 1945. The effects of these concepts upon the individual's development.

12. POLLAK, OTTO, and COLLABORATORS. *Social Science and Psychotherapy for Children.* New York: Russell Sage Foundation, 1952. Notable for the effort to utilize social science concepts in the conduct of casework. See particularly chapters ii, v, vi, and vii.

13. REDL, FRITZ. "The Concept of Ego Disturbances and Ego Support," *American Journal of Orthopsychiatry,* Vol. XXI, No. 2 (April, 1951). While this discussion relates to children, much of it is applicable to adults. Mr. Redl makes some penetrating and provocative comments on the state of our knowledge about the ego and on avenues for further exploration.

14. SAUL, LEON J., M.D. *Emotional Maturity.* Philadelphia: J. B. Lippincott Co., 1947. A non-technical exposition of personality development and dynamics.

15. SMALLEY, RUTH. "The Significance of the Family for the Development of Personality," *Social Service Review,* Vol. XXIV, No. 1 (March, 1950). Brief but pointed discussion.

16. TOWLE, CHARLOTTE. "Personality Development," *The Learner in Education for the Professions.* Chicago: University of Chicago Press, 1954. The development and adaptive functions of the ego are set forth succinctly and lucidly in Chapters iii and iv. While they are discussed in relation to the social work "learner," they are immediately applicable to considerations of the "learning" a client experiences.

### Chapter 3. The Problem

Accounts and discussions of the problems with which caseworkers help their clients and the problems which helping itself may create permeate the literature of casework. There are, however, few writings which give concentrated consideration to the general characteristics or implications of the kinds of problems with which social caseworkers deal. Three references that do so are:

1. APTEKAR, HERBERT. "Causality and Treatment," *American Journal of Orthopsychiatry*, Vol. IX, No. 2 (April, 1939). The contribution of this brief article (worth expansion) is the point that effects of problems are, in turn, causes of new ones and that the client's problem is part of a Gestalt.
2. RIPPLE, LILIAN, and ALEXANDER, ERNESTINA. "Motivation, Capacity, and Opportunity as Related to the Use of Casework Service: Nature of Client's Problem," *Social Service Review*, XXX, No. 1 (March, 1956). The development of a problem-classification scheme as part of a larger study is described here.
3. TOWLE, CHARLOTTE. *Common Human Needs: An Interpretation for Staff in Public Assistance Agencies.* ("Public Assistance Reports," No. 8.) Washington, D.C.: Government Printing Office, 1945. Republished by American Association of Social Workers, 1952. The common human problems, common human reactions to them, and their implications for casework are set forth here simply and tellingly.

Largely, the literature in casework on "problem" has focused upon particular types of interpersonal or social maladjustments, both to analyze their nature and to present the casework help that can be given. Within the past decade there has been a significant production by caseworkers of such writing, notable for its movement from the individual instance to groupings of cases and from specific treatment procedures to governing principles. The following are examples of these:

4. GOMBERG, M. ROBERT, *et al.* "Parent-Child Relationship Problems," in *Diagnosis and Process in Family Counseling*, ed. M. ROBERT GOMBERG and FRANCES T. LEVINSON. New York: Family Service Association of America, 1951.
5. HAMILTON, GORDON. *Psychotherapy in Child Guidance.* New York: Columbia University Press, 1947.
6. HOLLIS, FLORENCE. *Women in Marital Conflict.* New York: Family Service Association of America, 1949.
7. PECK, HARRIS B., M.D., and BELLSMITH, VIRGINIA. *Treatment of the*

*Delinquent Adolescent: Group and Individual Therapy with Parent and Child.* New York: Family Service Association of America, 1954.

## Chapter 4. The Place

1. AMERICAN ASSOCIATION OF SOCIAL WORKERS. "Code of Ethics," in *Standards for the Professional Practice of Social Work.* New York: The Association, 1951. A careful articulation of ethical principles and standards.
2. FOLLETT, MARY. "The Meaning of Responsibility in Business Management: The Illusion of Final Responsibility," in *Dynamic Administration,* ed. H. C. METCALF and L. URWICK. New York: Harper & Bros., 1942. "Authority and responsibility are derived from function" in social agencies as well as in business.
3. GOMBERG, M. ROBERT. "The Specific Nature of Family Casework," in *Family Casework and Counseling,* ed. JESSIE TAFT. Philadelphia: University of Pennsylvania Press, 1948. An exposition of the relation of the caseworker's operations to the function of the agency—in this case, the family agency.
4. HAMILTON, GORDON. "Agency and Inter-agency Practices," *Theory and Practice of Social Casework.* 2d ed. rev. New York: Columbia University Press, 1951. A useful and a considerably more complete coverage of this subject than the chapter in this book presents.
5. JOHNSON, ARLIEN. "The Administrative Process in Social Work," in *Proceedings of the National Conference of Social Work, 1946.* New York: Columbia University Press, 1947. Administration, a process "by which programs are transformed into reality," is seen as combining understanding of human relationships with mechanical structuring.
6. LOWRY, FERN. "Current Concepts in Social Case-Work Practice," *Social Service Review,* Vol. XII, No. 3 (September, 1938). "The setting . . . to a large measure determines the character of the philosophic concepts developed" is the thesis developed with vigor and clarity.
7. PERLMAN, HELEN HARRIS. "Generic Aspects of Specific Settings," *Social Service Review,* Vol. XXIII, No. 3 (September, 1949). Also in *Proceedings of the National Conference of Social Work, 1949: Social Work in the Current Scene.* New York: Columbia University Press, 1950. An attempt to identify likenesses in special settings which determine likeness in their casework practices.
8. ———. "The Social Components of Casework Practice," in *The Social Welfare Forum, 1953.* New York: Columbia University Press, 1953.
9. ———. "Social Casework Counseling," in *Psychotherapy and Counseling (Annals of the New York Academy of Sciences,* Vol. LXIII [November 7, 1955]).

Two articles in which this author attempts to identify the specific character of social casework by, among other factors, its social auspices and obligations.

10. TOWLE, CHARLOTTE. "General Objectives of Professional Education," *The Learner in Education for the Professions*. Chicago: University of Chicago Press, 1954. A nice discussion of the attributes professional education must seek to inculcate in the student.

11. ———. "Social Case Work in Modern Society," *Social Service Review,* Vol. XX, No. 2 (June, 1946). An examination of casework in the context of the profession of social work, of its society, and of various agency functions and structures.

12. WITMER, HELEN L. *Social Work: An Analysis of a Social Institution.* New York: Farrar & Rinehart, 1942. See especially chapter iii for a discussion of the institutional nature and the "material apparatus" of social work.

## Chapter 5. The Process

This chapter serves largely to introduce the idea of casework as a problem-solving process. All the chapters which follow elaborate and extend its content. Therefore, the reading references here are limited to those few which cast further light on the relationship between the "art" of casework and the "science" of a structured process.

1. DEWEY, JOHN. "The Natural History of Thinking," *Essays in Experimental Logic*. Chicago: University of Chicago Press, 1917.

2. ———. "Analysis of Reflective Thinking," *How We Think*. Rev. ed. New York: D. C. Heath & Co., 1933.

The thoughtful reader will find, in these two brief essays, discussions of intellectual problem-solving processes, much of which is transferable to his understanding of the forces at work in therapeutic problem-solving.

3. GARDNER, GEORGE E., M.D. "The Therapeutic Process from the Point of View of Psychoanalytic Theory," *American Journal of Orthopsychiatry*, Vol. XXII, No. 4 (October, 1952). Dr. Gardner's structuring of psychotherapy parallels the problem-solving idea proposed here.

4. IRVINE, MAY. "Communication and Relationship in Social Casework," *Social Casework*, Vol. XXXVI, No. 1 (January, 1955). Miss Irvine's thesis supports that presented here: The process of communication, fundamental to casework, has two inseparable aspects—"the rapport between worker and client . . . which is a matter of feeling" and "an ordering, structuring process." A well-ordered and well-structured article.

5. JAHODA, MARIE. "The Meaning of 'Psychological Health,'" in *The Social Welfare Forum, 1953*. New York: Columbia University Press, 1953. Also in *Social Casework*, Vol. XXXIV, No. 8 (October, 1953). Psychological health is associated with certain modes of problem-solving, and the stages of problem-solving are discussed.

6. PERLMAN, HELEN HARRIS. "The Basic Structure of the Casework Process," *Social Service Review*, Vol. XXVII, No. 3 (September, 1953). The thesis of this book is presented briefly in this article.

7. *Scope and Method of the Family Service Agency*. New York: Family Service Association of America, 1953. A statement from a major field of social work endeavor—family casework—of the essential aims and means in its helping process.

## Chapter 6. The Caseworker-Client Relationship

There is probably no article on casework that does not include some mention of relationship. The problem of choice, then, was one of an embarrassment of riches. The solution was to select only those writings which were exclusively devoted to the subject, which contained and extended what other like articles had included, and those which dealt with some particular aspect of relationship not developed elsewhere.

1. ACKERMAN, NATHAN W., M.D. "Psychotherapy and 'Giving Love,'" *Psychiatry*, VII (May, 1944), 129–38. An article, related as much to social casework as to psychiatry, which probes the question of the therapeutic relationship as a "love-giving" relationship, its limits and conditions. Of considerable interest and usefulness.

2. ALEXANDER, FRANZ, M.D., and FRENCH, THOMAS M., M.D. *Psychoanalytic Therapy*. New York: Ronald Press, 1946. Chapter v, "The Transference Phenomenon," defines and discusses reality and neurotic relationships in ways that are immediately useful to caseworkers.

3. APTEKAR, HERBERT. *Basic Concepts in Social Case Work*. Chapel Hill: University of North Carolina Press, 1941. In the chapter on "Relationship" the author discusses the makeup of the professional casework relationship in simple, common-sense terms.

4. GARRETT, ANNETTE. "The Worker-Client Relationship," *American Journal of Orthopsychiatry*, Vol. XIX, No. 2 (April, 1949). A clear, readily understood presentation of both the realistic and the irrational elements at play in caseworker-client relationships.

5. ROBINSON, VIRGINIA. *A Changing Psychology in Social Case Work*. Chapel Hill: University of North Carolina Press, 1930. This is a historically significant book in social casework, for Miss Robinson's perception and formulation of the dynamics inherent in the worker-client relationship opened what had been a stubbornly closed door to the means by which to motivate and engage the client and to the psychological import of the here-and-now contact between client and caseworker.

6. STUDT, ELLIOTT. "An Outline for Study of Social Authority Factors in Casework," *Social Casework*, Vol. XXXV, No. 6 (June, 1954). This

article is included because the authority elements in a professional relationship (whether in an authoritative setting or not) are dealt with
(pp. 232 and 233).

7. Towle, Charlotte. "Factors in Treatment," in *Proceedings of the
National Conference of Social Work, 1936*. Chicago: University of
Chicago Press, 1936. The factor of the client's capacity for purposive
relationship is given nice discussion here.

8. Wolberg, Lewis R., M.D. *The Technique of Psychotherapy*. New
York: Grune & Stratton, 1954. Chapter xxxi, "Establishing a Working
Relationship," presents many helpful points on the needs and interpretations patients (or clients) put into relationships and on ways by
which the relationship may be managed. As always, caseworkers reading in psychiatric literature need to take care to identify what does
and what does not hold for casework.

### Chapter 7. The Problem-solving Work

For this chapter the same reading references are suggested as
those listed for chapter 5, "The Process." See also, under chapter 2,
"The Person," Nos. 1, 2, 3, 6, 9, and 16, all dealing with ego functions
and operations. In addition, see:

1. Coleman, Jules V., M.D. "Psychotherapeutic Principles in Casework
Interviewing," *American Journal of Psychiatry*, CVIII (October, 1951),
298–302. This article, by a psychiatrist who has had long and productive experience with caseworkers, is one of the best and most affirmative presentations of the purposes, goals, and means of the social casework process. It is not limited to what its title suggests.

2. Marcus, Grace. Part I of "Helping the Client To Use His Capacities
and Resources," in *Proceedings of the National Conference of Social
Work, 1948*. New York: Columbia University Press, 1949. For comment see No. 5, below.

3. ———. "The Relation of Casework Help to Personality Change," in
*Family Casework and Counseling*, ed. Jessie Taft. Philadelphia: University of Pennsylvania Press, 1948. A discussion of the personality
changes which may come about through the caseworker's orientation
to the client's conscious ego and his aids to its problem-solving efforts.

4. Schmideberg, Melitta, M.D. "Needed: A Psychoanalytic Assessment of Environmental Factors," *Quarterly Journal of Child Behavior*,
Vol. IV, No. 4 (October, 1952). "Repeated everyday experiences are
as important as traumatic events." "Every environmental factor affects
a number of mental processes." These are ideas long known and often
spoken of in social casework, yet in some quarters there persists some
resistance to taking full measure of the client's environment. This is a
psychiatrist's plea to psychiatrists to do just this. Cf. Helen Harris

PERLMAN, "Mental Health Planning for Children," *Child Welfare*, Vol. XXVIII, No. 6 (June, 1949).

5. TOWLE, CHARLOTTE. Part II of "Helping the Client To Use His Capacities and Resources," in *Proceedings of the National Conference of Social Work, 1948*. New York: Columbia University Press, 1949. This and No. 2, above, are companion articles in which Miss Marcus emphasizes the client's responsibility in working on his problem with help from the caseworker, and Miss Towle focuses on the caseworker's responsibility and delineates the ways of enabling the client.

## Chapter 8. Person, Problem, Place, and Process in the Beginning Phase

1. ANDERSON, DELWIN M., and KIESLER, FRANK, M.D. "Helping toward Help: The Intake Interview," *Social Casework*, Vol. XXXV, No. 2 (February, 1954). The role of the caseworker at intake in this clinical setting is seen as helping the client to know and to want to use the agency's services for the problem he brings.

2. COLEMAN, JULES V., M.D. "The Initial Phase of Psychotherapy," *Bulletin of the Menninger Clinic*, Vol. XIII, No. 6 (November, 1949). The first interview(s) is focused upon helping the patient to know something of the relationship among him, his problem, and the treatment means and helping him to express his reactions, all of which is the primary material "worked" by the therapist. Useful for caseworkers' considerations.

3. COLEMAN, JULES, M.D., SHORT, GENEVIEVE B., and HIRSCHBERG, J. COTTER, M.D. "The Intake Interview as the Beginning of Psychiatric Treatment in Children's Cases," *American Journal of Psychiatry*, CV (September, 1948), 183–86.

4. DAWLEY, ALMENA. "Professional Skills Requisite to a Good Intake Service," in *Proceedings of the National Conference of Social Work, 1937*. Chicago: University of Chicago Press, 1937. One of the early articles to argue for a shift of focus from the client's problem to the client's wishes, will, and relation to agency function at intake. A "functional" point of view, it nevertheless affected general casework thinking on this subject.

5. FREUDENTHAL, KURT. "The Contribution of the Social Work Intake Process to the Psychiatric Treatment Situation," *Journal of Psychiatric Social Work*, Vol. XX, No. 1 (September, 1950). Because most of the patients coming to this clinic are not self-referred, the purpose of the intake interview is seen as that of engaging the client in wanting help, essentially the same purpose as is described in No. 1, above.

6. FROMM-REICHMANN, FRIEDA, M.D. *Principles of Intensive Psychotherapy*. Chicago: University of Chicago Press, 1950. The initial inter-

view with psychiatric patients is discussed in chapter v. Its structure is essentially that of beginning interviews in casework.

7. GILL, MERTON, M.D., NEWMAN, RICHARD, M.D., and REDLICH, FREDERICK, M.D. *The Initial Interview in Psychiatric Practice.* New York: International Universities Press, 1954. A careful study of the "first phase of contact," including a good review of the literature on initial interviews and a full bibliography which includes some pertinent social work literature. The authors conclude that diagnosis in this phase can better be made from various data in the immediate situation than from taking a history of the problem.

8. SCHERZ, FRANCES H. "Intake: Concept and Process," *Social Casework,* Vol. XXXIII, No. 6 (June, 1952). This writer's point of view is that "intake is a process designed to understand need, regardless of the nature of the request. . . . The emphasis is on understanding." Mrs. Scherz's article deserves careful reading, since it sets forth most clearly a point of view held by a number of caseworkers, yet markedly different from those expressed in this book and held by the other writers referred to who place more emphasis upon enhancing the *client's* understanding and motivation for taking help.

9. WOLBERG, LEWIS R., M.D. *The Technique of Psychotherapy.* New York: Grune & Stratton, 1954. In the section on "The Beginning Phase of Treatment" Dr. Wolberg discusses the objectives, content, and goals of the initial interview; much of his material is applicable to casework practice.

## Chapter 9. Content in the Beginning Phase

The small number of readings appearing below does not in any sense reflect a "content-less" casework! It indicates, rather, that content is all but inseparable from other aspects of casework and, therefore, is to be found in readings referred to under other chapters, especially chapters 7, 8, 10, and 11.

1. LOWRY, FERN. "Current Concepts in Social Case-Work Practice," *Social Service Review,* Vol. XII, No. 4 (December, 1938). This, the second of Miss Lowry's two articles on this subject (the first is annotated under chapter 4, "The Place"), deserves to be far better known than it is. It is one of the most lucid, compact, articulate organizations of the essential study, diagnostic, and treatment elements in casework.

2. MARCUS, GRACE. "The Relation of Casework Help to Personality Change," in *Family Casework and Counseling,* ed. JESSIE TAFT. Philadelphia: University of Pennsylvania Press, 1948. Noted under chapter 7, "The Problem-solving Work," this is recommended here for its discussion of the content of the client's decision to use the agency's help.

3. PERLMAN, HELEN HARRIS. "The Caseworker's Use of Collateral Infor-

mation," *Social Casework,* Vol. XXXII, No. 8 (October, 1951). Also in *The Social Welfare Forum, 1951.* New York: Columbia University Press, 1951. Considerations in the use of sources of information other than the client himself, with references to other relevant articles.
4. See also Nos. 1, 3, 5, 6, and 9 under chapter 8 for examples of agreement among caseworkers and psychiatrists as to certain common content in all beginning interviews.

## Chapter 10. Method in the Beginning Phase

The ways by which social caseworkers help their clients are abundantly recorded in the literature. Selected here are articles which present not individual examples of method but generalizations of methodology.

1. AUSTIN, LUCILLE N. "Trends in Differential Treatment in Social Casework," in *Principles and Techniques in Social Casework,* ed. CORA KASIUS. New York: Family Service Association of America, 1950. Also in *Journal of Social Casework,* Vol. XXIX, No. 6 (June, 1948). A classification and discussion of the major treatment emphases in casework, not mutually exclusive, as Mrs. Austin makes clear.
2. COLEMAN, JULES, M.D. "The Initial Phase of Psychotherapy," *Bulletin of the Menninger Clinic,* Vol. XIII, No. 6 (November, 1949). An article useful to caseworkers because of the many likenesses to be found methodologically between the psychiatric and casework interviewing processes.
3. FINESINGER, JACOB E., M.D. "Psychiatric Interviewing," *American Journal of Psychiatry,* CV (September, 1948), 187–95. The social casework reader need not be put off by Dr. Finesinger's stipulation that he is setting forth principles for "insight therapy." There is much in this article that will be found useful at any level of interviewing-toward-helping.
4. GARRETT, ANNETTE. *Interviewing: Its Principles and Methods.* New York: Family Service Association of America, 1942. The basic considerations in interviewing written simply and engagingly.
5. HOLLIS, FLORENCE. "The Techniques of Casework," in *Principles and Techniques in Social Casework,* ed. CORA KASIUS. New York: Family Service Association of America, 1950. Also in *Journal of Social Casework,* Vol. XXX, No. 6 (June, 1949). Classification and clear discussion of "means by which change was brought about" in casework practice. Cf. No. 1, above.
6. LEVINE, MAURICE, M.D. "Principles of Psychiatric Treatment," in *Dynamic Psychiatry,* ed. FRANZ ALEXANDER, M.D., and HELEN ROSS. Chicago: University of Chicago Press, 1952. Well-condensed and articulated presentation of the diagnostic consideration and treatment

modes in psychiatric practice, with an excellent bibliography. Here again the social casework reader must identify for himself that which is and that which is not applicable to his particular practice in his particular setting.

7. TOWLE, CHARLOTTE. "Client-centered Case Work," *Social Service Review*, Vol. XXIV, No. 4 (December, 1950). Essential aspects of social casework responsibility and process.

8. ———. Part II of "Helping the Client Use His Capacities and Resources," in *Proceedings of the National Conference of Social Work, 1948.* New York: Columbia University Press, 1949. Also in *Social Service Review*, Vol. XXII, No. 4 (December, 1948). The principles underlying casework method set forth with clarity and vigor.

## Chapter 11. Diagnosis: The Thinking in Problem-solving

Like the term "relationship," "diagnosis" is one which appears, and is given at least a nod to, in almost every article on social casework. The selection of readings from among the many pertinent articles on the subject becomes most difficult. I have winnowed out from among a mass of possible references three kinds: those which, to my mind, clarify the concept of diagnosis; those which present some provocative discussion of it, to stimulate the reader's further thought; and a few which present some facts on the subject.

1. ACKERMAN, NATHAN, M.D. "The Diagnosis of Neurotic Marital Interaction," *Social Casework*, Vol. XXXV, No. 4 (April, 1954). "In undertaking to diagnose marital relationships, we are not concerned in the first instance with the autonomous functions and pathology of individual personalities, but rather with the dynamics of the relationship, that is, with the reciprocal role functions that define the relations of husband and wife." This thesis of Dr. Ackerman's article shifts the center of diagnostic attention from the individual to the individual-behaving-in-some-social-role.

2. APTEKAR, HERBERT H. *The Dynamics of Casework and Counseling.* Boston: Houghton Mifflin Co., 1955. See pages 139–50 on "The Problem of Diagnosis." Aptekar's position throughout the book is that synthesis between major concepts of the diagnostic and functional schools is possible, although reviews by spokesmen for both schools deny this (see reviews by Florence Hollis and Ruth Smalley in *Social Service Review*, Vol. XXIX, No. 4 [December, 1955]). In relation to diagnosis, Aptekar believes that adherents of both schools diagnose but that content and method of their diagnosis differs.

3. ASH, PHILLIP. "The Reliability of Psychiatric Diagnoses," *Journal of Abnormal and Social Psychology*, Vol. XLIV, No. 2 (April, 1949).

A study of psychiatrists' agreements and disagreements on interviewing and diagnosing fifty-two cases shows that agreement upon *specific diagnostic categories* obtained in only 20 per cent of the cases seen by three psychiatrists. Agreement upon *major* categories (including "mental deficiency" and frank psychosis) occurred in 45.7 per cent of the cases among the three psychiatrists. The author states that these results are consistent with those of other studies. The data in this study and in No. 11, below, suggest that present-day clinical diagnosis is still "in the rough."

4. CAMERON, D. EWEN, M.D. "A Theory of Diagnosis," in *Current Problems in Psychiatric Diagnosis,* ed. PAUL HOCH and JOSEPH ZUBIN. New York: Grune & Stratton, 1953. Dr. Cameron states his basic propositions thus: "that the diagnosis is a design for action; that it is greatly affected by the existing premises concerning power [that is, power which moves and affects the personality]; that the concept of diagnosis is in a period of major transition." A stimulating, thought-provoking essay.
5. DEWEY, JOHN. *How We Think.* Rev. ed. New York: D. C. Heath & Co., 1933. See especially chapter vii, "Analysis of Reflective Thinking," for an analysis of the process of diagnosis.
6. GOMBERG, M. ROBERT. "Principles and Practices in Counseling," *Diagnosis and Process in Family Counseling.* New York: Family Service Association of America, 1951. See pages 21, 22, and 23 for a statement which combines several approaches to diagnosis.
7. HAMILTON, GORDON. *Psychotherapy in Child Guidance.* New York: Columbia University Press, 1947. See chapter ii, "The Diagnostic Process in Child Guidance," where diagnosis of emotional and behavioral disturbances of children is discussed and a helpful classification of such disorders presented.
8. ———. *Theory and Practice of Social Casework.* 2d ed. rev. New York: Columbia University Press, 1951. See chapter viii, "Diagnostic and Evaluation Processes," in which the author sees diagnosis as "concerned with causal interaction," evaluation with "social purpose." This separation expresses some difference from my point of view, which proposes that the items of causal interaction to be sought and analyzed are determined by the particular social purposes being pursued.
9. HOLLIS, FLORENCE. "Casework Diagnosis—What and Why?" *Smith College Studies in Social Work,* Vol. XXIV, No. 3 (June, 1954). Sets out to particularize casework diagnosis. Argues for making a clinical diagnosis as part of the broader diagnosis which includes current functioning, total family picture, nature of personality disturbance, "especially its structure, depth, and degree," "relative strength of the ego," "nature of individual's libidinal maturity," "ego defense mechanisms," etc. The "what" of casework diagnosis here poses the all-too-

common dilemma for the caseworker: what to select out for use in a given kind of case and to what problem does this apply?

10. ——. "The Relationship between Psychosocial Diagnosis and Treatment," *Social Casework*, Vol. XXXII, No. 2 (February, 1951). In this earlier article Miss Hollis gives a nice definition of the purpose of diagnosis, its content range and limits.

11. HUNT, WILLIAM A., WITTSON, CECIL L., and HUNT, EDNA B. "A Theoretical and Practical Analysis of the Diagnostic Process," in *Current Problems in Psychiatric Diagnosis,* ed. PAUL HOCH and JOSEPH ZUBIN. New York: Grune & Stratton, 1953. A study which finds that in the examination of 794 navy men there was a 93.7 per cent agreement between two teams of psychiatrists as to which men were not suitable for service but only a 32.6 per cent agreement on the specific clinical diagnosis. One of the questions this study raises is of the usefulness and accuracy of clinical classification as a design for action.

12. LEHRMAN, LOUIS. "The Logic of Diagnosis," *Social Casework*, Vol. XXXV, No. 5 (May, 1954). The scientific method underlying diagnosis.

13. LEVINE, MAURICE, M.D. "Principles of Psychiatric Treatment," in *Dynamic Psychiatry,* ed. FRANZ ALEXANDER, M.D., and HELEN ROSS. Chicago: University of Chicago Press, 1952. Good definitions of types of diagnosis. The caseworker reader needs to remember that, in the context in which Dr. Levine writes, the disease is the problem.

14. RAWLEY, CALLMAN, "The Use of Diagnosis in Vocational Service," *Jewish Social Service Quarterly*, Vol. XXXI, No. 1 (Fall, 1954). This article sparked a series of responses, disagreeing and qualifying, by Hamilton, Rawley, Boehm, and Smalley. See the ensuing issues of this quarterly (Winter, 1955; Summer, 1955; and Spring, 1956) for Mr. Rawley's redefinitions and the reactions of the above-named readers. A healthy, lively debate.

15. REYNOLDS, BERTHA. "Is Diagnosis an Imposition?" *Social Work and Social Living*. New York: Citadel Press, 1951. The essential plea in this chapter is for the diagnostic recognition of external reality factors in the client's life.

16. RICHMOND, MARY. *Social Diagnosis*. New York: Russell Sage Foundation, 1917. See especially chapters iii and v.

17. SHERMAN, SANFORD N. "Psychosocial Diagnosis and Its Relationship to Treatment," *Diagnosis and Process in Family Counseling*. New York: Family Service Association of America, 1951. A strong statement of the psychic and social factors included in casework diagnosis with particular emphasis upon the client's use of the casework relationship as a diagnostic indicator.

18. SYTZ, FLORENCE. "The Development of Method in Social Casework," in *Principles and Techniques of Social Casework,* ed. CORA KASIUS. New York: Family Service Association of America, 1950. A review of

the literature on diagnosis in casework stimulated by the opposing "diagnostic" and "functional" views, with some astute points made and some synthesis achieved.

19. WHITEHORN, JOHN C., M.D. "The Concepts of 'Meaning' and 'Cause' in Psychodynamics," *American Journal of Psychiatry*, CIV (November, 1947), 289–92. "The techniques of personality dissection are easier and more spectacular than those of plastic reconstruction. If we fail to keep the young psychiatrist clearly oriented to current issues and attitudes in the patient's life, we are likely to develop a crop of probe-pushers, clever in case presentations but not very competent in actual management and therapy of real patients." Dr. Whitehorn stresses the need to observe, draw out, and deal with the meaning to patients, the theme, of their symptoms and reactions rather than pushing for etiology.

20. *A Comparison of Diagnostic and Functional Casework Concepts.* New York: Family Service Association of America, 1950. A presentation by two committees of two points of view, uneven and apparently not entirely satisfactory to either school of thought (as reviewed in several professional journals).

21. *Diagnosis and Treatment of Marital Problems.* New York: Family Service Association of America, 1947–49. Within these eight articles by seven casework authors may be found many general agreements about diagnosis but also many differences of emphasis and of principle, varying from "whether the appropriate treatment method is within casework competence should not affect the diagnostic formulation; it is a secondary consideration" (Patricia Sacks) to "there is no definite division between diagnosis and treatment" (Regina Flesch). This pamphlet is cited as illustration of the different conceptions of diagnosis which hold even among confirmed "diagnosticians" in casework. Compare Flesch's comments, for example, with Rawley (14, above), with Ackerman (1, above), with Sherman (17, above).

22. *The Functioning of Psychiatric Clinics in New York City: A Study towards the Prevention of Waste.* New York: New York City Committee on Mental Hygiene of the State Charities Aid Association, 1949. Among the findings: Of patients whose first four interviews consisted largely of psychiatric examination (formalized questions to secure diagnostic information), 44 per cent dropped out before the fifth visit, as compared with 16 per cent drop-out of patients whose first four interviews focused on discussion of changes in feelings, attitudes, behavior, or circumstances.

## Chapter 12. The Client's Workability and the Casework Goal

1. BLENKNER, MARGARET. "Predictive Factors in the Initial Interview," *Social Service Review*, Vol. XXVIII, No. 1 (March, 1954). Apropos

of motivation and capacity, this study found (among other factors) client's insight, discomfort, and resistance associated with his movement following intake.

2. FRENCH, THOMAS M., M.D. *The Integration of Behavior,* Vol. I: *Basic Postulates.* Chicago: University of Chicago Press, 1952. In the context of this chapter, notable particularly for the author's discussion of motivation and goal.

3. GREEN, SIDNEY L., M.D. "Psychoanalytic Contributions to Casework Treatment of Marital Problems," *Social Casework,* Vol. XXXV, No. 10 (December, 1954). In his discussion of ego structure and function the author lists qualities of capacity comparable to those in this chapter.

4. HUNT, J. McV. "Measuring Movement in Casework," *Journal of Social Casework,* Vol. XXIX, No. 9 (November, 1948). In this brief article, forerunner of his full studies on testing and measuring results in casework, Mr. Hunt sets forth the criteria for "movement" or change agreed upon by the caseworkers co-operating in his study. Of note is the fact that "change," not "adjustment," was the working concept.

5. MITCHELL, HOWARD E., PRESTON, MALCOLM G., and MUDD, EMILY H. "Anticipated Development of Case from Content of First Interveiw Record," *Marriage and Family Living,* Vol. XV, No. 3 (August, 1953). Apropos of predictive possibilities in observation of behavior, this study of factors in the client's behavior as observed in one interview shows persistent projection of blame as an important prognosticator of poor capacity to work on marital problems.

6. MURRAY, HENRY A., and KLUCKHOHN, CLYDE. "Outline of a Conception of Personality," in *Personality in Nature, Society, and Culture,* ed. CLYDE KLUCKHOHN, HENRY A. MURRAY, and DAVID M. SCHNEIDER. 2d ed. rev. New York: Alfred A. Knopf, 1953. On pages 24–26 criteria of ego strength are offered.

7. POLLAK, OTTO, and NEUMANN, FREDERIKA. "Limited Treatment Goals," in *Social Science and Psychotherapy for Children,* ed. OTTO POLLAK *et al.* New York: Russell Sage Foundation, 1952. Discussion of considerations which might help caseworkers set realistic, achievable goals.

8. RIPPLE, LILIAN. "Motivation, Capacity, and Opportunity as Related to the Use of Casework Service: Plan of Study," *Social Service Review,* Vol. XXIX, No. 2 (June, 1955). This is the first of a series of articles on this study done at the Research Center of the School of Social Service Administration of the University of Chicago, examining the proposition that "the client's use of casework service is determined by his motivation, his capacity, and the opportunities afforded him both by his environment and by the social agency from which he seeks help." Within the context of this chapter the schedule items hold particular interest, since they seek to identify client capacity and moti-

vation from case records. From the completed study some predictive factors as to degree and nature of motivation and capacity to use case-work help may be anticipated.

9. TOWLE, CHARLOTTE. "Factors in Treatment," in *Proceedings of the National Conference of Social Work, 1936.* Chicago: University of Chicago Press, 1936. Among the factors are the client's capacity for relationship. The signs by which this may be gauged are carefully delineated here.

10. WOLBERG, LEWIS R., M.D. *The Technique of Psychotherapy.* New York: Grune & Stratton, 1954. On pages 551–56 Dr. Wolberg discusses "practical" goals relevantly.

*INDEX*

# INDEX

Acceptance; *see* Relationship
Ackerman, Nathan, quoted, 165 n.
Adaptation
  versus "adjustment," 200
  appraisal of, 192
  ego functioning described, 14–17
  modes of, 129–30
  as occurring in problem-solving work, 61–62, 85–100
  in past, 176
  as result of relationship, 73–74, 86–87
Adjustment, meaning of, 53; *see also* Adaptation
Advice, 161–63; *see also* Method
Agency
  caseworker as representative of, 44, 50–51
  classification and character of, 40–43
  client's view of, 44
  helping client engage self with, 149–51
  identified as "place," 14
  as living organism, 49
  misuses of conditions in, 133
  primary and secondary, 41–42
  professional standards of, 52
  program and function of, 45–46
  public and private, 40–41
  relation of, to problem focus, 32–33
  specialization of function of, 42–43
  structure, policies, procedures of, 46–48
  as used by client and caseworker, 109–10, 130–32
  as will of society, 43–44
Alexander, Franz, quoted, 8, 87
Ambivalence
  dealing with, 153–54, 157
  defined, 121
  toward use of help, 133–34
Anxiety
  in relation to advice, 162
  in relation to asking help, 106–8
  in relation to beginning phase, 110
Austin, Lucille, ix
Authority
  in casework relationship, 69–70
  as delegated to casework position, 46

Beginning phase
  agency in, 109–10
  aim of, 105, 113
  caseworker in, 110–12
  client in, 105–8
  content of, 114–38
  help given in, 111–12
  problem as dual, 109
  process as prototype of the whole, 111
  significance of agency to client in, 110–11

Behavior
  conditions which affect, 13–36
  as expression of personality, 9–17
  purpose and meaning of, 7–9
  *see also* Personality
Browne, Marjorie, 80 n.

Cameron, Ewan, quoted, 163 n.
Capacity for problem-solving
  emotional, 189–92
  as Gestalt, 196–97
  intelligence and, 192–96
  physical, 196
  related to problem-solving, 189
  tests of, 130, 135, 188, 197, 198
Casework, social
  aim and means of, 5, 7, 58
  defined and described, 3–5
  as implementing agency functions, 42
  as intervention, 39
  as problem-solving, 58–59
  *see also* Problem-solving
Casework process
  intent and means of, 58–60
  as problem-solving, 53, 63
  *see also* Problem-solving; Relationship
Caseworker
  as member of profession, 51–52
  as representing agency, 50
  as seen by client, 108, 110–11
  self-awareness of, and management by, 81–83
Caseworker-client relationship; *see* Relationship
Causal factors, 33, 36, 37, 126–28, 175–79
Change, factors in, 129
Choice; *see* Decision-making
Clarification, 88–90, 141–44
Client
  in beginning phase, 105–11
  identified, 4
  problem of being, 37–39
  related to his problem, 119
  *see also* Person
Clinical diagnosis; *see* Diagnosis
Coleman, Jules V., quoted, 160 n.
Comments; *see* Questions and comments
Communication, capacity for, and values, 193–95

Conditions
  of agency help, 152–53
  of eligibility, 110
Conflict, 13–14
  in carrying social roles, 23–24
Constants, in casework, need to identify, v–x
Coping; *see* Adaptation
Countertransference; *see* Relationship
Culture, as determinant of behavior, 22–25
Current life-experience
  as affecting personality, 17–20
  in diagnosis, 171
  feelings about, 120–21
  as part of casework inquiry, 116–19
  as vital to adjustment, 19, 20

Decision-making
  choice and decision, 131
  deterrent to, 156–57
  as ego's executive action, 95–98
  as part of problem-solving, 60, 92, 95–99, 135
  *see also* Ambivalence
Defenses
  appraisal of, 192
  purposes and uses of, 8, 15, 16, 192
  *see also* Adaptation; Ego
Dewey, John, quoted, 159 n., 172, 242
Diagnosis
  in beginning phase, 116, 180
  as by-product of problem-solving, 62
  of client's responses, 95
  clinical, 170, 172–75
  content of, as threefold, 168–70
  defined and described, 164–66
  difficulties in way of, 165–68
  dynamic and psychosocial, 170–72
  etiological, 170, 175–80
  as "intellectual and empathic," 166–67
  as logical thinking, 179
  as process and product, 164–67
  as product of casework study, 115–16
  purpose of, 164–68, 179–80
  shared, 95, 125
  of "workability," 183–98
Discomfort, as motivating force, 186, 187
Dynamic diagnosis; *see* Diagnosis
Dynamic stability, 8; *see also* Adaptation; Defenses

Ego
  as affected by external forces, 85–86, 100
  assets and liabilities of, 184
  concept of, 10–17
  enabled by partializing, 148
  executive action of; *see* Decision-making
  limited capacities of, 99
  perceptive, defensive, adaptive, and executive functions of, 14–16, 86
  as problem-solving apparatus, 16–17, 85, 95–98
  as strong or weak, 17
  *see also* Adaptation; Decision-making; Id; Perception; Superego
Ego ideal, concept of, 13
Eligibility, in beginning phase, 110
Emotion
  as affecting person's functioning, 56–57
  as affecting problem, 35
  as bond in relationship, 64
  as capacity, 189–92
  as shared and dealt with by caseworker, 90, 120–21, 125, 143–44
  stress of, in being client, 25, 26, 37, 39
Enabling, defined and described, 163, 197
Environment
  as dynamic, 18–20
  related to ego powers, 99–100
  as treatment means, 62–63
Etiology; *see* Diagnosis
Executive action of ego; *see* Decision-making
Expectation, in culture and social roles, 22–23; *see also* Relationship

Facts
  as basis of problem-solving, 60, 88–90
  in casework study, 115–16
  from client and collateral sources, 122–23
  defined, 88
  obstacles to learning, 117–19
  subjective and objective, 116, 119–22
  therapeutic value of exploring, 88–91

Family-centered project, 156 n.
Family diagnosis, 171 n.
Family relationships, in molding personality, 18
Feelings
  helping client to express, 143–44
  in regard to asking and taking help, 38–39
  *see also* Emotion
Focus
  definition of, 145
  guides to, 136–38
  of problem, 28–32
  *see also* Partialization
Focusing, methods of, 145–47
Freud, Sigmund, 242
Function; *see* Agency
Functional contributions, xi
Future orientation, 20–22; *see also* Hope

Goals
  adjustment versus adaptation, 198–200
  as evolving, 201–3
  as limited and individualized, 200–201
Gomberg, M. Robert, ix
Green, Sidney L., quoted, 189 n.

Hamilton, Gordon, ix, 242
Help, in beginning phase, 111–12
Helping process; *see* Casework, social; Problem-solving
History-taking, 178; *see also* Diagnosis, etiological
Hollis, Florence, ix
Hope, as motivating force, 20–22, 186, 187

Id
  concept of, 10–11
  relation between, and other functions of personality, 13–17
  *see also* Ego; Superego
Identification, of client with caseworker, 73
Individual; *see* Person
Individualization, 140
  and classification, 175
  of goals, 201
  purpose of, 7
  in relation to agency conditions, 157
Information, and counsel, 159–60; *see also* Methods

Inquiry; *see* Facts; Questions and comments
Intake, changes in practice of, 131; *see also* Beginning phase
Intelligence, as capacity, 192–96

Jevons, William, quoted, v

Levine, Maurice, quoted, 167

Macdonald, Mary E., xiii
Maladaptation
as caused by personality problems, 13–16
due to external conditions, 99, 100
in relation to emotions, 191
in relationships, 74–78
as seen in poor problem-solving, 55–57
Marks, Rachel, xiii
Menninger, Karl, quoted, 174 n.
Method
advice, information, and connsel in, 159–62
of dealing with resistance, 154–55
of focusing and partializing, 144–47
of helping client to tell and clarify troubles, 141–43
nature of techniques of, 157–58
questions and comments in, 159–61
responsiveness to client's feelings, 143–44
as therapeutic attitude, 140–41
Motivation
of acquiescent client, 153–54
of ambivalent and unmotivated clients, 153–56
discomfort and hope as, 186–87
signs of "willingness" in, 187–88
tests of, 130, 135, 188, 197, 198
"wanting" and "willing" as, 185–86

Objectivity, caseworker's achieving, 81–83
Osborn, Phyllis, xiii
Overton, Alice, 155 n.

Partialization
criteria for, 149
and ego functions, 148
of problem, 147–49
*see also* Focus
Participation, by client, 58–61, 109, 124, 151, 156

Partnership; *see* Participation
Perception
as affecting adaptation, 85–86
as capacity, 193
clarified by casework, 89
distortions of, in relationship; *see* Relationship
as ego function, 14
problems in, 85
Person
behavior of, and personality functions, 7–17
as having roles and status, 22–25
identified, 4
as molded by past, present, future, 17–23
as product-in-process, 6
under stress, 26
*see also* Client
Personality
definition and description of, 9–10
functions of, 10–17; *see also* Ego; Id; Superego
*see also* Person
Physical well-being, as related to problem-solving capacity, 55–56, 196
Place, identified, 4; *see also* Agency
Policies and procedures; *see* Agency
Problem
of being client, 37–39
causal and chain reactions in, 33–35, 37
causes of, 126–29
facts involved in, 116–24
focus, criteria for, 29–33
identified, 4
nature of, in casework, 27–28
objective-subjective interactions of, 35–37
of personality, 36–37
as sharing idea of, 125–26
Problem-solving
aims of, 58
ascertaining and clarifying facts in, 88–90
blockings in, 55–58
conscious and unconscious, 86–88
decision-making in, 95–97
and direct questions, 142
ends and means in, 5, 58–60, 200
essential operations of, 60–61
exemplified, 206–37
"helping client to tell his troubles," 141–44

identified, 4, 5
as normal life-process, 53–54
as relating to client's feelings, 143–44
in relation to ego functions, v, 85–86
in relation to tangible resources, 62–63
and thinking through facts, 90–95
*see also* Beginning phase; Method
Prognosis, 180
as tested in current responsiveness, 183
Psychosocial diagnosis; *see* Diagnosis

Questions and comments, 92–93, 142, 145–46, 159–61; *see also* Method

Relationship
as acceptance and expectation, support and stimulation, 67–68
authority in, 69–70
bonds of emotion in, 120
and caseworker's role, 72, 140
client's capacity for, 189–90
complications in client's use of, 74–75
conditions which promote, 71
defined and described, 64
management of, by caseworker, 78–83
as nurture to normal human growth, 64–65
purposiveness in professional, 68–69
therapeutic values of, 72, 86, 87
transference and countertransference in, 76–78, 81
Resistance; *see* Ambivalence; Motivation
Resources, 55, 58, 62
as ego support, 100
use of, with unmotivated client, 156
Richmond, Mary, vii, 242
quoted, viii, 179 n.
Ripple, Lilian, xiii
Robinson, Virginia, quoted, 166 n., 242
Role, conflicts and gratifications of, 23–25; *see also* Person

Schour, Esther, xiii
Selby, Lola, xiii
Self-determination
concept of, 60

as promoted by caseworker, 124, 132, 135
Services; *see* Resources
Settings, primary and secondary, 41; *see also* Agency
Sherman, Sanford, quoted, 181
Skill
definition of, 166 n.
techniques of, 157
Social agency; *see* Agency
*Social Casework,* cited, 173 n.
Social casework, defined, 4; *see also* Casework, social
Social caseworker; *see* Caseworker
*Social Diagnosis* (Mary Richmond), vii, viii
Social study, content in beginning phase of, 115–16; *see also* Facts
Solutions
as problematic, 38–39
sought and explored, 130–35, 149–51
*see also* Decision-making
Specialization of agency functions, reasons for, 27–28, 43
Status; *see* Person; Role
Stephens, James, quoted, 73
Stress, and defenses, 25–26; *see also* Anxiety; Emotion
Structure
of content, 139
of problem-solving process, 60–61
of social agency, 46–47
Study-diagnosis-treatment, viii, 61
Subjectivity; *see* Objectivity
Superego
concept of, 10–14
relation between, and other functions of personality, 13–17
*see also* Ego; Id
Support
of debilitated clients, 99
of ego functions, 86
and stimulus, in relationship, 67, 68

Techniques, defined and discussed, 158–63; *see also* Method
Thinking
as adaptation, 92–94
as capacity, 195
in diagnosis, 164–66, 179
in problem-solving work, 60, 90–95
Towle, Charlotte, ix, xii, 242

Transference; *see* Relationship
Treatment
  defined, 181
  as yielding diagnosis, 165, 181; *see
    also* Capacity for problem-solv-
    ing, tests of; Motivation, tests of
  *see also* Goals; Method; Problem-
    solving; Relationship

Whitehead, Alfred North, quoted, xi,
  179

"Workability"
  assessment of, as product of treat-
    ment, 198
  defined and discussed, 183–84
  as diagnostic content in beginning
    phase, 180–82
  as related to use of help, 184
  *see also* Capacity for problem-solv-
    ing; Motivation
Wright, Helen R., xii